DARE TO BE CHRIST

Homilies for the Nineties

WALTER J. BURGHARDT, S.J.

PAULIST PRESS
New York/Mahwah

also by Walter J. Burghardt, S.J.
published by Paulist Press

GRACE ON CRUTCHES
LOVELY IN EYES NOT HIS
PREACHING: THE ART AND THE CRAFT
SEASONS THAT LAUGH OR WEEP
SIR, WE WOULD LIKE TO SEE JESUS
STILL PROCLAIMING YOUR WONDERS
TELL THE NEXT GENERATION
TO CHRIST I LOOK

The excerpt from "In Praise of Diversity" by Phyllis McGinley is taken from *Love Letters of Phyllis McGinley,* copyright © 1953 by Phyllis McGinley. Used by permission of Viking Penguin, a division of Penguin USA.

Illustrations by Nancy R. Myette.
Cover by Tim McKeen.

Library of Congress Cataloging-in-Publication Data

Burghardt, Walter J.
    Dare to be Christ : homilies for the nineties / Walter J.
    Burghardt.
        p.   cm.
    Includes bibliographical references.
    ISBN 0-8091-3222-2
    1. Church year sermons. 2. Occasional sermons. 3. Catholic Church—
Sermons.   4. Sermons, American.   I. Title.
    BX1756.B828D37   1990
    252'.02—dc20   90-24859
                                                                       CIP

Published by Paulist Press
997 Macarthur Boulevard
Mahwah, NJ 07430

Printed and bound in the
United States of America

In reverent remembrance of
Ignacio Ellacuría, S.J.
Joaquín López y López, S.J.
Amando López Quintana, S.J.
Ignacio Martín-Baró, S.J.
Segundo Montes Mozo, S.J.
Juan Ramón Moreno Pardo, S.J.
and their lay associates
Elba Julia Ramos
Celina Maricet Ramos
martyred in El Salvador
November 16, 1989
because they dared to be Christ
and
lived the faith that does justice

TABLE OF CONTENTS

ORDINARY TIME

WEDDINGS

MEDLEY

PREFACE

The six collections of my homilies which the Paulist Press graciously published during the 1980s have enjoyed a gratifyingly warm welcome—not only from harried clergy in quest of a homiletic hint but from all manner of Christian folk hungering for a contemporary spirituality. Letters from the latter suggest that three approaches pervading these homilies have an especial appeal: the effort (1) to retell the scriptural story, especially the parables of Jesus, in a contemporary idiom; (2) to deepen our understanding of the Word with the insights of today's theology; and (3) to link all this to a "faith that does justice," i.e. life lived for "the other," particularly those who experience more of Christ's crucifixion than of his resurrection.

These approaches, I believe, continue to characterize the homilies in this volume. Hence my title and subtitle: the challenge to follow in the footsteps of the Crucified and Risen One in the context of a new decade, still plagued with poverty and pain, with indignity and injustice, yet unexpectedly, from East to West, "born anew to a living hope" (1 Pet 1:3).

Walter J. Burghardt, S.J.

Advent

1
REMEMBER, REPENT, REHEARSE
First Sunday of Advent (A)

- Isaiah 2:1–5
- Romans 13:11–14
- Matthew 24:37–44

As far back as memory takes me, Catholics have been confused by
Advent. We get mixed signals—from Rome and the local pastor, from
the readings and the local homilist. We are told in Matthew, "Keep
your eyes open, for you do not know on what day your Lord is coming" (Mt 24:42). But I was told he's coming on the 25th. No, that's his
first coming, back there in little old Bethlehem. You can't look forward to something that's already happened—like the first footsteps
on the moon. What you don't know is when the Lord is *returning*,
trailing clouds of glory. But how do you keep your eyes open for
that—and why in God's name around Christmas, when we're
surrounded not by clouds but by cribs, not by an all-powerful judge
but by a powerless baby in straw?

Through John the Baptist in camel's hair the Church commands
us, "Prepare the way of the Lord" (Mt 3:3). What way? Surely not the
road Joseph and Mary took to Bethlehem. Surely not outer space, a
satellite for Judge Jesus at the end of time. Or do you ready your soul
for dying, because the Church warns us in Advent that "the Son of
man is coming at an hour you do not expect" (Mt 24:44)?

If you weren't confused before, you should be now. What are
these four short weeks all about—this month that climaxes in Christmas? Let me clarify Advent with three memorable verbs. They have to
do with the past, the present, and the future—with yesterday, today,
and tomorrow. (1) We remember. (2) We repent. (3) We rehearse. A
word on each.

I

First, we remember. For Christmas has a past. To prepare for Christmas, we dare not live "business as usual" and expect to wake up on the 25th with Bethlehem's star in our eyes. I am not asking you to forget the turkey and the tree, to give up on semester exams, to leave the office early, to forgo the diamonds that are for ever, to spend four weeks on your knees. I do submit that we who celebrate D-Day and birthday, Presidents' Day and Memorial Day, with such rich recollections, such a sense of history, must look back even more gratefully and thoughtfully on C-day, the supreme event in human history.

On a night we now take for granted, the whole of history was turned upside down. Something happened that had never happened before, that would never happen again, that blows the human mind, that no one in his right mind would have predicted. God's own Son entered our world. Not an angel, not another prophet; God's Son, the Second Person of the Blessed Trinity. Not as we would have written the scenario: in the capital city of the Roman Empire, with all the majesty of a king, surrounded by an army and adored by millions. He entered our world as we entered it: out of a young woman's body. He had been there for nine months—very much like us—growing, feeding, breathing, moving. He entered our world in our flesh—our mind and our marrow, our blood and our glands. He entered our world in a forgotten corner of the earth, in a feeding trough for animals, with only one man and one woman to see. He entered our world as powerless as we were—what someone called "omnipotence in bonds." I suspect he cried, felt cold till Mary gathered him in her arms, didn't quite know what to make of the shepherds, hardly heard the choir of angels singing "Glory to God."

We remember that night because when Jesus touched this earth with his flesh, life would never be the same again. Oh yes, on the surface much seems the same. Hate still hounds us and wars wound us; children still starve and the elderly are oft forgotten; cancers riddle our flesh and death never takes a holiday. But that human birthday was a divine promise: In Christ Jesus men and women need no longer be slaves to sin and Satan, evil is less powerful than good, each one of us can be one with God, one with one another, now and for ever. In the ceaseless declaration of early church writers, "God became human to make us divine." To give us a share in God's own life; to make it possible for us to believe what is beyond belief, to hope against hope, to love as Jesus loved.

So then, if you want to prepare for Christmas, remember! Some years ago Elie Wiesel, that remarkable Jewish storyteller who feels guilty because he survived the Holocaust, reminded us that, for Jews, to forget is a crime against justice as well as memory: If you forget, you become the executioner's accomplice. For us Christians, the type of memory most exhilarating *and* most painful is memory of the birth and death of Christ. Exhilarating because God was born and died *for us;* painful because it makes demands on us that would change our lives.

II

This brings the past into the present, summons up my second point: In Advent we repent. You see, important as memory is for the Christian, our memory of Christmas ought not to mean that we live in the past. To live in the past is to begin dying. The miracle of Christmas is that Jesus' birth was not a solitary historic event in the "little town of Bethlehem"; it was a beginning. Christmas is now. These four weeks, paradoxically, we prepare for what already is, prepare for the present. Let me explain.

Very simply, for all the countless cribs that will dot the Christmas scenery, Jesus no longer lives in a crib. With the angel at the tomb we must proclaim, "He is not here, for he has risen" (Mt 28:6). Not simply to return to his Father in heaven. "If [you] love me," Jesus declared, "[you] will keep my word, and my Father will love [you], and we will come to [you] and make our home with [you]" (Jn 14:23). Jesus rested in a crib not for his own sake; he rested in a crib because he wanted to rest in us.

"If you love me. . . ." Do you want to awaken on Christmas murmuring with the apostle Peter, "Lord, you know that I love you" (Jn 21:17)? Do you want to make sure that the first Christmas has come to birth in you? Then your Advent must be a conversion. To convert means to turn: to turn *from* something *to* someone. Concretely, to turn from self to Christ. Sometimes the turning is quite radical. So it was for one of the criminals crucified with Jesus: "Jesus, remember me . . ." (Lk 23:42). So it was for St. Augustine in a Milanese garden, his intellect captured by Christ, his will still prey to pleasure, his prayer still "Grant me chastity and continence, but not yet."[1] And then that remarkable moment when the words you just heard St. Paul address to the Christians of Rome spoke to his tears: "not in reveling and drunkenness, not in debauchery and licentiousness, not in quarreling and jealousy, but put on the Lord Jesus Christ, and make no provision for the flesh, to gratify its desires" (Rom 13:13–14). "In that instant, with the very ending of the sentence, it was as though a light of utter confidence shone in all my heart, and all the darkness of uncertainty vanished away."[2] So it was for Dorothy Day, saint of the homeless and hopeless, moving from Communism to Christ.

Such radical repentance is not rare. But may I suggest that, for such as you and me, for us who cradle Christ on hands or tongue day in and day out, Advent calls for a different kind of conversion? I mean where Christ is indeed there, rests within us, but we react strangely. I take him for granted; I give him less time than I allot the Charlotte Hornets;[3] I do just what I have to do to avoid serious sin; I play fast and loose with business expenses ("everybody does it"); the less I remember of a beer bash, the better it must have been; chastity is for squares and Mother Teresa; nobody goes to confession any more; I'm apologetic about being a Catholic, tell friends it's not as bad as they think; if I've earned the money, who's to tell me how to spend it?

Advent is the season to cut compromise out of my Catholicism, to stop being halfhearted about church and religion, about morality and love, to face up to the frightening words spoken by the Lord God in the Book of Revelation to the bishop of the proud and wealthy city of Laodicea: "I know your works: You are neither cold nor hot. Would that you were cold or hot! So, because you are lukewarm, and neither cold nor hot, I will spew you out of my mouth" (Rev 3:15–16).

Advent is the time to take the barnacles off my Catholic bottom —the obstacles that keep me from being enthusiastic in my faith and hope and love, too sophisticated to love God with all my mind and heart, all my soul and strength, too self-centered to love my brothers and sisters as much as I love myself. For a remarkable rabbi, Abraham Joshua Heschel, the question of religion was not what we do with our solitude; the question of religion was what we do with the presence of God. Here God is, St. Paul told the Athenians, "not far from each one of us" (Acts 17:27). Here the God-man is—not a mere memory but a living presence: here in the Word proclaimed to you; here in the tabernacle that houses him "body and blood, soul and divinity"; here deep inside of you through his grace; all around you in the men and women who share your turf and beg for bread and a bed, for shoes and a word of love, runaway youngsters by the thousands pimped and prostituted. How shall we live in this wondrous, this tragic presence of God? In rapture and fear, in awe and near despair—or carefree disregard, "no sweat," don't get involved?

III

Third, we rehearse. To rehearse is to go through privately what will take place more formally, publicly. I rehearse a homily; you rehearse a play; Santa Claus rehearses his "Ho, ho, ho" for the children who will lounge in his lap at Belk's.[4]

Advent is a splendid time to rehearse for a final coming of Christ. He came to us first in our fragile flesh almost 20 centuries ago; he comes to us now when we love him, when we receive him in Communion, when we open our arms to him in the oppressed; he will come once more when time is about to end, when he will come to judge the living and the dead, when, as Paul puts it, "he delivers the kingdom to God the Father" (1 Cor 15:24).

But how do you prepare for something as awesome, as unimaginable, as futuristic, as unpredictable, as science-fictionish as the ultimate coming of Christ—no longer in swaddling clothes but in the glory of God? I have one simple suggestion, two monosyllables: as if. Live Advent as if Christ were coming in majesty this December.

How would I react if Express Mail reached me today with this short message: "Expect my Son on the 25th. Will come not in a crib, but trailing clouds of glory. This is the end. Repeat: This is the end. Prepare for his arrival. It'll be sheep at his right hand, goats at his left. No regrets accepted. Signed, Father/Mother"? I suspect my Advent would be different. How about you?

In my younger Jesuit days, a pious story circulated about a canonized saint. In the midst of a tennis match his opponent asked: "If you knew right now that you were going to die today, what would you do?" Racquet in hand, the saint responded: "Serve!" Legend or not, the story is instructive. Instructive not because I ought to start worrying whether Christ is actually about to arrive. Instructive because the way I live now should be the way I want to look whenever Christ comes for me.

It's not a question of giving up all that is dear to you—work and play, family and sex—and heading naked for Mount Mitchell[5] to welcome Christ. It's rather, how Christlike am I where I am, in what I do, with the people whose lives I touch? How do I handle the three main goals all too many young Americans admit to: money, power, fame? How do I relate to Christ crucified today—crucified in the 25 percent of U.S. children who live in poverty, in the 2.5 million elderly who live on $104 a week?

So then, a three-part program for Advent. (1) Contemplation: a long loving look at the past, at the Son of God born of a woman out of love for me. (2) Conversion: a turning to Christ today that is total—no longer a lukewarm, tepid, indifferent, dishwater-type Catholicism, but St. Paul's cry from ground level, "What do you want of me, Lord?" (Acts 22:10). (3) Concern for tomorrow, for what I shall look like when Christ returns—a concern that translates into looking like that now, inside myself, in the way I touch others, in my closeness to Christ.

We remember, we repent, we rehearse. A lifetime project, you protest? I agree. All the more reason for starting today. Especially if you can credit Christ's caution, "You do not know on what day your Lord is coming" (Mt 24:42).

St. Peter's Church
Charlotte, N.C.
December 3, 1989

Lent

2
A PENCIL IN GOD'S HAND
Saturday after Ash Wednesday (A)

- Isaiah 58:9–14
- Luke 5:27–32

In the brief time at our disposal,[1] let me (1) tell you a story, (2) relate the story to the reading from Isaiah, and (3) move from Isaiah to Lent.

I

In December 1989, *Time* magazine ran a short but stimulating interview with Mother Teresa. In her typically humble fashion she said:

> People are responding not because of me but because of what we are doing. I think that before people were speaking much about the poor, but now more and more people are speaking to the poor. That is the great difference. Before, nobody bothered about the people in the street. We have picked up from the streets of Calcutta 54,000 people, and 23,000-something have died in that one room (at Kalighat).

Then came four swift questions, four remarkable responses:

> **Q.** Humble as you are, it must be an extraordinary thing to be a vehicle of God's grace in the world.
> **A.** But it is his work. I think God wants to show his greatness by using nothingness.
> **Q.** You feel you have no special qualities?
> **A.** I don't think so. I don't claim anything of the work. It is his work. I am like a little pencil in his hand. That is all. He does the thinking.

He does the writing. The pencil has nothing to do with it. The pencil has only to be allowed to be used. . . .

Q. What is God's greatest gift to you?

A. The poor people.

Q. How are they a gift to you?

A. I have an opportunity to be 24 hours a day with Jesus.[2]

II

Teresa turns us to Isaiah, to the powerful passage proclaimed to us this morning. The six verses are the conclusion of chapter 58, a chapter on true and false fasting. What sort of fasting is acceptable to the Lord? Not when Israelites fast and at the same time "seek [their] own pleasure and oppress all [their] workers" (v. 3). Not when they fast "only to quarrel and to fight and to hit with wicked fist" (v. 4). What, then, is the fast the Lord chooses?

> [Is it not] to let the oppressed go free,
>   and to break every yoke?
> Is it not to share your bread with the hungry,
>   and bring the homeless poor into your house;
> when you see the naked, to cover him,
>   and not to hide yourself from your own flesh? . . .
> If you pour yourself out for the hungry,
>   and satisfy the desire of the afflicted,
> then shall your light rise in the darkness
>   and your gloom be as the noonday.
> And the Lord will guide you continually,
>   and satisfy your desire with good things,
>   and make your bones strong;
> and you shall be like a watered garden,
>   like a spring of water,
>   whose waters fail not.
>   (Isa 58:6–7, 10–11)

In itself, fasting is no more deserving of praise than is eating. So much, Isaiah insisted, depended on why an Israelite fasted and what else an Israelite did or did not do. The prophets made it limpidly clear that incense and sacrifice, sackcloth and ashes, festivals and prayers, the melody of harps and even the gift of a first-born were an abomination in God's sight if the people turned their face from the oppressed, if they claimed to love God and yet hid themselves from their own flesh.

III

Teresa and Isaiah turn us to Lent. I am not a foe of fasting, not an enemy of abstinence. If weight-watching can help you keep a commandment of the Church, no sweat: Stick to the raw carrots and the cottage cheese. I simply submit that the age-old Catholic practice of "giving up for Lent" demands refining. All well and good to surrender the Scotch, deny the dessert, forgo the film. Better still to surrender the selfishness in me, to deny myself, give up the self, give the self, my self, to others.

Isaiah and Teresa turn us to the untold millions who are in so many ways "poor." The homeless and the hopeless, indeed, those who hunger for bread or for justice, for the touch of a human hand or a sign that somebody cares, the AIDS-afflicted and the crack-enchained. But beyond these, the "haves" who have not. Have not peace, because they are ceaselessly lusting for more: more riches, more power, more fame. Have not security, because they rest their hopes not in God but in man and woman, build not on rock but on sand. Have not love, because today the race is to the swift and the savage, and they dare not love anyone else as much as they love themselves.

You need not fly to Teresa in Calcutta. The "poor" surround us, work with us, live with us, share our blood. We need only senses sensitive to the world around us: eyes that see beneath the grime the face of Christ; ears awake to each unspoken plea or protest; a touch attuned to the ambivalence of adolescents and the anxieties of the aging. In Lent you and I need to give new life to an age-old monosyllable: We need to care.

If you really care, you will share Mother Teresa's gift: "an opportunity to be 24 hours a day with Jesus." All God asks is the most difficult gift of all: Let go . . . let go of yourself. Be a little pencil in God's mighty hand.

The Oratory
Rock Hill, S. Carolina
March 3, 1990

3
FAITH IN THE SHADOW OF A CROSS
Second Sunday of Lent (A)

- Genesis 12:1–4
- 2 Timothy 1:8–10
- Matthew 17:1–9

Today I want to talk about a man, a woman, and a congregation. A man long dead, a woman amazingly alive, a congregation balancing death and life. I want to talk about Abraham, about Thea, about you and me.

I

First, a man long dead, a man who lived 18 centuries before Christ. I mean the Abraham proclaimed briefly to you some moments ago. "The Lord said to Abraham, 'Go from your country and your kindred and your father's house to the land that I will show you' " (Gen 12:1). So what? Why make a federal case out of a divine command to leave Mesopotamia?

The New Testament Letter to the Hebrews tells us why: "By faith Abraham obeyed when he was called to go out to a place which he was to receive as an inheritance; and he went out, not knowing where he was to go" (Heb 11:8). Not knowing where he was to go. Abraham typifies faith—the faith the same letter defines as "the reality of things we hope for, the proof of things we cannot see" (v. 1).[1]

Abraham did not know where he was to go. Not only the strange new country that would be his. He did not know what would happen to him along the way: the famine that would drive him into Egypt; his wife Sarah taken into Pharaoh's harem because Abraham, afraid of being killed, said Sarah was his sister. What he did know was that God was calling him—calling him, at age 75, to leave the land he loved, leave Mesopotamia, and settle wherever God might choose.

16

Abraham marks a significant point in the story of salvation. This is the ancestor of Israel, the man who was the very first to worship the true God. This is the man who believed God's promise of innumerable descendants: "I will make of you a great nation" (Gen 12:2)—a faith that was put to a terrible test when God commanded him, "Take your son, your only son Isaac, whom you love, and go to the land of Moriah, and offer him there as a burnt offering . . ." (Gen 22:2). This is the man who had the knife poised to slay his son when God stopped him: "Do not lay your hand on the lad or do anything to him; for now I know that you fear God, seeing you have not withheld your son, your only son, from me" (Gen 22:12).

This is the man the early Church saw as model, pattern, exemplar of our faith. Faith not only as intellectual assent, yes to whatever God *says*. Faith in its fulness, as the gift of my total self, yes to whatever God *wants*.

II

Second, a woman amazingly alive. Her name is Thea Bowman. She is black, a Franciscan Sister of Perpetual Adoration. In 1984 she was diagnosed as having cancer. The cancer has spread to her skull and most of her other bones; she gets around in a wheel chair. "I have pain," she admits. "Pain is a constant." A well-known evangelizer, Thea Bowman travels whenever she can because "I might not get better."

Last June Thea addressed a national conference of U.S. bishops gathered at Seton Hall University in New Jersey, to tell them what it means to be black and Catholic in this country. Addressing bishops did not faze her. "I feel grateful for the opportunity to speak to the Church assembled. Since I was a child, people have said I have a mouth." For her, "They are my brothers; they are my pastors; they are the hierarchy of my Church—but they are my brothers and I thank God for them."

After her talk, Thea had the bishops stand up, cross arms, hold hands, sing "We Shall Overcome"—and sway while doing it. The bishops, God save the mark! Too often, she said, Catholics leave their bishops and priests alone. "We isolate them. We need to love them into life."

One of the gifts that African Americans bring to a Catholic Church that is universal is a closeness. Our houses were crowded, our churches were crowded, and our neighborhoods were crowded. We like to touch. We need to find a way to reach out and touch . . . being in solidarity and holding on to one another. There are so many forces trying to divide us.

Afterwards, in a warm room, resting under a blanket and a quilt, this 51-year-old nun quoted a spiritual: "I keep so busy serving my master, I ain't got time to die."[2]

A woman who has left behind everything save her God and her blackness. A woman bent on sharing her God and her blackness with an American church that is still uncomfortable with black bishops and priests, with gospel choirs in the sanctuary, with clapping and swaying and "amen-ing" during a sacred ceremony. A woman who "ain't got time to die" because there is so much healing to do—because she must heal . . . you and me.

III

You and me. This leads directly into my third point: a congregation. Abraham and Thea combine to preach—to me as well as to you—a basic Lenten homily: faith in the shadow of a cross. Not that the pilgrimage of Abraham and the cancer of Thea have to be copied, must be reproduced literally, in your life and mine. Why, we don't imitate even Jesus slavishly. There are facets of our living that Jesus did not and could not experience. He was a man, not a woman. He was a teacher, but not a scholar. He did not experience old age or Alzheimer's disease. He did not even live to be a Jesuit! Each of us must indeed live faith in the shadow of a cross, but each in his or her own way, the way God wants us to walk. Let me explain.

There is a dreadful danger in the manner many think of Jesus. Oh yes, he learned from Joseph how to shape a plow, but it must have been make-believe: Wasn't he God? Yes, he grew hungry, but his stomach couldn't really growl: Wasn't he God? Yes, he suffered on the cross, actually died, but it wasn't all that bad, because he knew he would rise again: Wasn't he God?

Yes, Jesus was God's only Son. But the marvel of the Incarnation is that this same Son of God was as truly human as he was divine. As a man, he was not only born of a woman, not only sweated and slept, not only winced under insult, not only feared to die, not only died a criminal's death. He lived by faith; with faith he died. This man did not step onto our turf with a day-to-day scenario, detailing every episode from Bethlehem to Calvary. He had to live by faith. I mean with confidence, with trust, in his Father's love. This faith came to a climax on the cross. That dying the remarkable theologian Karl Rahner described poignantly in his own dying years:

> . . . Jesus surrendered himself in his death unconditionally to the absolute mystery that he called his Father, into whose hands he committed his existence, when in the night of his death and God-forsakenness he was deprived of everything that is otherwise regarded as the content of a human existence: life, honour, acceptance in earthly and religious fellowship, and so on. . . . [E]verything fell away from him, even the perceptible security of the closeness of God's love, and in this trackless dark there prevailed silently only the mystery that . . . has no name and to which he nevertheless calmly surrendered himself as to eternal love and not to the hell of futility. . . .[3]

This man died not with an unassailable syllogism, logical proof that he would rise again. He died as he had lived, died as we die: with a lively hope. For all that he was God, this man too died not with experience of resurrection; he died with faith in his Father, with hope of life for ever. He died murmuring, "Father, into your hands I entrust my spirit" (Lk 23:46). My whole self, all that I am, I rest with confidence in your love.

What was true of Jesus, what was true of Abraham, what is true of Thea, that must be life-and-death reality for every Christian. That is why the 40 days of Lent are so important. Not an annual intrusion into pleasant living, not a long-faced price you have to pay for Easter, not a providential period to thin out for the beach. Here is where you and I renew our Christian identity: a hope-full faith in the shadow of a cross.

Two teeth-grinding monosyllables: faith and cross. In our technocratic culture the word "faith" gives off a bad odor. Faith is a placebo, a sugar-coated pill you give or take when God fails to appear under our microscope or through linguistic analysis, a rabbit you pull out of your Christian hat when rational argument "sucks." I have news for you. Living faith, loving faith, is the most remarkable gift God gives any of us in this life. After a half century of study, of research, of scholarship, I have high regard for what the human mind can uncover—from Aristotle to Einstein, from Aquinas to Jonas Salk. And yet, if push came to shove, I just might trade it all in for the unreflective faith of my dear mother, for the faith that simply exclaims with the apostle Thomas before the wounds of the risen Christ, "My

Lord and my God!'' (Jn 20:28). Why? Because a living faith is my unreserved response, my graced yes, to a living God, to the risen Christ: God addressing me through Old Testament and New, through church and conscience; God alive in me through grace and the Bread of Life. Faith is not weakness; faith is power—the power of God.

But faith must be lived in the shadow of a cross. By "cross" I do not mean simply the final breath I shall draw, the ultimate stroke, the last agony. Dying in a theological sense begins when living begins; we share in Jesus' dying by sharing his cross through the whole of our lives. Whatever makes for pain—pain of flesh or of spirit—should be part and parcel of our Christian dying. Acne or anxiety, diverticula or disappointments, schizophrenia or the wrenching of my heart, dying hopes or the death of a dear one, drug addiction or AIDS, the insecurities of youth and the trembling of the aging—whatever it is that pricks my pride, that assails my lustiness, that intimates my mortality, that takes the joy from my very bones—in all these brief or drawn-out episodes of what Rahner called "dying in installments,"[4] we confront a crucial question: How am I to cope with them? Do I merely put up with them, endure them, sit back and sulk, wait for a better tomorrow? Do I protest, cry out to heaven in anger, ask with Judas "Why this waste?" Do I cling all the more desperately to what has not yet been taken from me? Do I despair? Or . . . do I see in such breakdowns "events of grace," the hand of God fashioning me to a closer imaging of Christ—the reason why I exist?

Of course it takes faith! Not a casual creed on Sunday, but a ceaseless struggle to find the face of God, dark nights of the soul, times when a man or woman resonates to Rod Steiger in that powerful old film *The Pawnbroker:* "Everything I loved was taken away from me . . . and I did not die."

Tough stuff indeed. The paradox is, faith in the shadow of a cross is the only sure way to lasting joy. Not "lasting joy" only as heaven following on a vale of tears. I am not telling you, "Buck up, stiff upper lip, it will all be over before you know it, and then you can strum a harp with angels." No. I mean joy now, profound joy in the midst of sorrow. Even in your anguish, as novelist Edith Wharton phrased it, you will be "conscious of that lift of the heart which made one of the saints declare that joy was the inmost core of sorrow."[5]

Joyful faith on a cross? Ecstasy within agony? Impossible, you say? Athletes experience it day after day—gymnasts and marathoners, pugilists and weight lifters, Redskins and Capitals. You'll never really know unless you try it, unless you try to live it. Lent is a splendid spot for a test case. Take a cross, small or immense, that actually has you nailed—in flesh or spirit or both—and sweat and pray till you can say, and mean it, "Into your hands, Lord, I entrust all this, entrust my whole self." Or, with Jesus in the garden of agony, "Father, if you would, remove this cup from me; nevertheless, not my will but yours be done" (Lk 22:42). For Lent with Jesus, it sure beats surrendering the suds on your Buds or contemplating your navel.

Dahlgren Chapel
Georgetown University
and
Holy Trinity Church
Washington, D.C.
March 11, 1990

4
LISTEN, LET GO, LAUGH!
Second Sunday of Lent (C)

- Genesis 15:5–12, 17–18
- Philippians 3:17—4:1
- Luke 9:28–36

All through this decade I have been privileged to share Lent with you. Largely because of you I have struggled to deepen my grasp on these 40 days. Thousands are the words I have winged your way; varied are the visions I have evoked for you. At this point I want to extract from those many utterances three themes that strike me as uncommonly crucial for your Lent and for your life.[1] These three themes take seriously the command of Jesus that we "repent," but take just as seriously the first Lenten Preface, which describes these 40 days as "this joyful season." These three themes amount to three Lenten penances. (1) For your Lenten penance, listen! (2) For your Lenten penance, let go! (3) For your Lenten penance, laugh!

I

For your Lenten penance, listen! Begin by listening to one another, to the earthbound humans whose lives touch yours. Not easy. Most conversations are not conversations at all. Either they are monologues: I wait patiently till you have finished—since civility demands it—and then I say exactly what I would have said if you had not spoken. Or they are debates: I do indeed listen, but only for that inept word or false phrase at which I proceed to intercept and destroy. No. To listen is to give yourself totally, for that moment or that hour, to another, to put yourself into the other's mind, the other's heart. It means you hear not naked words but a flesh-and-blood person.

Remember our Lady? She listened: to an angel in Nazareth and angels in Bethlehem, to shepherds and wise men from the East. Remember Helen Keller? Blind, deaf, mute, she "listened" to Annie Sullivan as if her life depended on it (it did indeed). Remember St. John Vianney, famous parish priest of Ars in France? Twelve hours a day in the confessional, he listened—not simply to sins but to fractured hearts. I remember my remarkable mentor in early Christianity at Catholic University: "I learn as much from my students as my students learn from me."[2]

The problem? To listen is to risk. It takes your precious time, often when you can least afford it. You take on other people's problems, when you have enough of your own. You must pay attention to folk less brilliant than you—like students. If you're a good listener, people "dump" on you. If you listen, someone may fall in love with you—and that can be a burden you do not care to bear.

But the risk will be matched by a matchless joy. For listening, really listening, is an act of love; and so it is wonderfully human, splendidly Christian. I used to think, in my youthful arrogance, that what I had to offer the Catholic world was a hatful of answers. No. I come to others as I am, with my own ignorance, weakness, sinfulness, my own fears and tears. I share not words by myself; I am there. And that, dear friends, is my Christian mission and yours: to be where another can reach out to us.

Second, listen to Jesus. That was the Father's command from the cloud: "Listen to him!" (Lk 9:35). Why? Because here is God's Revelation in flesh, the Word God speaks. How does Jesus speak to us now? Vatican II rings loud and clear: "[Christ] is present in his word, since it is he himself who speaks when the holy Scriptures are read in the church."[3] Do you believe that? Do you really believe "This is the word of the Lord"? If you do, how do you listen? As breathlessly as Moses listened to the Lord on Sinai? As open to God's word as was the teen-age Mary of Nazareth? Do you "marvel," like his townspeople, at "the words of grace" that fall from Jesus' lips (Lk 4:22)? Do you exclaim, as the two disciples exclaimed on the road to Emmaus, "Did not our hearts burn within us while he talked to us . . . while he opened the Scriptures to us?" (Lk 24:32). Or has repetition dulled your appetite, made J.C. less exciting than J.R.?[4]

Third, listen to the world around you. God speaks to you through the things He has shaped. For God could fashion nothing unless it imaged some perfection of His. There is no blade of grass that does not speak of Him. The whirlwinds reflect His power, the mountains mirror His majesty, surging waves His irresistibleness, a star-flecked sky His breath-taking loveliness. If I miss their message, it is because I am not tuned into God, am not listening.

God speaks to me through history, through human events. The cry of the blacks for freedom was a cry of God, "Let my people go!" From the ovens and gas chambers of Dachau, the God of Abraham is talking to a world that would like to forget its inhumanity to Jewish man and woman. From Appalachia to Calcutta it is the voice of Jesus that begs for bread and human dignity. But I need him to put his fingers into my ears and murmur "Be opened" (Mk 7:33–34).

Good friends: If you want to "do" something for Lent, if you want to share in the dying-rising of Jesus, rise above Oprah Winfrey and the Optifast diet. Simply listen: Listen to one another, listen to Jesus in the proclaimed word, listen to the Lord speaking through the things and people that surround you. For your Lenten penance, please . . . listen!

II

For your Lenten penance, let go! Suppose we begin with the Word of God rather than the word of Burghardt:

> Though of divine status,
> [Jesus] did not treat like a miser's booty
> his right to be like God
> [his right to appear like Yahweh in glory],
> but emptied himself of it,
> to take up the status of a slave
> and become like men;
> having assumed human form,
> he still further humbled himself
> with an obedience that meant death—
> even death upon a cross!
>
> (Phil 2:6–11)

Moving, poignant words. A liturgical hymn sung in ancient Christian liturgy. But what does the hymn say to us? Not only did Jesus himself journey to Jerusalem; he commanded us to follow him on that journey. It is a journey that goes to life through death; and death gives life not only when we breathe our last, but all through our Christian existence.

In our journeying to life, we die in two ways; for death comes to us from two sources. Death comes, first, from sin—from the sins of our own fashioning and from "the sin of the world," all the weight and burden of human transgression from Adam to Antichrist. And "the wages of sin is death" (Rom 6:23). Not the soul leaving the body; not some abstract absence of God. The results of radical sin, of "mortal" sin, are within me. It unmakes me, undoes me, unravels me, misshapes me. In radical sin I am a different person; for Life has left me.

To the death that is sin we have been dying since our baptism. And the dying is never ended. For dying to sin is not something negative; dying to sin is turning to Christ, and turning to Christ is a constant conversion. If sin is rejection, dying to sin is openness: I am open to God's presence poured out on me through every flower that opens its chaliced petals to me, every breeze that caresses my skin, every man or woman whose eyes meet mine, the awesome presence of the Holy One Himself tabernacled within me. In dying to sin, we live to God.

Death comes to us in a second way: from the very shape of the human journey—even apart from sin. For your human journey to go forward, to move ahead, you must let go of where you've been, let go of the level of life where you are now, so as to live more fully. Whether it's turning 21, 40, or 65, whether it's losing your health or your hair, your looks or your lustiness, your money or your memory, a person you love or a possession you prize, yesterday's rapture or today's applause—you have to move on. Essential to the human pilgrimage, to the Christian journey, is a self-emptying more or less like Christ's own emptying: Time and again, from womb to tomb, you have to let go. And to let go is to die a little. It's painful, it can be bloody; and so we hang on, clutch our yesterdays like Linus' blanket, refuse to grow.

But no, it will not do—especially for a Christian. You are commanded to let go. Not invited—commanded: "Follow me!" It is a risky thing, this letting go of yesterday, if only because you cannot be certain where it will lead, except that the journey is in the tracks of one who laid aside his divine glory to clothe himself in our flesh, let go of Nazareth and his mother, the hill of Transfiguration *and* the garden of Gethsemane, the sinners he had touched with his forgiveness and that unpredictable band of mixed-up apostles—let go of the very miracle of being alive.

The comforting thing, the thrilling thing, is that you let go for a purpose. Emptying, dying, is not its own end. You let go of yesterday because only by letting go, only by reaching out into a shadowed future, can you grow into Christ, grow in loving communion with God, with the crucified images of God, with the breath-taking beauty of God's creation.

Only by dying, not only to sin but to yourself, can you come fully to life. You don't *forget* your yesterdays; they are part of who you are today. You simply refuse to live in them, to wallow in them, to pretend that there, in some near or distant yesterday, there life reached its peak or died its death.

No, good friends, die a little, to live more richly. Let your yesterdays be yesterdays, the joys and the sorrows, so that *today* you may listen to the Lord's voice (cf. Ps 95:7), receive his flesh and blood for *today's* food and drink, go out to a little acre of God's world where anguished women and men need so badly a Christian who has died to sin and self, who lives to God and for others . . . today.

For your Lenten penance, please . . . let go!

III

For your Lenten penance, laugh! In the famous Abbey of Lérins, on an island off the southeast coast of France, there is an unusual sculpture. It may go back to the 12th century, and it has for title *Christ souriant,* "The Smiling Christ." Jesus is imprisoned on the cross; his head is leaning somewhat to the right; his eyes are closed—in death, I think; but on his lips is a soft, serene smile.

Now the Gospels never say that Jesus smiled or laughed, as they twice testify that he wept—over Jerusalem and Lazarus, over his city and his friend. But I do not understand how one who was like us in everything save sin could have wept from sorrow but not laughed for joy. How could he fail to smile when a child cuddled comfortably in his arms, or when the maître d' at Cana wondered where the good wine had come from, or when he saw little Zacchaeus up a tree, or when Jairus' daughter wakened to life at his touch, or when Peter put his foot in his mouth once again? I refuse to believe that he did not laugh when he saw something funny, or when he experienced in the depths of his manhood the presence of his Father.

But granted that Jesus smiled, is there room for the smiling Christ these 40 days? Yes, but only if in Lent you refuse to pretend. In Lent you dare not make believe that Christ is not yet risen, that you have to wait for Easter to enjoy his rising. Even in Lent you and I are *risen* Christians. Oh yes, during these weeks we re-present the stages of our Lord's journey to Jerusalem, his way to the cross; but we do it as risen Christians. That means we do right to reproduce in our own Lent, on our own cross, the smiling Christ of Lérins. The cross is victory, not defeat; and we need not wait for that victory, wait for Easter to dawn.

But we cannot pretend the other way either. Simply because we have risen with Christ in baptism, we cannot make believe that Lent is unreal. Risen we are, but not yet *fully* risen. That is why we must ceaselessly reproduce Jesus' journey to Jerusalem, not only in liturgy but in our flesh and bones. That is why our laughter is not yet full-throated, why it is often through tears that we smile, why we still pray "Father . . . remove this cup from me" (Lk 22:42). We have not been transformed completely into the risen Christ; that transformation will take place only if we go up to Jerusalem with Jesus. The smiling Christ rests on a cross.

Is Lent for laughing or for crying? I say, for both. But I am stressing the laughter of Lent because it is so far removed from our spirituality. It is almost as hard to find a smiling Christian on Good Friday as it is to find a smiling Christ in crucifixion art. Little wonder we have the philosopher Nietzsche's cutting critique of Christians: You "do not look redeemed."

How look redeemed? I suggest that you give up something tastier than nachos, smokier than Kents, perhaps more destructive than sin. I mean an absorption in yourself—where you take yourself all too seriously, where the days and nights revolve around *you*. I ask you to see yourself as you really are: a creature wonderfully and fearfully made, a bundle of paradoxes and contradictions. You believe and doubt, hope and despair, love and hate. You are exciting and boring, enchanted and disillusioned, manic and depressive. You are "cool" on the outside and you hurt within. You feel bad about feeling good, are afraid of your joy, feel guilty if you don't feel guilty. You are trusting and suspicious, selfless and selfish, wide-open and locked in. You know so much and so little. You are honest and still play games. Aristotle said you are a rational animal; I say you are an angel with an incredible capacity for beer!

If it is the incongruous, what does not fit, that makes for humor, you can indeed smile at yourself. St. Ignatius Loyola has a rule for Jesuits: Our "whole countenance should reflect cheerfulness rather than sadness." If *we* don't obey Ignatius, you should!

Your smile will turn to lusty laughter if you only realize how lovable you are. Not because of anything you've made of yourself, but because God loves you, because God died for you, because God lives in you . . . now.

Then, with your new-found delight in yourself, minister the smiling Christ to others. Not far from you is someone who is afraid and needs your courage; or lonely and needs your presence; or hurt and needs your healing. So many feel unloved and need your touching, are old and need to feel that you care. Many are weak in so many ways and need for support your own shared weakness. You will rarely know greater happiness than when through you a smile is born on the face of someone in pain; you will have given birth to a smiling Christ.

Christianity needs men and women who repent of their smallness, fast from their selfishness, abstain from isolation. Lent calls for risen Christians, men and women like the hero of Eugene O'Neill's *Lazarus Laughed*—the Lazarus who has tasted death and sees it for what it is, whose joy in living is irresistible, whose invitation to the world is his infectious cry:

> Laugh with me!
> Death is dead!
> Fear is no more!
> There is only life!
> There is only laughter![5]

Unreal? In a sense—when you look at the Middle East, Northern Ireland, Southeast Asia; when you touch bellies bloated with hunger or shriveled from cancer. But where does the Christian start—start to overcome fear and death? Here, right where you are; now, not after Easter. By bringing the smiling Christ, the joy of Jesus, to one man, woman, or child reliving his passion. Who knows? It just might be your own healing, your own salvation.

At any rate, if the crucified Christ can look redeeming, the crucified Christian can at least look redeemed. For your Lenten penance, therefore, please . . . look . . . redeemed! For your Lenten penance, please . . . laugh!

Dahlgren Chapel
Georgetown University
and
Holy Trinity Church
Washington, D.C.
February 19, 1989

5
EXPLAIN YOURSELF, FATHER!
Fourth Sunday of Lent (C)

- Joshua 5:9a, 10–12
- 2 Corinthians 5:17–21
- Luke 15:11–32

You have just heard perhaps the greatest short-short story of all time, from the lips of surely the greatest storyteller of all time. Rembrandt has painted it, Balanchine choreographed it, Prokofiev set it to music, Nietzsche philosophized about it. But it's not just a great story, a superb piece of fiction, of which William Faulkner or Flannery O'Connor or J. D. Salinger might well be envious. Here is the gospel of Jesus Christ in a nutshell; this is what God's Son took flesh to do; here is your Christian hope. Sound exaggerated? Then muse with me on (1) the parable itself, (2) its Christian significance, (3) your response and mine.

I

First, the parable itself, with a bit of embellishment by Burghardt.[1] The first character on stage is a lad just out of his teens. His father is well off; not a Donald Trump, still he owns a large farm or at least lots of land. But the youngster is restless, unhappy at home. It's Dullsville, and he craves action, a few fleshpots. So he asks and gets his share of the property—by Palestinian custom, one third. He converts it into cash, gets as far over the border as he can. He squanders his money in lewd living. How lewd? Jesus does not say, but the lad's older brother will complain later that he spent a good bit in "the best little whorehouse"[2] outside Palestine. Down to his last shekel, he is hit by a famine. In desperation, he hires out to a Gentile, who sets him to the

29

ultimate in degradation: a Jew feeding pigs! Remember the rabbinic saying, "Cursed be the man who raises pigs. . . ."[3] He sinks so low that he longs to fill his belly with what the swine are swilling; but hogfood disgusts him, and no one will give him anything else.

Now he comes to his senses. Not simply because he's flat broke and starving, and the cuisine is more savory back home. He wakes up to what he has done, what he has become, and he is filled with remorse. "I shall . . . go to my father and say to him: 'Father, I have sinned against God and against you; I no longer deserve to be called your son; treat me as one of your hired hands' " (Lk 15:18–19); let me work for you as a day laborer.

Back he goes. Enter character number 2, head of the house. He spies his son while the lad is still a good ways away. Does he rock in his rocker, clamp down on his cheroot, nod knowingly: "Well, well, well —the kid's back. I always knew if he got hungry enough he'd come crawling back to the old man. Now let him squirm"? No. Compassion fills his heart; he runs to meet his son, runs as fast as his varicose veins will let him. The prodigal can hardly get his apology out. His father hugs him, kisses him, not just in welcome but in tearful forgiveness, as once King David kissed Absalom (2 Sam 14:33). Treat him like a hired hand? Not on your life! Treat him like an honored guest. Dress him in a Burberry suit, a Hermes tie, Gucci shoes. Phone the neighbors and get a party started.

Out in the fields, sweating with a vengeance, is character number 3, son number one. Coming to the house, he cannot believe his ears: dance music from the Sinai Show Stoppers. He summons a servant boy: "What in God's name is going on?" The boy tells him. He's outraged. A party for the prodigal, the lazy lout who washed his hands of the estate, who treated his dad like dirt, the sexed-up neurotic who fornicated a third of the family's fortune? His father comes out, pleads with him to join the party. "No, sir; not on your life. Frankly, I'm mad as hell. Here I've been slaving for you ever since I grew muscles, never disregarded a single command of yours. Have you ever thrown a party for me? What kind of father are you?" His father gently chides him: "Son, you are always with me. All that I have is yours. But your brother—yes, he's been stupid, he's sinned against God and against me; he's been as good as dead. But, son, your brother has come alive again; he's changed; he's a man now, a new man. Why shouldn't we make merry?"

Did the elder brother ever join the party? We'll never know. But I can imagine him sulking on a post fence, nursing a bitter Bud Light, hearing the heavy metal and resenting every single note.

II

My second point: What is the Christian significance of the parable, its religious meaning? To grasp that, you must grasp what is somewhat hidden: Who is the leading man in the story, the main character? No, not the prodigal son. In neon lights is the father. For before all else the parable preaches a striking set of truths about God. Three truths in particular.

1) Our God is not a God of vengeance, waiting to pounce on you as soon as you stray from the straight and narrow. Our God exemplifies to the nth degree what you would expect of a father or mother. Do you remember how the Israelites in bondage cried in anguish, "The Lord has forsaken me, my Lord has forgotten me"? Do you recall the Lord's reply? "Can a woman forget her sucking child, that she should have no compassion on the son of her womb? Even these may forget, yet I will not forget you. Behold, I have graven you [like a tattoo] on the palms of my hands" (Isa 49:14–16). Do you imagine that God's own Son took your flesh to wreak vengeance on it? He could have done that from outer space. Can you conceive that he was joking when he murmured through crucified lips, "Father, forgive them" (Lk 23:34)? The primary principle of the parable is crucial for your Christianity: God loves the sinner while he or she is still a sinner!

2) Not only does God forgive; God takes the initiative, the first step, in forgiveness. God doesn't wait, aloof and aloft in solitary splendor, stroking a gray beard like a shrewd psychiatrist, till you come to your senses. Your Father runs to meet you. Before you can actually say "I have sinned against you," God who knows your heart kisses you in forgiveness, dresses you in new garments of innocence, throws a party for you among the angels. For, in our Lord's own assurance, "there is joy before the angels of God over one sinner who repents" (Lk 15:10).

3) A truth as consoling as it is frightening: Unless God took the initiative, the first step, in forgiveness, you could never come to God. Here the parable could be misleading. You cannot decide all by yourself, "This life of sin is for the pigs; I'm hurrying home." What makes it possible for you and me to crawl out of the pigpen, to eat the Bread of angels, is God's love. Without that we're dead, and we would stay

dead. We did not ask the Son of God to hide his glory in our feeble flesh. We did not ask the earthly Christ to wean us from sin by a bloody cross. We did not ask the risen Christ to keep interceding for us with his Father till time is no more. It's all God's own wild idea. But unless Christ had done all this, if he did not continue to draw us by his love, you and I would still be lusting for the carob pods of pigs.

III

Finally, what might our response be? Actually, I cannot speak for you. Your best bet is to listen to the Lord; for the best of Burghardt is not necessarily the cream of Catholicism. I can only tell you what *I* have learned for my own life.

Lesson number 1: I have learned, slowly yes, to relate to God as my loving Father. (By the way, if the word "Father" sticks in your throat, prevents your profiting from the parable, then whenever I say "Father" you may murmur "Mother"; the First Person of the Trinity is not a male—nor a female.) What does "loving Father" mean to me? Several things. My God is not the God of the Deists, a cold Creator who shaped the world and then let us go our merry way, uncaring, unheeding, unhelpful, waiting for us to appear before Him for just judgment. He is, as I pray each day, "our Father." Not just the Father of Jesus Christ; our Father. My Father. In God's sight I am not a faceless cipher; I am unique. I was shaped by a Father's eternal love, reshaped by His Son's crucified love.

True, I cannot explain Him. Somehow He lets things happen I would not expect of a father: a devastating earthquake in Soviet Armenia, infants starving in Ethiopia, two world wars, a unique Holocaust that gassed six million Jews, schizophrenia and Alzheimer's and AIDS. But neither can I explain why He sent His own Son to die for me, why He still cares for me when I say no to His love, why He wants me to share His life for ever.

My response is no longer "Explain yourself, Father! Tell me, in simple monosyllables, how you can be God and let the innocent suffer, the wicked prosper!" For all my problems with God, God does not sit in a D.C. court cringing under the whiplash of Judge Burghardt. "If you can justify your actions and your omissions, then I shall treat you like a father. If you cannot, I shall put you away from me till you repent." Hogwash! I begin with my basic belief: God is Love. Without that, the whole Christian edifice crumbles. I begin not with a question but with an act of trust—the same trust a Godforsaken Christ forced through parched lips: "Father, into your hands I entrust my spirit" (Lk 23:46). The movement is not from knowledge to love; the movement is from love to knowledge. The more I love God, the better will I know God.

Lesson number 2: I have learned, through years of experience, not to play the elder brother. (Here too, if the word "brother" sticks in your throat, then whenever I say "brother" you may substitute "sister"; God won't mind.) Yes, the elder brother will get to heaven all right. After all, he's done everything his father has told him to do. What's left? A little item called mercy. He wants his kid brother to get what he deserves: strict justice. He sinned; give him the wages of sin: death. A touch of capital punishment.

I have learned not to resent the Mafia-type who has mangled most of the Commandments and with a fatal bullet in his hairy chest makes a perfect act of contrition. I no longer turn up my nose at "foxhole Christians," those who cry to God in desperation, whether in war or final exams. I refuse to judge "born-again Christians," Pentecostals, store-front religions. I can even live with Jimmy Swaggart's tears on TV. Why? Because I know from my own life that God's mercy is limitless, not bounded by our myopia.

I rejoice that my heavenly Father does not treat me as I deserve. I laugh in gladness when Christ leaves the 99 righteous and goes looking for me. I thank the Lord that a single sincere expression of sorrow out of love can set me right with God again.

Lesson number 3: Of the three personae in the parable, I identify best with the prodigal. Not that I've had his brand of fun or landed in his pigpen. Rather because I recognize in him, far more than in his brother, our human condition. For all our apparent strength, of ourselves we are frail creatures. We chafe under restrictions, rebel against authority, sulk when slighted, go off into our own far countries. We take our Father all too lightly, give Him the time left over from more important events, even leave His house, the Church, when we don't like what's going on. We toy with temptations, but only when they're attractive. We can be awfully small, self-centered, disagreeable. At times we come slinking back, embarrassed, to our Father: "I have sinned against heaven, against you." If you've never experienced any of this, please write me about it!

But this I have learned above all: The prodigal's "I have sinned" is not just an admission of guilt, it's an act of love. The prodigal could just as effectively have said, "Father, I love you." If sin is rejection, repentance is acceptance: I accept God's love for me, and I return love for love.

Several months ago, on the West Coast, a Jesuit priest I had taught died. Died in agony. Died of AIDS. Several years ago he told his people publicly that he had contracted AIDS from sex with a homosexual; he asked their forgiveness. Many a Catholic was scandalized that this prodigal had made so public a confession; others were shocked that he was allowed to continue ministering to God's people. Are *you*?

Dahlgren Chapel
Georgetown University
and
Holy Trinity Church
Washington, D.C.
March 5, 1989

6
WHO IS IT THAT STRUCK YOU?
Passion/Palm Sunday (A)

- Isaiah 50:4–7
- Philippians 2:6–11
- Matthew 26:14—27:66

During World War I, a British Episcopalian minister composed a poem he entitled "Indifference." Terribly forceful in its very simplicity, the poem ran like this:

> When Jesus came to Golgotha,
>   They hanged him on a tree.
> They drove great nails through hands and feet,
>   And made their Calvary.
> They crowned him with a crown of thorns;
>   Red were his wounds and deep.
> For those were crude and cruel days,
>   And human flesh was cheap.
>
> When Jesus came to Birmingham,
>   They simply passed him by;
> They never hurt a hair of him;
>   They only let him die.
> For men had grown more tender;
>   They would not cause him pain.
> They only passed him down the street,
>   And left him in the rain.
>
> Still Jesus cried, "Forgive them,
>   For they know not what they do!"
> And still it rained a winter rain
>   That drenched him through and through.

> The crowds went home and left the streets
>   Without a soul to see,
> And Jesus crouched against a wall
>   And cried for Calvary.[1]

To open this sacred week, let me unfold my thoughts in three stages: (1) the cross on Calvary, (2) the cross erected over history, (3) the cross in your life and mine.

I

First, the cross on Calvary. I shall not dwell on the distressing details of our Lord's passion. You know them all too well: the bloody sweat in Gethsemane and the bloodless kiss of Judas, Caiaphas blasting Jesus for blasphemy and Pilate washing his hands of him, a murderer released in his stead and a crowd clamoring for crucifixion, the whips lashing his back and the thorns piercing his brow, the cross on his shoulder and his shoulders on the cross, the darkness that covered the earth and the darkness in Jesus' soul, the last loud cry to heaven: "Father, into your hands I entrust my spirit" (Lk 23:46).

I shall not dwell on these because, believe it or not, there is something more important, a vexing three-letter word: Why? Why? St. Paul phrased the answer in two momentous monosyllables: ". . . the Son of God loved me and gave himself for me" (Gal 2:20). For me. Everybody can repeat those words: Adam and Abraham, Mary and Judas, Attila the Hun and Hitler of the Holocaust, Henry the Eighth and Joan of Arc, Mother Teresa and the Reverend Moon . . . you and I.

But the question persists: Why me? St. Paul saw the problem: "While we were yet helpless, at the right time Christ died for the ungodly. Why, one will hardly die for a righteous man or woman—though perhaps for a good person one will dare even to die. But God shows His love for us in that while we were yet sinners Christ died for us" (Rom 5:6–8). God's love for us. The evangelist John expressed it in unforgettable phrases: "God so loved the world that He gave His only Son, that whoever believes in him should not perish but have eternal life" (Jn 3:16).

But what is so lovable about us sinful folk that the Son of God should take our flesh from a Jewish girl, touch our earth in a stable, walk our dust for three decades, sweat our sweat, and die our death?

Nothing we have made of ourselves. Left to ourselves, to naked human nature, we would have to agree with poet Francis Thompson's "Hound of Heaven":

> "Strange, piteous, futile thing!
> Wherefore should any set thee love apart?
> . . . Thou knowest not
> How little worthy of any love thou art!
> Whom wilt thou find to love ignoble thee
> Save Me, save only Me?"[2]

Why God should love any of us, why God should love sinners, love men and women who reject God with a curse or pass God "down the street," is hidden ultimately in the mystery that is God. Oh yes, we can speculate, surmise, imagine. Perhaps God, looking on Adam and Eve exiled from Eden, saw traces of the man and woman He had shaped in the image of divinity, had made like God. Perhaps. But whatever drew God's love, it does not explain why the Son of God drew our love by crucifixion. He could have saved us in so many simpler, bloodless ways: a single breath of Bethlehem's breeze, the hidden years in backwater Nazareth, his baptism by John, his compassionate "Your sins are forgiven you," the kiss of Judas, one soldier's slap of his cheek. Any one of these would have been enough.

Then why Calvary? Frankly, we do not know. And we do not know because we cannot fathom three slender syllables in the First Letter of John: "God is Love" (1 Jn 4:8). God not only loves; God *is* Love. That alone begins to make some sense out of Calvary, out of a God-man pinned to a cross for sinners, for you and me. All through human history love has made sacrifices beyond the power of sheer intelligence to grasp. Out of love our father in faith, Abraham, was willing to sacrifice his only son, Isaac. What Calvary tells us is that God will not be outdone even in sacrifice, that even God can sacrifice His only Son.

Don't ask, "Why me?" If God offers you crucified love, offers God's Son on a cross for you, the least you can do is accept it. Welcome the mystery and move on from there.

II

The cross on Calvary moves me to the cross erected over history.[3] You see, the cross on which Christ hung did not disappear after Joseph of Arimathea took his body down from it. I do not mean that those two beams of wood were actually rediscovered; the stories surrounding such rediscovery[4] belong to legend. I mean rather that crucifixion, mental and physical anguish, is writ large over human existence and that it calls for a Christian response.

I am not bringing you news when I contend that crucifixion is woven into the very texture of human living. In large ways and small. Newsprint spells it out for you each day, TV flashes it before your eyes: the Hammer and Sickle poised over Lithuania; Christians at one another's throats in the north of Ireland; apartheid in South Africa; Latin America living in degradation, wallowing in Third World debt; six Jesuits brutally murdered in El Salvador; one in four American children growing up below the poverty line; the plague of AIDS racking untold thousands; drugs and alcohol destroying minds and bodies; black and white sundered in hostility and hate; all our ills from stroke through cancer to schizophrenia; and hovering over each one of us, the spectre of death.

So what? On broad lines, two reactions—not somewhere in outer space, but right here on our fragile earth. For some, all that I have described is simply fact, ills that flesh is heir to. We are born as and when chance would have it. If we are lucky, happiness attends most of our days; if not, tough apples: "Grin and bear it." And sooner or later we die—swiftly or slowly.

For others, things are more complex: God enters the picture. A God who is a question or an answer, a problem or a solution. In the Christian vision, basic to human crucifixion is a striking sentence in St. Paul's letter to the Christians of Colossae in Asia Minor: "I rejoice in my sufferings for your sake, and in my flesh I complete what is lacking in Christ's afflictions for the sake of his body, that is, the Church" (Col 1:24).[5] Not that the work of Christ was somehow insufficient to redeem the world from sin. Rather that the passion of Christ is not instant salvation, heaven for the asking no matter how we live; his suffering must be shared by all who claim the name Christian. All of us can apply to ourselves what Jesus said to the two discouraged disciples on the way to Emmaus after the crucifixion: "Was it not necessary that the Christ should suffer these things and [so] enter into his glory?" (Lk 24:26). That is why Paul can speak of himself as "always carrying in the body the death of Jesus, so that the life of Jesus may also be manifested in our bodies" (2 Cor 4:10).

For the Christian, pain, agony, anguish, grief is not something we sheerly suffer because there is no relief save aspirin or morphine,

sleep or suicide. In our sin-stained situation suffering is indeed here
to stay. But in our redeemed reality the cross erected over history
need not be waste. If Calvary reveals anything, it declares the central
Christian paradox: From death springs life. Not only from Christ's
dying; from our own dying from womb to tomb. No, I cannot explain
infant stomachs shriveled from starvation in the sub-Sahara, innocent
newborns ravaged by AIDS, the bad things that happen to good people. But as a Christian, I must believe that there is no human torment
that cannot be touched to the cross of Christ, no death that does not
bring life, if only Christians carry in their bodies the death of Jesus.
More profoundly than author Antoine de Saint-Exupéry intended,
there is no pain, no passion, that does not radiate to the ends of
the earth.

III

This leads to my third point: the cross in your life and mine. I
suggest that there are two ways in which Jesus comes not to Calvary,
not to Birmingham, but to our home town—where we live and move
and have our being. Correspondingly, two ways in which we can crucify Christ again. Two ways that summon up the cynical question lev-
eled at a blindfolded Christ, "Who is it that struck you?" (Mt 27:68;
Lk 22:64). Two ways we can pass Christ "in the rain." Two ways we can
reveal crucifying indifference.

The first is my approach to my own suffering. From the acne of
the adolescent to the Alzheimer's of the aging, how do I look at the
ailments that do or might afflict me? Do I simply endure them like an
ancient Athenian Stoic, conforming myself to a relentless destiny? Do
I avoid pain like the plague—not only the infirmities of the flesh but
suffering of the spirit as well? Is disease for me an enemy, death the
archenemy?

Understand me. I am not condemning tylenol or naprosyn, colo-
noscopy or the CAT scan, chemotherapy or heart transplants. Health
is a gift; God expects us to nurture it; a high-octane body can build the
kingdom. I am concerned about an unchristian mind-set where suffering is severed from spirituality, where sickness is never a grace, where
the ailing are always to be pitied. I mean a mind-set where suffering is
not sanctified because it is not linked to the nailed hands of Christ.

No, good friends, to follow Christ, to be his disciple, is to share
not only the joy he promised "no one will take from you" (Jn 16:22)

but the cross he said you must "take up" if you are to be worthy of him (Mt 10:38). You don't have to search for it; it hangs over you.

The second way we can pass Christ "in the rain" is to pass by his crucified images, those he called "the least of my brothers and sisters" (Mt 25:40, 45).[6] Not that Christ is to be found only in the hungry or the thirsty, only in the stranger and the naked, only in the sick and the imprisoned. Rather that these needy image more obviously the help-less Christ of Calvary. To be a genuine disciple of Jesus is to be pro-foundly engaged with the mystery of the cross, and that mystery is, as Jesus put it, a life given in "ransom" for others (Mt 20:28; Mk 10:45).[7] I am not a genuine disciple of Jesus if, like Luke's priest on the Jericho road, I see a human "half dead" and "pass by on the other side" (Lk 10:30–31).

Let me close with a true story. It is the story of a lady who linked her sufferings to Christ and to the poor of Christ.[8] Penny Lernoux was a Catholic journalist who moved from observer-reporter to an impassioned advocate for the underprivileged, the impoverished, the degraded and desperate of Latin America. The church of the poor was no longer simply an important story; it became the focus of her faith and professional life. She wrote courageously of courageous people. In the ugly class conflict that is Latin America she took sides —with the poor. Her books, like *Cry of the Poor*,[9] detailed the ways powerful people and institutions oppress the powerless of that conti-nent. She documented U.S.-supported persecution, examined the weight of foreign debt on the poor, looked critically at questionable Vatican policies. She not only wrote of suffering; she suffered with those of whom she wrote.

In early September 1989 Penny discovered she had cancer. The primary cancer was in her lungs, but it spread into her bones and liver. Chemotherapy did not help. Two weeks before her death she wrote:

> I feel like I'm walking down a new path. It's not physical fear or fear of death, because the courageous poor in Latin America have taught me a theology of life that, through solidarity and our com-mon struggle, transcends death. Rather, it is a sense of helplessness —that I who always wanted to be the champion of the poor am just as helpless—that I, too, must hold out my begging bowl; that I must learn—am learning—the ultimate powerlessness of Christ. It is a cleansing experience. So many things seem less important, or not at all, especially the ambitions.[10]

On October 8, one month after the dread diagnosis, Penny Lernoux died. As we enter this sacred week, let us pray that we too may come to sense deep within us the helplessness of Christ, the helplessness of so many Christs, and ultimately our own helplessness with Christ. For therein lies our salvation. Then never again will I have to ask in fear, "O Christ, who is it that struck you?" It's too close to Judas' question, "Is it I, Master?" (Mt 26:25).

Sage Chapel
Cornell University
Ithaca, New York
April 8, 1990

Easter

7
BORN ANEW TO A LIVING HOPE
Second Sunday of Easter (A)

- Acts 2:42–47
- 1 Peter 1:3–9
- John 20:19–31

One of the most moving Gospel stories after the crucifixion tells of two of Jesus' disciples walking the seven miles from Jerusalem to Emmaus. They are two sad sacks; Calvary is all too vivid in their memories. Jesus joins them, but they do not recognize him. Asked why so depressed, they recount gloomily how this "prophet mighty in deed and word before God and all the people" (Lk 24:19) was condemned to death and crucified. "But we had hoped that he was the one to redeem Israel" (v. 21).

"We had hoped. . . ." That epitaph on human hopes echoes down the ages—over tombstones and ambitions, over dashed desires and wasted flesh: "We had hoped." In harmony with this Easter season, let me develop three related ideas: (1) the hopelessness that overshadows human hearts, (2) the hope that rose from Calvary's rock, (3) the challenge to you and me. Put differently, I shall speak successively of today, of yesterday, of tomorrow.

I

I begin with today, with hopelessness. By hopelessness I mean an absence of genuine hope. Here I limit myself to four threats to hope. First, psychiatrists report that many men and women today are suffering from an unconscious despair.[1] Why? They are afraid—afraid they are becoming an appendage to, a subordinate part of, the machine. They sense that we have less and less to say about our destiny, about how we live and what we shall become. Beneath this unrest lies a profound fear: Some day technological progress may annihilate our species. Sheer survival is a problem, is questionable. Why? Because we seem incapable of controlling the technology we have created. Look back on Hiroshima and the Holocaust; look now at our air polluted and our waters poisoned, acid rain and global warming; look ahead to the threat of a nuclear winter.

A second threat to hope is our conscious fears. So many are afraid of growing old. Not only firm flesh yielding to telltale wrinkles, not only sex "not what it used to be." More fearful still, fear that I will change inside, lose a high-paying job, be forced to retire, see my nearest and dearest die, be babied or bullied in a nursing home, endure a long-drawn-out and painful illness, be unable to "do" anything, to be productive. There is fear of God's anger over my sinfulness—the fear that my sin is too great to be forgiven. And there is death itself: How can I face it?

A third threat to hope stems from scientists. Not science, not even all scientists. But read a Nobel Prize winner, geneticist Jacques Monod. In his best seller *Chance and Necessity*[2] he proclaims that science has finally shown that human effort is meaningless. What you and I do is no more significant than what the legendary King Sisyphus of Corinth was condemned to do in the lower world. Over and over again he had to keep pushing a huge rock up a hill, only to have it immediately roll down into the valley. For such as Monod, the human species is a freak, a product of pure chance. It is time for men and women to realize that, like gypsies, they live "on the boundary of an alien world. A world that is deaf to [their] music, just as indifferent to [their] hopes as it is to [their] suffering or [their] crimes."

A fourth threat to hope distresses me mightily. You see, I am not unflappable; I can be disturbed. Not only by nuclear research in Iraq and summary execution in Iran; not only by inhuman apartheid in South Africa and unchristian warfare in Northern Ireland; not only by crack across my city and "heavy metal" on my campus. On another level, I am perturbed by a mushrooming mind-set among Christians. Increasingly I hear and read that it doesn't really matter much whether there is life after death. Perhaps there is, but there's no proof of it. These Christians—Catholics among them—remind me of an Old Testament author who reflects the skeptical side of Israelite wisdom: "There is nothing better for a man [or woman] than to eat and drink, and find enjoyment in his [or her] work. This also, I saw, is from the hand of God. . . . [But] who knows whether the spirit of man [or woman] goes upward and the spirit of the beast goes down to the earth?" (Qoh 3:22, 21).[3]

II

Those four threats to hope today draw me back to yesterday, compel my second point: the genuinely Christian counterpole to unconscious despair over technology, to that host of conscious fears, to the charge that life is meaningless, to the mind-set that eternal life really doesn't matter. It was proclaimed to you short moments ago, the mind-shivering Easter affirmation from the First Epistle of Peter. Listen to it again, this time with Easter ears:

> Blessed be the God and Father of our Lord Jesus Christ! By His great mercy we have been born anew to a living hope through the resurrection of Jesus Christ from the dead, and to an inheritance which is imperishable, undefiled, and unfading, kept in heaven for you, who by God's power are guarded through faith for a salvation ready to be revealed in the last time. In this you rejoice, though now for a little while you may have to suffer various trials, so that the genuineness of your faith, more precious than gold which though perishable is tested by fire, may redound to praise and glory and honor at the revelation of Jesus Christ. Without having seen him you love him; though you do not now see him you believe in him and rejoice with unutterable and exalted joy, obtaining as the outcome of your faith the salvation of your souls.
>
> (1 Pet 1:3–9)

Here is the heart of the Christian mystery: "By [God's] great mercy we have been born anew to a living hope through the resurrection of Jesus Christ from the dead" (v. 3). It begins with resurrection. St. Paul put it pungently: "If Christ has not been raised, your faith is futile and you are still in your sins. If for this life only we have hoped in Christ, we are of all men and women most to be pitied" (1 Cor 15:17, 19).

Make no mistake. If Jesus did not really come back to life, forget it! Go home, turn on the Movie Channel, revel in violence or sex or whatever turns you on. But don't waste your time on a Christ who simply lives in our memories, simply in our hearts, simply in a picture frame. That Christ deserves to stay dead.

No, our Christ is alive. Alive now. More alive that you and I have ever been. Alive in his Godhead and in the humanity God's Son borrowed from us for ever. Alive for us, for you and me; alive for what the Letter of Peter calls a rebirth. What does it mean to be "born anew"? Basically, it means you have a new life. You know what it means, what it feels like, to be humanly alive. You can think, shape an idea, argue a point, listen to Mozart or Michael Jackson. You can do things. I mean, you can work and play, dance and sing, laugh and cry, walk on the beach or sway to aerobics.

Something similar happens when you are gifted with new life in Christ. You can believe what passes proof. I mean, you can take God's word for it that God loves you and lives in you, that God died for you and rose for you, that life does not end at 40 or 90, that death is a prelude to life without end. And you can do things not possible unless Christ had died and risen for you. You can love God more intensely than man ever loved woman, love your sisters and brothers as Jesus himself loves them. Take Jesus' word for it: "If you have faith as a grain of mustard seed, you will say to this mountain, 'Move hence to yonder place,' and it will move; and nothing will be impossible to you" (Mt 17:20).

Briefly, in that extraordinary sentence proclaimed to you from the First Epistle of Peter, "Without having seen [Jesus] you love him; though you do not now see him you believe in him" (1 Pet 1:8). This is what it means to be alive in Christ. But the same letter trumpets not only faith and love; it claims "we have been born anew to a living hope" (v. 3). Not an Anglo-Saxon "stiff upper lip, old boy." No. Christian hope is a gift of God. Not wishful thinking: I hope Israel and the PLO can come to peaceful terms; I hope Washington will not be humid this summer; I hope I can combine a 4.0 with a "max" of Michelob. Christian hope is confident expectation—confidence that a God who is ceaselessly faithful despite my infidelities will always be there for me—will be there for me in the here-and-now, will be there for me in the hereafter. Such is the hope that marks a follower of Christ. Such is the hope that marked the earthly Jesus—a Jesus who was afraid, did not want to die, begged his Father in the garden of agony to take this cup from him: "Father, don't let me die!" Still, "not my will but thine be done" (Lk 22:42). And an angel came from his Father, gave him strength to carry his cross to Calvary, strength to murmur with parched lips to a Father who seemed to have forsaken him, "Into your hands I entrust my spirit" (Lk 23:46). Such is the hope that left Calvary's tomb empty.

III

Third, what of you and me, your fears and mine? What of tomorrow? The First Letter of John declares, "There is no fear in love, but perfect love casts out fear" (1 Jn 4:18). It's a fact: Perfect love can destroy all fear. You see it all through Christian history—from the original apostles leaving the threatening council "rejoicing that they were counted worthy to suffer dishonor for the name" (Acts 5:41), through Joan of Arc at the stake and Thomas More on the scaffold, to Mother Teresa and her 3000 Missionaries of Charity touching plague and AIDS with love. They are men and women who are afraid of nothing. Not that they are masochists, take pleasure in pain. Pain hurts them as much as it hurts us. But unreserved love enables them to put into everyday practice the promise of Paul, "God is faithful . . . will not let you be tried beyond your strength, but with the trial will also [enable you] to endure it" (1 Cor 10:13).

But I suspect that most Christians are not able to destroy all fear. Fear is instinctive, nestles in our bones, strikes when we least expect it. What then? Hope; Christian hope. With hope, you can cope, cope with fear. I mean, confront fear, eyeball to eyeball, live, even joyously, with your fears.

Let me be uncommonly honest. I am not running towards death with open arms; in fact, I'm dragging my feet. I cannot yet bring myself to echo St. Paul, "My desire is to depart [to die] and to be with Christ" (Phil 1:23). Why? Several reasons. I'm afraid of pain; I fear a lingering illness; I am morbidly mindful of my mother's six years in a nursing home—six years without memory, without mind. And I love this life so passionately that I resonate to poet Francis Thompson's "Hound of Heaven":

> . . . though I knew His love Who followed,
>   Yet was I sore adread
> Lest, having Him, I must have naught beside.[4]

Still, of one thing I am confident, that when illness and dying do strike, God will be there: a Father who is especially then a Mother, a Christ who rose from the rock for my resurrection, a Holy Spirit whose other name is Love.

As for you, Easter, the resurrection of Jesus, trumpets an incredibly consoling truth. Whoever you are, whatever your pain or problem, anxiety or affliction, frustration or failure, you need never despair. Not that pain will be converted into pleasure, problems conveniently solved, failure turn to instant success. Simply that the promise of Jesus can come true: "So you have sorrow now, but I will see you again and your hearts will rejoice, and no one will take your joy from you" (Jn 16:22).

I say the promise of Jesus *can* come true. For living hope is not something automatic: Press H on your computer and out comes

Christian hope. Hope was indeed infused in you when baptismal waters bathed your brow. But that gift has to grow, has to be nurtured like a delicate flower. And it grows best if your relationship to Jesus is the prayer lyricized in the musical *Godspell:* "This, Lord, I pray: to see you more clearly, love you more dearly, follow you more nearly." It is less than Christian to treat Christ only as a God of foxholes, a Savior of final exams, someone you can call on when living gets desperate, when human help is helpless. The God of your hope is deep inside you, closer to you than you are to yourself. To live with living hope is to live lovingly with the source of hope, the Jesus who died and rose precisely to give you hope.

In sum, good friends, I am simply stressing what is surely known to you intellectually but may not have gotten into your Christian guts. The hope we need to face up to our most profound fears is not in the power of man or woman to provide. I am not defaming the psychiatrist's couch or the philosopher's portico; these have proven their human value, can even help us become more Christian. But in the last analysis the hope you and I need to live like Christ is a gift of God, a gift that is actually part of our Christian make-up, a gift we paradoxical people leave untapped, allow to rust. The only remedy I know for such rusting is an injection of love. Get closer to Christ; rest, like the Beloved Disciple at the Last Supper, "close to the breast of Jesus" (Jn 13:23); humbly place in his hands your specific helplessness, your experience of hopelessness. Get closer to this earth's images of Christ, especially the hopelessly crucified; touch one of them in selfless love.

And so my Easter prayer for you is the prayer of Paul for the Christians of Rome: "May the God of hope fill you with all joy and peace in believing, so that by the power of the Holy Spirit you may abound in hope" (Rom 15:13).

Dahlgren Chapel
Georgetown University
and
Holy Trinity Church
Washington, D.C.
April 22, 1990

8
LET CHRIST EASTER IN US
Second Sunday of Easter (C)

- Acts 5:12–16
- Revelation 1:9–13, 17–19
- John 20:19–31

The Jesuit poet Gerard Manley Hopkins wrote an ambitious poem entitled "The Wreck of the Deutschland." It commemorates the quasi martyrdom of five Franciscan nuns drowned on the German ship *Deutschland* at the mouth of the Thames in the winter of 1875. One half-line especially intrigues me: "Let him easter in us."[1] Let Christ "easter" in us. A rare verb indeed, but it suits this sacred season, and it is the heart of my homily. How does Christ easter in us? In three wondrous ways: (1) By a faith that rises above doubt. (2) By a hope that conquers despair. (3) By a love that does justice. A word on each.

I

First, let Christ easter in you by faith. Here the unforgettable character is dear doubting Thomas. A paradoxical apostle. Before Calvary, instant loyalty. When Jesus was bent on going to Jerusalem, into the camp of his enemies, enemies threatening to stone him, then you heard Thomas blustering with bravado to his fellow apostles, "Let us also go, that we may die with him" (Jn 11:16). After Calvary, not nearly as loyal. Between Good Friday and Easter Sunday he apparently deserted the disciples—perhaps to drown his disappointment with some Manischewitz. The result? He missed the disciples' encounter with Jesus on Easter evening. And now, when the disciples shout at him, "We have seen the Lord," Thomas lays down nonnegotiable conditions on when he will believe: "Unless I see in his hands the print of the nails, and place my finger in the mark of the nails, and

51

place my hand in his side, I will not believe" (Jn 20:25). Jesus invites him to do just that. To his credit, Thomas adopts a hands-off policy. He simply exclaims, in Scripture's most startling act of faith, "My Lord and my God!" (v. 28).

"Why startling?" you ask. "What else could he do, with Jesus standing before him? Easy as breathing, with resurrection staring him in the face, wounds open for all to see." Not so fast! Remember the remark of St. Paul, "No one can say 'Jesus is Lord' except by the Holy Spirit" (1 Cor 12:3). Lazarus rose from the dead; Thomas did not cry, "My Lord and my God!" Thomas' confession a week after Easter went far beyond the evidence. His outburst is a gift—a gift only God can give. He addresses Jesus the way Israel addressed Yahweh. In the Gospel of John this is the climax of faith; to these five words the Gospel has been moving. Thomas speaks for the first Christian community.

And what of you? "Blessed are [you] who have not seen and yet believe" (Jn 20:29). What indeed have you seen? A wafer cradled in your palm or on your tongue—and you murmur, "Lord, I am not worthy to receive you." What have you seen? A bloodied body on twin beams of wood—and you cry with the centurion on Calvary, "Truly this was the Son of God" (Mt 27:54). What have you heard? Stories about angels and apostles, mysteries and miracles, prodigals and prostitutes, a crib and a cross—and you respond, "This is the Word of the Lord." An incredible gift. If ever you are tempted to think yourself nothing, a slimeball, stow it! You have become what Jesus asked of Thomas before all else, what Jesus enabled Thomas to become: "Become a believer" (Jn 20:27). A gift that is yours not because you are bold or beautiful, high or mighty, but only because God for some strange reason loved you with a lavish love.

Do you ever get doubts? If you're anything like me (a dreadful thought), probably you do. You're never too old to doubt. Every so often I wake at night and wonder how the Christian thing makes human sense. How a God can even be. How an all-powerful God who doesn't need me can wear my flesh. How a God-man can die for me, rise from death for me. How I can feed on his flesh and wet my lips with his blood. How I can share his life now. How I can possibly live for ever, in joy days without end. And I shiver, for it doesn't make human sense. All I can do is bend at my bed and beg with the father of the Gospel epileptic, "I believe; help my unbelief" (Mk 9:24). And, thank God, I do believe. Like Thomas, a leap in the dark—a leap that is God's gift to me.

Does science shake me, technology? At times. Till I remember that science is my servant, not my master. Till I remember that with my mind and heart I can do what a billion computer bytes can never do: I can touch God—as God has touched me. With my faith I need not envy *Discovery* on its flight to outer space. I can reach God—in an instant. And then I thank God—for the marvels of creation yes, but even more for my God. *My* God. Dear Christ, continue to easter in me.

II

Second, let Christ easter in you by hope. Here there is something basic you must get straight. Christian hope is not wishful thinking: I hope the Soviets will free their satellites; I hope my true love will come riding in on a white charger; I hope the Shi'ites will release the American hostages, the Ayatollah moderate his wrath against writer Rushdie, Botha grant equality to black South Africa, the Jesuits give Georgetown to Cardinal Ratzinger. Christian hope is clear, precise, unwavering. I firmly trust, I confidently expect, that God will give me all I need to live like Christ, all I need to die in the peace of Christ, all I need to enjoy God and my dear ones literally for ever.

To live like Christ. Aye, there's a tough one. Not only the quiet Christ of Nazareth, but the refugee Christ in Egypt. Not only the Christ who manufactures miracles, but the Christ whose relatives think him mad. Not only the Christ who strengthens the broken-hearted, but the Christ who cannot save himself when crucified. Not only the Christ who loves his mother, but the Christ who wills her to John on Calvary. Not only the Christ who multiplies bread so that others may eat, but the Christ who hungers in a desert, thirsts on a cross. I confidently expect that God will grace me with all the courage I need to live like him in a world where megabucks coexist with a billion hungry; where freedom rings while millions pine in political prisons; where you and I can joy in being alive while death stalks our streets, our children crash on crack and coke, and little but fear keeps the superpowers from nuking one another. To live like Christ in a world where I cannot promise myself that tomorrow will be as peaceful as today; where I just might, like my mother, lose my mind and my memory; where AIDS and cancer are everyday words; where a stroke can change my life in a split second.

Christ easters in me because I trust that, whatever happens, God still cares for me, God will always be there. Such trust is indeed Christ's resurrection gift to us—begun in baptismal water, fed with his flesh, recovered in the sacrament of reconciliation.

With the gift of hope, I confidently expect that I will die in God's peace. Death is not an event most of us care to dwell on. Frankly, I don't look forward to it. Every so often I resonate to what a respected medical doctor wrote in a respected medical journal: ". . . death is an insult; the stupidest, ugliest thing that can happen to a human being."[2] But I force myself to remember that death is more than doom. Death will be my final, most significant act of faith. Just as it was for Jesus—Jesus who died not with unassailable proof of resurrection but with hope, confident trust in his Father's love: "Father, into your hands I entrust my spirit" (Lk 23:46). With this prayer on my lips I hope to die.

With the gift of hope, I confidently trust that death is not an end but a fresh beginning. Christ easters in me whenever I proclaim the Preface of the Mass for the Dead: "For those who believe, life is not ended, life is merely changed." Is this your hope? Not a wistful wish—a confident conviction? It should be; for this is what Christ died and rose to give you. Otherwise you share the despair of the two disciples on the road to Emmaus after the crucifixion, lamenting to a Christ they did not recognize: "We had hoped. . . ." (Lk 24:21). No, we do hope—right now. We trust like crazy—because Christ risen from the dead easters in us.

III

Third, let Christ easter in you by love. Remember St. Paul's summary: "Faith, hope, love abide, these three; but the greatest of these is love" (1 Cor 13:13). Why the greatest? Paul again: "If I have all faith, so as to remove mountains, but have not love, I am nothing" (v. 2). And recall those frightening words in the New Testament Letter of James: "You believe that God is one; you do well. Even the demons believe—and shudder" (Jas 2:19). I can hope, trust confidently, that God will take care of me; but if I have not love, my confidence is not Christian hope but pagan presumption. Without love, faith is dead and hope is arrogance.

Here I concentrate on a love terribly concrete. I take for granted that Christ easters in you in that you love God more than anyone or anything on earth. Without that love, the first commandment God lays on you, you're in deep trouble. But I want to focus on the commandment Jesus claimed is "like" the first (Mt 22:39), the love that goes out to your less fortunate sisters and brothers, the love that does justice. Now the very power to love others as you love yourself is already within you. It came to you from Christ's rising from Calvary's rock, from your rising into Christ from the Church's font. The question is, are you using the power that lies within you?

I can recall no period of history when this gift you have has been more urgent. Each year the haves have more and the have-nots have less. Each year the AIDS-afflicted and the drug-addicted mushroom. Each night a billion so-called humans fall asleep hungry. Catholics and Protestants bloody one another in Northern Ireland, Palestinians and Israelis in the Middle East, blacks and whites in South Africa. Afghanistan, Iraq, Iran—all are bleeding from the wounds of war. Who knows how many millions are rotting in Soviet concentration camps? Our own D.C. is dividing up the turf for crack and coke. Terrorists hold airlines and countries hostage. And there is always the bloodless, hidden pain: the aging who feel unloved, the Alzheimer who knows not what the next moment will bring, the homeless who hope only for a warm grate.

How focus your love? Mull over Mother Teresa. Whether she is bouncing an abandoned baby in bomb-blasted Beirut or nursing a starving old man in Calcutta, her attitude is ever the same: The greater the need, the greater her love. A very practical love. Some years ago, when she visited Washington, a District official asked her rather skeptically how she expected to feed the thousands of hungry here. Her answer? "One by one."

Oh yes, think big, love large. Press the powerful on the Hill to humanize our horrifying housing, to crush the drug empire at its source, to bring the warring to peace tables, to treat refugees like people and not political footballs, to reverence the earth before it rises up to destroy us. But think small as well, love little. I mean, let your head, your hand, your heart go out to one man, one woman, one child who desperately needs what you have to give. It's Jesus all over again. While saving a world, he still had time for individuals: Peter's fevered mother-in law, Peter sinking beneath the waters, a hemorrhaging woman, a woman horribly crippled, a woman taken in adultery, an epileptic boy, a small child in his arms, a speechless demoniac, a blind man by the roadside, a rich young man lusting for life, a lifeless Lazarus, a dead 12-year-old, a mother burying her only son, a widow giving her last penny to the temple, Simon the leper, a robber crucified with him, his mother beneath his cross.

They're still out there, you know, closer than you realize. Sometimes they're sitting next to you, or lying wounded where you pass, mutely pleading for bread or a word, for justice or a smile, for some small sign that you care. Of one thing I can assure you: Rarely in your life will you experience such profound joy as when through you and your love a smile is born on a crucified face. It is then that Christ will easter in you as never before: when through you he easters in another.

Dahlgren Chapel
Georgetown University
and
Holy Trinity Church
Washington, D.C.
April 2, 1989

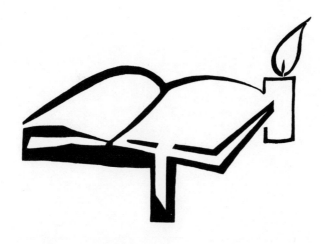

Ordinary
Time

Ordinary
Time

9

SET THE SPIDER WEB A-TREMBLE
Second Sunday of the Year (A)

- Isaiah 49:3, 5–6
- 1 Corinthians 1:1–3
- John 1:29–34

One of Cardinal John Henry Newman's many perceptive sermons is titled "The Religion of the Day."[1] In every Christian age, he observed, what he called "a religion of the world" has fastened on one or other characteristic of the gospel, and by neglecting the rest of Christian doctrine "has distorted and corrupted even that portion of it which it has exclusively put forward."[2] In a "rude and fierce" age, for example, what the world stressed was a religion of fear, to the neglect of a God of love. "Superstitions abounded, and cruelties. The noble firmness, the graceful austerity of the true Christian were superseded by forbidding spectres, harsh of eye, and haughty of brow; and these were the patterns or the tyrants of a beguiled people."[3]

In his own day, Newman noted, in the second half of the 19th century, "the world's religion has taken the brighter side of the Gospel,—its tidings of comfort, its precepts of love; all darker, deeper views of man's condition and prospects being comparatively forgotten."[4] What remained was "a religion *natural* to a civilized age." Its characteristics? A general decency and grace over the face of society; beauty and delicacy of thought; courteous manners; no pain or offense to anyone; vice was unseemly, "out of taste." Conscience, which tells of guilt and punishment, disappears, and with it Scripture's fearful images of divine wrath. "Every thing is bright and cheerful. Religion is pleasant and easy; benevolence is the chief virtue; intolerance, bigotry, excess of zeal, are the first of sins. Austerity is an absurdity. . . ."[5]

In line with today's Gospel (Jn 1:29–34), in line with John the Baptist's exclamation "Look! Here is the Lamb of God who takes away

59

the world's sin" (v. 29), I shall suggest that today's corruption of the gospel revolves around the word "sin." I shall argue, however, that the corruption is not all bad, because it has yielded a fresh facet of sin terribly neglected before our time. As usual, then, three stages to my homily, three questions: (1) What have we lost? (2) What have we gained? (3) Therefore what?

I

First, what is it we've lost? In my prolonged adolescence, in my seminary days, in my young years as a priest, a sense of sin pervaded Catholic existence. Confession was a must; a good many Catholics would not dream of receiving Communion without first going to confession. Our prayer books prepared us for confession with an extensive laundry list of sins. Nuns (none of whom can be held responsible for my warped psyche) impressed that list on our consciences. Parish retreats pictured the fiery effects of sin in hellish rhetoric. And high place among sins was held by that old devil sex.

In the turbulent 60s that sense of sin began to disappear. So much so that in 1973 a remarkable psychiatrist, Karl Menninger, wrote an unexpected book entitled *Whatever Became of Sin?*[6] Dr. Menninger was not afraid to speak of sin. He did not hesitate to quote the First Letter of John: "If we say we have no sin, we deceive ourselves, and the truth is not in us" (1:8). Not so for American Catholics on the whole.

Much of it was an understandable reaction. The word "sin" had exercised a tyranny over Catholic living. It had almost replaced "love" as the symbol of our Christianity. Our textbooks of morality spent far too much space arguing how many ounces of meat added up to a mortal sin on Friday; how much of Sunday Mass you could miss without having to go to another; how long a kiss might last before it entered the confessional.

The reaction made good Catholic sense. What did not make sense was the extreme to which we carried it. We put a basic Christian gospel on the back burner. Sin is part and parcel of our human make-up. Not that we are always sinning; not that we are dominated by sin. Only that the tendency to say no to God and neighbor, yes to self, did not wash out with our baptism. Only that hate and violence, lying and insider trading, whoring after another's wife or goods are not limited to pagans and Protestants. Only that, granted "guilt trips" keep psychiatrists in business, there are actions we *ought* to feel guilty about.

After all, if the seven deadly sins have disappeared from our memory, they have not fled from our lives. Catholics are still plagued by envy and anger, pride and lust, greed and gluttony, spiritual sloth. Nor do I believe St. Paul was speaking only to the Christians of Galatia when he warned against impurity and idol worship, selfishness and strife, dissension and drunkenness (cf. Gal 5:19–21).

Regrettably, we have forgotten that confession, the sacrament of reconciliation, reconciles us not only to God but to the community against which we offend by sinning.

II

So much for what we've lost: a hard-nosed sense of personal sin. We have lost not only a destructive guilt; we have lost a realistic recognition of what the New Testament Letter of James remarks so simply, "All of us sin in many ways" (Jas 3:2). But even if any one of you is by God's extraordinary favor an exception to that affirmation, don't leave now. You might still profit from my second point: What have we gained? What facet of sin, neglected before the 60s, have we come to see with new eyes?

The answer is an expression I never heard till the late 60s or early 70s: "sinful structures." What can that possibly mean? It means that

> by the power of sin injury and injustice can penetrate social and political institutions. That is why . . . even situations and structures that are unjust have to be reformed. Here we have a new consciousness, for in the past these responsibilities could not be perceived as distinctly as they are now.[7]

Very simply, sin infects not only individuals, you and me; sin infects institutions. Examples? (1) A government like Noriega's in Panama. It is not only Noriega who was corrupt. Corruption had invaded the whole system, making for death squads, drug industry, desperate poverty. And it was not only vicious animals who followed his lead. Good people, without realizing it, were destroying lives and liberty. (2) Genocide. Hitler's program to annihilate the Jews was not only built into a structure; it could not have gassed six million Jews without the help of uncounted Christians. (3) Prejudice. For centuries white Americans have imbibed a bias with their mothers' milk: Blacks are inferior, to be feared, to be kept "in their place." It was not the gospel but the Supreme Court that declared their civil rights. And even fine folk like me, who never did anything bad to them, have found it terribly difficult to cross the color line, to go beyond "Some of my best friends are black." Apartheid, racial segregation, is not restricted to South Africa. (4) Business. Big business, business people tell us, operates on two basic principles: greed and fear. Day after day we read of corporate manipulation, of profit as an end in itself, of bureaucracy as the source of endless corruption. (5) Landowners. Specifically, landowners in Latin America and the Philippines who keep 90% of the people in economic slavery. (6) A male-dominated society. Not only in Iran but on several American levels women are second-class citizens.

Please understand me. I am not saying that every Panamanian soldier, every German of the 30s and 40s, every white American, every man or woman in business, every landowner, every American male has committed or is committing a personal sin. No. The point is, all of us are in some measure part of structures that do harm, that inflict injustice, that hurt our brothers and sisters.

If the phrase "sinful structures" causes confusion or a "guilt trip," think rather of "wounded communities." You and I are all part of larger groups: a city, a state, a nation; a parish, a diocese, a universal church; a job, an industry, a multinational corporation; a platoon, a regiment, an army; a color, a culture, a civilization; a classroom, a university, an educational system; a law school, "L.A. Law,"[8] the legal profession; a medical school, a hospital, the healthcare complex; the Georgetown Jesuit community, the Jesuits of the United States, the Jesuit order; a male or female sex. All of these, for all the good they do, fall under a phrase the Second Vatican Council used of the Catholic Church: "always in need of reformation."[9] All these are not just saintly structures with a handful of "bad apples"; they are wounded communities. They are not the structures they ought to be, the communities God wants them to be. If you fail to see this, you haven't been reading the front page—or even the comics.[10]

III

So then, we are wounded by sin—as individuals and in our community existence. This leads into my third point: Therefore what? Wounds call primarily not for guilt but for healing. And yet you know as well as I, to heal a wound, you must know where the wound lies. No point giving you an aspirin for bone cancer. Where does the disease lie in our personal lives and in the systems we share?

Fortunately, our awareness is growing. The Georgetown University Law Center now publishes a scholarly journal on legal ethics. Hospitals increasingly have ethics committees. Business schools offer courses in ethics. The media deplore day after day the scandals on Wall Street, in government agencies, in Congress, in religious bodies. Self-criticism is an integral part of educational institutions. Splendid! But let me try to uncover a single basic wound and suggest antibodies.

At the root of most of our American diseases is what sociologist Robert Bellah identified as a resurgence of late-19th-century rugged individualism.[11] Of supreme importance today is for me to get to the well first before it dries up; when the chips are down, the one reality that matters is myself; here is *numero uno,* here my ultimate responsibility. Nice guys finish last.

You might expect that the counteragent to rugged individualism would be a body numbering over 900 million, a body that proclaims with St. Paul, "The head cannot say to the feet, 'I have no need of you' " (1 Cor 12:21). But, sympathetic researchers report, our Catholic body has been more influenced by the dominant culture than an influence upon it.

The first stage in community healing is to heal myself. A community is ailing because its members are not whole. Wherever our vocation takes us—to Congress or courtroom, to healthcare or Housing & Urban Development, to industry or Internal Revenue, to postal service or priesthood—that community is wounded to the extent that you and I are not living the second great commandment, in the measure that we who share its life do not love every other as much as we love ourselves—love especially the impotent and impoverished.

If this is my constant effort, if I am refashioning myself in the image of Christ, then I can lay a healing hand on the community within which I work. A business man or woman, I can help my corporation live the affirmation of Dayton Hudson, one of our largest retailers: "The business of business is serving society, not just making money; profit is our reward for serving society well. . . . [P]rofit is . . . not an end in itself."[12] A lawyer, I can help my prestigious firm serve the down-and-out as effectively as it serves the moneyed. Hospital administrator, doctor, or nurse, I can help bring not only the paying sick to our hospitals but our hospitals to the surrounding community, help medical research discover and apply not so much what it *can* do as what it *ought* to do: Give life and not hasten death. Male or female, I can help responsible feminists reform the thought systems that undergird a social order still terribly unjust where women are concerned. A Washingtonian, I can help the capital city of our nation destroy its image as the crime capital of America. A Catholic Christian, I can help our Church become gradually a home where the enslaved find freedom, the poor experience food for their flesh and solace for their spirits. A citizen, I can help our political leaders pursue right rather than might, human rights before selfish interests.

I realize that these recommendations are terribly broad. To bridge the gap between the abstract and the concrete, between the wild blue yonder and the blood and guts of everyday living, I suggest a practical principle: Think globally, act locally. Think globally. Know the wounds that afflict our world's communities, what needs healing at home and abroad, from Wall Street to El Salvador, from Georgetown to Rome, from the U.S. Congress to multinational corporations, from the plague of AIDS to the pollution of your air, from cocaine cartels to panic in the streets, from the rip-offs of the powerless to the ceaseless rape of the poor. Think globally—not to end up in despair, but to rise up in rage. Perhaps more importantly, to see your Christian vocation in context. For, to paraphrase a friend, unless you see your community from the moon, you don't see it in focus. Then act locally. Select a single wound in a community to which you belong, and never stop tending and mending it—ejecting the poison, binding the wound, healing the hurt. One community, one wound.

A remarkable Presbyterian preacher/novelist compared humanity to an enormous spider web: "if you touch it anywhere, you set the whole thing trembling. . . . As we move around this world and as we act with kindness, perhaps, or with indifference, or with hostility, toward the people we meet, we too are setting the great spider web a-tremble. The life that I touch for good or ill will touch another life, and that in turn another, until who knows where the trembling stops or in what far place and time my touch will be felt. Our lives are linked. No man [no woman] is an island. . . ."[13]

Holy Trinity Church
Washington, D.C.
January 14, 1990

10
WHAT WE DON'T HAVE IS TIME
Third Sunday of the Year (C)

- Nehemiah 8:2–4, 5–6, 8–10
- 1 Corinthians 12:12–30
- Luke 1:1–4; 4:14–21

Several weeks ago I experienced an exhilarating evening. By a fortunate coincidence, I was privileged to sit entranced at the Kennedy Center's Terrace Theater while a superb songstress thrilled us with her pure soprano timbre. So much that Barbara Cook sang moved me mightily, but nothing so profoundly as two lines in a song I believe was composed in part by a long-term AIDS victim:

> Love is all we have for now,
> what we don't have is time.[1]

Such is my song today. It is not simply a plea from the darkening twilight of one preacher's existence. It is not a commercial for one-night love boats. What Barbara Cook sang with such soft anguish to a theater audience, St. Paul wrote with a passionate pen to the Christian community in Corinth. My three movements are three Cs: Corinth, Christianity, and Cook.

I

My first C: Corinth. You've just heard a reading "from the First Letter of Paul to the Corinthians." I'll bet any of you dollars to doughnuts—or bourbon to bagels—that the word "Corinthians" said absolutely nothing to you. And yet St. Paul was not writing a term paper from a beach at Ephesus, not penning an episcopal pastoral with a peaceful plume to just anybody and everybody. He was writing to an explosive city called Corinth. Explosive indeed; for Corinth in Paul's time could be a showcase for D.C. and L.A., New York and Las Vegas, Paris and the Riviera all lumped into one.

What do I mean? Corinth was cosmopolitan—folks flocked there from all regions of Rome's empire. Corinth was Washington in miniature—a center of government, a primitive Pentagon. Corinth was commerce writ large, made for merchants. For sports, Corinth could compete with Seoul 1988; its Isthmian games rivaled the Olympics. For lust and license, Corinth would make today's Sin City look like a Trappist monastery. "To live like a Corinthian" came to mean "wallow in immorality." Corinth's patron saint? Aphrodite, goddess of love—her temple serviced by a thousand prostitutes. Wealth? In Corinth Donald Trump would have had a field day. Bud Light? In one small area diggers have discovered 33 taverns.[2]

This was the city to which Paul had carried Christianity back in 51. Within 18 months he had an exciting community of converts. Five years later he had to write them a vigorous letter—the letter that was announced in the short selection read to you. Why did he write? In large measure because he was upset. In large measure because Corinth's newborn Christians were torn by cliques, coteries, factions. Perhaps as many as four. A better-educated minority was entranced by Apollos: He knew the Old Testament inside out, and he hypnotized his hearers. A second group boasted a particular empathy with Peter, prince of the apostles. A third crowd, the majority, poor freedmen and slaves, rocked and rolled for Paul, apostle of dear old Corinth. A fourth faction seemed to think they were closer to Christ than anyone outside their graced little group.[3]

II

That situation summons up my second C: Christianity. How does Paul react to Corinth's cliques? In two ways. First, he lets them "have it," right from his Christian spleen. Factions founded on favorite ministers of Christ? "I belong to Paul," "I belong to Apollos," "I belong to Peter"? And some Christians "belong to Christ"? "Is Christ divided? Was Paul crucified for you? Or were you baptized in the name of Paul?" (1 Cor 1:12–13).

Less angrily, Paul tells the Corinthians what he told you today.

You "were all baptized into one body" (1 Cor 12:13). And that one body is the body of the one Christ. All of you together are like the human body—the body of a man or a woman—like your own body. Take a look at yourself. Recognize it or not, that body is a work of art. And it's a work of art precisely because it is many-splendored, precisely because you're shaped of so many different parts. Picture yourself as all hands or feet, all heart or liver, all bone or blood, all rib or rump. Not only would you look funny; it just wouldn't work.

What Paul is saying in nonmedical language is that each of you is a single body because all your members, whatever they are, have a role to play in that body. Your blood system, if laid end to end, would circle the equator four times;[4] but even your pinkie, if fractured, would play havoc with your jump shot. Three million sweat glands cool your body; but even the mucus that lines your stomach keeps you from eating yourself alive.[5]

So, Paul tells his Corinthian converts, so is it with the body of Christ, with the Church. No one of you can say to any other, "I have no need of you" (1 Cor 12:21). Of course there are different roles: "Are all apostles? Are all prophets? Are all teachers? Do all work miracles? Do all possess gifts of healing? Do all speak with tongues? Do all interpret?" (vv. 29–30). Obviously not; but, my cherished Corinthians, each of you is an important part of this one body, this one Christ—"no discord," only "the same care for one another" (v. 25). It reminds me that a century ago some cynic asked Cardinal Newman what good the laity were for. "Well," answered the Cardinal with devastating simplicity, "the Church would surely look strange without them."

But at this point—having listed the prominent positions, the center-stage functions, in the Church—Paul rocks Corinth with a master stroke, utterly unexpected: "I will show you a still more excellent way" (v. 31). More important than any of the offices, any of the gifts, he has just listed. More important than being Peter or Paul; more important for the Church than being pope; more important, believe it or not, than being a Jesuit! And what is that?

III

You're asking for my third C: Cook. Paul's "more excellent way" is the couplet that Barbara Cook winged into my heart that Friday evening:

> Love is all we have for now,
> what we don't have is time.

Two pithy, poignant expressions here. First, "love is all we have for now." Now, composers and chanteuse were quite aware that there is more to living than loving. All you need for proof is to lift your eyes to South Africa and Soviet Armenia,[6] to the Middle East and the north of Ireland, to Wall Street and the Bowery. What I find in their song, perhaps read into their words, is a realization that the words are more profound than they sound. Whether it's AIDS or your career, whether it's cancer or Christianity, when the chips are down and you're talking about life-and-death, when it's a question of what it means to be human, then what makes the difference is love. St. Paul put it another way to the Corinthian Christians: "So faith, hope, love abide, these three; but the greatest of these is love" (1 Cor 13:13).

It's "the greatest" for your world and for your Church. For your world. You see, love is the one gift that can make any area of this world more human than was Corinth. Other gifts can help: economics and education, health and housing, equal rights and Medicare. But without love—unless deep down we care; unless Wall Street is more than a countinghouse, Georgetown more than a springboard for success; unless love of law is subordinate to the law of love, medicine less for profit than for people; unless competition is less compelling than compassion, technology not simply science but the art of aiding; unless money and power and fame serve not self but the other; and yes, unless we live Christ's command, "Love the Lord your God with all your heart . . . love your neighbor as [you love] yourself" (Mt 22:37, 39)—the most powerful nation on earth will be little more than a contemporary Corinth.

And love is "the greatest" for your Church, for the body of Christ. We have our differences, God knows—differences that threaten to tear one Church into more factions than Paul ever imagined. A pulpit is not the place to argue those differences—from contraception to the kiss of peace, from women's ordination to homosexual activity. But a pulpit *is* the place to proclaim this gospel: If our differences destroy our love, we are no longer Christians. I may indeed go to church, receive Christ in hand or on tongue, but without love the rest of it is a charade, play-acting. And when the final judgment is passed on me, it will rest on one four-letter word: Did you really love?

With that question goes the second line of the couplet: "what we don't have is time." That's true not only of the AIDS-afflicted; it harasses all of us. Not in an obvious sense. After all, I can move from hate to love in an hour, a moment; God's grace is not measured by a clock. And some folk for some reason are given decades to discover love. The point is, I cannot promise myself time. Neither could the 50,000-plus who perished in Soviet Armenia's earthquake. Neither can you—however young, however strong.

More positively, I lay before you the urgent plea in Psalm 95: "O that today you would hearken to [God's] voice!" (Ps 95:7). Today. Etch that word on your mind and heart. You can remember yesterday; you can imagine tomorrow; today alone can you live. It's the supreme importance of the present moment. We are tempted to tolerate the routine or rupture of the present, with an eye to the rapture of the future; to endure today's travail, in hope of tomorrow's ease. Never for a day have I forgotten a framed sign I read decades ago in a convent chapel: "Priest of God, say this Mass as if it were your first Mass, as if it were your last Mass, as if it were your only Mass." Something similar can be said to each of you each day: "Child of God, live this day as if it were your first day, as if it were your last day, as if it were your only day."

So too for your loving. Not a tension-packed day into which you crowd all your caring; that way madness lies. To be aware that "what we don't have is time" is rather to realize that each dawn ushers in a new creation; each moment is a fresh chance to be Christlike; each human you touch, an invitation to be better than you are. It makes so much more sense than two blood sisters refusing to speak to each other for half a century. It alone makes impossible another Auschwitz, another *Mississippi Burning*.[7] It alone makes the difference between a jungle and a city, between people and educated animals, between marriage and an armistice, between a Catholic collegiate community and a campus clogged with six thousand intellectuals hell-bent on self-satisfaction.

Good friends: A well-known singer and bandleader, now 81, wrote in his autobiography: "Women, horses, cars, clothes. I did it all. And do you know what that's called, ladies and gentlemen? It's called living."[8] Wouldn't it be more satisfying if someday you could say about yourself: "People—those I liked and those I didn't—all people, but especially the homeless and the hopeless, the naked and the hungry, the lonely and the unloved, the brown and the black, the drug-addicted and the AIDS-afflicted. I did *not* do it all, but I did what I could. And do you know what that's called, ladies and gentlemen? It's called . . . loving."

> Love is all we have for now,
> what we don't have is time.

Dahlgren Chapel
Georgetown University
and
Holy Trinity Church
Washington, D.C.
January 22, 1989

11
CHOOSE LIFE . . . IN CHRIST
Sixth Sunday of the Year (A)

- Sirach 15:15–20
- 1 Corinthians 2:6–10
- Matthew 5:17–37

Suppose someone among you were to pose this pointed problem to me: "I should like to expand my Catholic existence, deepen my spiritual life. Right now I'm what you'd call a good average Catholic. I rarely miss Mass, even when I sleep in on Sunday and the Redskins are playing that afternoon. I keep all Ten Commandments, however sticky the sixth. I listen respectfully to pope and bishops, though the contraception bit is a corker and the pastoral on the economy is hard to swallow. I'm a reliable family man, though my teen-age children think I'm a cross between Hitler and Danny De Vito. I'm honest in my business dealings, no matter what my colleagues do. I'm generous at collection time, even try to support my pastor in the style to which he'd like to become accustomed. But I'm dissatisfied; there's something missing. Sometimes I feel I'm that Pharisee in the temple recording his virtues; for all his fidelity to the law, the Lord was not happy with him. How does a busy man or woman begin to be better than he or she is?"

Where to begin? I suggest that today's three readings can be uncommonly helpful if we want to know Christ *more* clearly, love him *more* dearly, follow him *more* nearly. And so my three points are simply (1) Sirach, (2) Paul, (3) Jesus.

I

First, Sirach. Here is a book of Israelite wisdom, written about 180 B.C. The author? A respected, well-traveled teacher who ran an academy for young Jewish men. He tells you that the Lord has shaped you with a fearful power: the power to choose. "If you will, you can keep the commandments, and to act faithfully is a matter of your own choice" (Sir 15:15).[1] You cannot blame God for the bad choices you make, for the sins you commit.

The heart of your power to choose? The critical decision for every human person: "Before [you] are life and death, and whichever [you] choose will be given to [you]" (v. 17). It recalls the Lord's words to Israel in Deuteronomy: "I have set before you life and death, blessing and curse; therefore choose life, that you and your descendants may live" (Deut 30:19).

"Choose life." But "life" here does not mean merely x-number of years, does not mean "Choose to be 80 or 90 or 100." "Life" here means "loving" God, "obeying" God, "cleaving to" God (Deut 30:20). This it is to be genuinely alive. And "death" here is not a fatal stroke, heart arrest. "Death" here is idolatry in its thousand shapes— putting any creature on a pedestal and worshiping it: money in the millions or sex on demand, power over your brothers and sisters or the applause of the masses.

If life is what you really want, then you have the Lord's promise through Moses: "The Lord your God will circumcise your heart . . . , so that you will love the Lord your God with all your heart and with all your soul, that you may live" (Deut 30:6). Is this what you really want? Then God will work in you the change, the conversion, that makes it possible to fulfil the law of love. In fact, if you really want it, God is already at work in you.

II

So much for Sirach: Choose life. What the apostle Paul adds is a Christian dimension: The life you choose is life in Christ. It goes back to what Paul calls the "secret and hidden wisdom of God . . . [which] none of the rulers of this age understood" (1 Cor 2:7–8), a wisdom so profound that only Paul's "mature" (v. 6) can grasp it, men and women who have been taught by the Holy Spirit.

What is this "hidden wisdom" which Paul declares "God has revealed to us through the Spirit" (v. 10)? Very simply, it is God's plan of salvation—how a God whose name is Love planned to recapture our love, recapture the love of a sinful humanity, not by force but by the crucifixion of God's own Son. It is a plan, a love, that sheer human reason, however brilliant, could never conceive or believe. In fact, in an outburst of fascinating imagination, Paul declares that if the authorities who crucified Jesus had known that God's plan would be realized through the humiliating death of Jesus, "they would have tried to frustrate it by letting him live."[2]

By the death of Jesus you and I are alive. Not alive in the sense that I can eye the sky at night and hear the harmonies of Haydn or Lena Horne, smell a spider lily and drool over Domino's pizza, touch my fingers to a face I love. That life I can live without Christ and his Calvary; that life is open not only to Mother Teresa but to Rambo and James Bond. The life I cannot live save through a crucified Christ is a threefold power: the power to believe what the eye cannot see, to hope for what the heart can hardly imagine, to love as Jesus loved. It is Paul's passionate cry to the Christians of Galatia: "I have been crucified with Christ; it is no longer I who live, but Christ who lives in me; and the life I now live I live by faith in the Son of God, who loved me and gave himself for me" (Gal 2:20).

III

Now all that is quite broad; it doesn't tell me what to *do* if I choose life. What Sirach and Paul propose on the level of principle—choose life, live life in Christ—Matthew brings down to bone-and-blood reality. Here we have part of the Sermon on the Mount. Now don't think of the Sermon as a single event where Jesus proclaims at one sitting all that Matthew has in three chapters—all those beatitudes and biddings, commands and counsels that occupy 105 vibrant verses. A masterful editor, Matthew has pieced together all sorts of material from different sources, from different pronouncements of Jesus—stitched them into a coherent whole that confronts the Christian with what it means to follow Jesus.[3]

Today's extract from the Sermon includes three injunctions in which Jesus takes us a giant step beyond the covenant struck on Sinai: how to fulfil, how to perfect, commandments five, six, and eight.[4] On Sinai God proscribed murder, adultery, and false witness. On the mountain of the Beatitudes Jesus demands a good deal more: "Unless your uprightness, your holiness, exceeds that of the scribes and Pharisees, you will never enter the kingdom of heaven" (Mt 5:20). And don't think of the scribes and Pharisees as lax; quite the contrary. The lifeblood of the Pharisees was the law of Moses: not only the written Torah but the oral as well, interpretations of the written law after the Exile. A Jew would be saved, the nation made holy, only by knowing the law thoroughly and following it exactly: Sabbath and feast days, ritual purity, tithing, dietary laws—all 613 imperatives. The Pharisees were strict; Jesus is stricter still.

Take commandment five: "You have heard that it was said to men and women of ancient times [to the generation that first heard the law from Moses], 'You shall not murder; and whoever murders shall be liable to judgment.' But I say to you that everyone who is angry with his brother [or sister] shall be liable to judgment . . ." (Mt 5:21–22). What is Jesus doing? He "shifts the ground from the act of murder to the emotional prelude to murder, anger."[5] He is trying to get inside us, get at the roots of immoral activity, at the emotion that triggers the fatal act. That is why Jesus insists: before worship, friendship; before litigation, reconciliation. That is why he would agree with St. Paul, "Don't let the sun set on your anger" (Eph 4:26).

Now Matthew's five verses are not a rounded treatise on anger. Jesus does not distinguish a righteous anger, an anger justified by circumstances, the anger he himself experienced when he drove the buyers and sellers from the temple, the anger with which he looked at the hardhearted worshipers in the synagogue so ready to accuse him for curing the sick on the Sabbath. He does not discuss neurotic repression of anger, the kind of repression psychologists say leads to mental illness. He does not explain how you reconcile with someone who spurns your outstretched hand. He does not put a time limit on parents' anger when their daughter is gang-raped. He is simply trying to lift his followers from a narrow legalism to a new integrity, a gospel wholeness. He wants us to be aware how dangerous anger can be, justified or not. If you don't believe it, you haven't been watching your Movie Channel or the nightly news. Violence and murder— these stem not only from cold-blooded Mafia types but from the anger, the rage, the hatred of good people.[6]

Take commandment six: "You have heard that it was said, 'You shall not commit adultery.' But I say to you that everyone who looks at a woman lustfully has already committed adultery with her in his heart" (Mt 5:27–28). Wow! If this doesn't wake you up, nothing in the Gospels will. And if you are unhappy with the text, you have only three alternatives: (1) Jesus never really said it. (2) He said it but didn't really mean it. (3) He meant it but not for a sophisticated culture like ours. Don't waste valuable energy on any of the three. Jesus said it; Jesus meant it; Jesus meant it not only for Peter and Judas but for cultured dudes like you and me.

What is Jesus trying to do? Once again, he wants to (a big word) interiorize a command of the law, internalize it. I mean, he goes from the external act to the internal stimulus. It is not only the visible act of forbidden intercourse that is destructive; just as destructive is the lustful heart—perhaps even more destructive. For, as Jesus said on another occasion, "Out of the heart come evil thoughts, murder, adultery, fornication, theft, false witness, slander" (Mt 15:19). "To look at a woman as an object of lust is to violate the respect due a human person."[7] To look lustfully is worlds apart from looking lovingly.

Once more Jesus is raising his followers, raising you and me, to a gospel wholeness. Disordered desire in any human context is unchristian: in money as well as sex, in power as well as fame. Look within, Jesus counsels you; find out what drives you, what motivates you, what triggers the deeds you do.

Take commandment eight: "You have heard that it was said to men and women of ancient times, 'You shall not swear falsely, but shall perform to the Lord what you have sworn.' But I say to you, Do not swear at all. . . . Let what you say be simply 'Yes' or 'No' " (Mt 5:33–34, 37). Here Jesus is combining two commandments: (1) You shall not take the name of the Lord in vain; (2) You shall not bear false witness. On Mount Sinai God forbade perjury. On the mountain of the Beatitudes Jesus moves far beyond perjury. In your everyday living, he says to his followers, be straight-out honest. Say yes when you mean yes; say no when you mean no.

No need for angst, for anxiety. Presidents can still swear to uphold the Constitution; courts can still administer oaths about "the truth, the whole truth, and nothing but the truth"; Jesuits can still vow poverty, chastity, and obedience. In our sinful, imperfect world we still need a certain number of public binding oaths. This is not Jesus' concern. He is saying to his disciples, to such as have chosen to follow him, to you and me: Your sincerity, your honesty, your freedom from hypocrisy, as well as your respect and love for one another, should "make a simple 'yes' or a simple 'no' a sacred expression of truth."[8] Ethicists may still reason about mental reservations, discuss when a lie is not a lie, even contend that sometimes a lie is legitimate. Jesus is not lecturing Jerusalem on moral theology. He is telling us what it means to follow him, to be his disciple: With God's grace we can do more than avoid sin; we can struggle to be other Christs, to live the Sermon on the Mount. It may take a lifetime, but what else is a Christian lifetime for?

Good friends all: I have set before you three examples of "Choose life," three facets of high Christian living, three ways of living that stretch three of the Ten Commandments. The problem is, these three examples are just that—examples. The Sermon on the Mount is chock-full of the paradoxes that make up "life according to Christ." When Lent comes later this month and you're searching for a penance with teeth in it, you might mull over Matthew 5–7. Discover what it means to be poor in spirit and a peacemaker, meek and merciful; what it means to turn the other cheek and love your enemies; what it means to serve God and not money, not to be anxious about tomorrow, not to judge another, to enter life by the narrow gate, to build your house not on sand but on rock.

I make no apology for these hard sayings, simply because the spirituality I suggest stems not from me but from *numero uno* among homilists, our Lord Jesus Christ. I set such spirituality before you because to do otherwise is to deceive you, to mislead you into thinking that Catholicism is a creed you repeat each Sunday, a homily with three sugar-coated points, Bethlehem's crib without Calvary's cross. I set it before you because you are capable of living it. I set it before you because you are not ordinary men and women. You believe: I mean you affirm that the Word you hear is God's Word, proclaim with an amen that the wafer in your hand and on your tongue is Christ the Lord. You hope: I mean you confidently expect that the life in and with Christ that is yours now will never end. You love: I mean you try to live not for your individual selves but for the God who shaped you to a divine image, try to live for every Lazarus who lies outside your gate pleading for the crumbs from your table.

If that is so, then the Sermon on the Mount is your charter for Christian living, for Christian choosing, for choosing life. It's tough, I admit—but not much tougher than Wall Street or "L.A. Law."[9] No need for despair; quite the contrary. If you choose life, if you choose Christlife, you start with Christ in you—Life with a capital L. Enjoy it; enjoy . . . him.

Dahlgren Chapel
Georgetown University
and
Holy Trinity Church
Washington, D.C.
February 11, 1990

12

SEE MORE CLEARLY, LOVE MORE DEARLY, FOLLOW MORE NEARLY
Trinity Sunday (C)

- Proverbs 8:22–31
- Romans 5:1–5
- John 16:12–15

For you good folk, Trinity Sunday is not an ordinary Sunday. Trinity is the name of your parish. Moreover, the Trinity is arguably the most profound of Christian mysteries. And yet, uncounted parishioners might vote to change the parish name to St. Ignatius Loyola or Our Lady of Georgetown. Holy Trinity doesn't grab you; and as for the mystery, to quote one old Jesuit brother, "For all practical purposes, we've got three Gods."[1]

For all its mystery, the Trinity must be preached. Why? Because it tells us something about God, something about ourselves, and because God took flesh to tell us that something. But a homily is not a lecture. A homily does not prove that God is One in Three; it starts with that, because God-in-flesh told us it is so. A homily does not argue abstruse Trinitarian theology; it touches the mystery to Christian living.

That said, where do we go from here? I suggest a remarkable prayer-song from *Godspell*, probably modeled on a prayer attributed to 13th-century Saint Richard of Chichester: "Dearest Lord Jesus, Saviour and friend, three things I pray: to see thee more clearly, love thee more dearly, follow thee more nearly, day by day." Let's see how we might (1) see our triune God more clearly, (2) love such a God more dearly, (3) follow that God more nearly.

I

First, see more clearly. Not solve the mystery, in good old P. D. James style.[2] Despite half a century devoted to God-talk, I shall not

77

send you from this sacred spot with God's own key to the Trinity. But what can we say, from God's self-revealing? First, a neat summary on the lips of Jesus, his final command to his disciples in Matthew's last paragraph: "Go, therefore, and make disciples of all nations, baptizing them in the name of the Father and of the Son and of the Holy Spirit" (Mt 28:19).

From the New Testament, the privileged book of Christians, we emerge with a mind-blowing truth: God is Father (no sex or gender here), God is Son, God is Spirit. Not an Alec Guinness playing three roles. No, three distinct persons: The Father is not the Son, the Son is not the Father, neither Father nor Son is the Holy Spirit. And still there is but one God. It's beyond our experience; it's off the human wall. But there it is, a fact, guaranteed by God.

But if that were all God told us, we would only be mystified. Far more passionately, far more personally, God's Word proclaims three magnificent monosyllables: "God is Love" (1 Jn 4:8). God, this trinity of living persons, not only loves; God *is* Love. If you're looking for the perfect realization of perfect love, the model-without-beginning for every love that has ever begun, look at God. Am I serious? Never been more serious. That God is Love we discover in two stunning ways: in the secret life of God and in the life God shared with us.[3]

We discover it in God's secret life. Love, you see, is a we: a you and an I. Whether I love God or another human being, I never cease to be myself. Mystic Teresa of Avila, caught up in God, never ceased to be Teresa, never became God, Romeo, forsaking his very name for Juliet, never became Juliet. Love demands "I" and "thou."

But love forbids "mine" and "thine"—what St. Augustine called "those ice-cold words." If to love is to give, to love perfectly is to give till there is nothing left to give. Only then do the two, remaining two, become perfectly one.

The astounding truth about the Trinity? There is "I and thou" without "mine and thine." Father, Son, and Spirit—each is a real person, an "I," an ego. And still there is no egoism. The Father gives to the Son literally all that He Himself has, all that makes Him God, all that makes Him Love. The Son, perfect image of the Father, loves the Father to selfless perfection. And, marvel beyond human grasping, the love with which Father and Son love each other, that love is a person. That love *is* the Holy Spirit!

But God's love does not hide in outer space. Perfect love has touched our earth; we discover it in the love God shared with us. A single Gospel sentence sums it up: The Father "so loved the world that He gave His only Son, that whoever believes in him should . . . have eternal life" (Jn 3:16). The Son, Paul rhapsodizes, did not think divine glory a prize to clutch (cf. Phil 2:6). He took our bone and blood, our skin and sinews. Not because He needed them. He took what is ours only to give us what is His, to let us share God's life. And the Holy Spirit? The Spirit is not only the very private love between Father and Son; the Spirit is God's Gift to you and me. "If I leave you," Jesus promised the night before Calvary, "it is only to send you my Spirit, to be with you always, to teach you all truth, to be my Presence among you, my Presence within you" (cf. Jn 16:7–15).

II

But Christian living is not just seeing more clearly. Seeing, knowing, should lead to loving. It is Thomas Aquinas' keen reminder on two ways of desiring knowledge. One way is to desire knowledge as a perfection of myself; the other is to desire it not merely as a perfection of myself but because through this knowledge the one I love becomes present to me. In fact, the most profound knowing, the kind of knowing John's Gospel proclaims, implies loving. "This is eternal life," Jesus prayed to his Father, "that they may know you, the only true God, and Jesus Christ, whom you have sent" (Jn 17:3). Not intellectualism pure and simple; rather, "immediate experience and intimacy."[4] Hence my second point: Love our triune God more dearly. But how do you do that?

A homily is not the place for a treatise on love—certainly not from a confirmed bachelor, and a Jesuit at that. Instead, I refer you to a fairly reliable authority on loving: the Second Person of the Trinity wearing our very flesh, the night before he died: "If you love me, you will keep my commandments" (Jn 14:15). It's the succinct message that has come down the ages: Love is shown not so much in words as by deeds. Not that the words are unimportant. Many a marriage has miscarried because a macho husband or a self-centered spouse never uttered those three incomparable monosyllables . . . "I love you." The point is rather, words can be cheap, can fall too facilely from fluent lips. I cannot recall that my immigrant father ever explicitly said to me, "I love you." But year after year, six or seven days a week, he worked from three in the morning till three in the afternoon, on a milk wagon drawn by a horse that once split his chin with a well-placed kick, hauled heavy milk cans to feed me, clothe me, give me the education he never had.

And so it is with God. An "act of love" is simple enough on the tongue: "Dear God, I love you above all else. Bye now, I'm off for another Bud." But an "act of love" that stems from my life, ah, that's loving. Mother Teresa cradling an orphaned infant in the ruins of Beirut; Father Damien of Molokai bringing love to lepers, until one day he began his sermon with "We lepers"; the four chaplains in World War II who drowned arm-in-arm because they had given their lifebelts to others; my dear deceased friend Perry, who seated his wife at table for 60 years without fail, remembered each wedding anniversary with not only roses (one, two, ten, 50) but always a love letter—here is genuine love, in good times and bad, in sickness and health, in poverty and wealth.

How know if you really love God? Do what God wants you to do. It's as simple as that—and as difficult. From the second great commandment: Love the human images of God "as [you love] yourself" (Mt 22:39)—through the Sermon on the Mount: not only no killing but no anger, care and prayer not only for friends but for enemies, not only no adultery but no lustful eye—down to a whole gospel way of life: preference for the poor, compassion for the crippled in flesh or spirit, respect for rain forest and robin redbreast and endangered species, tears for 14 million refugees, a powerful protest against war on the womb—so do you reveal if you actually love God or are using words as a smoke screen.

All this and so much more is hidden in the first great commandment: "You shall love the Lord your God with all your heart, and with all your soul, and with all your mind" (Mt 22:37). Love—for the things of God, for the people of God, for God Three in One—love is not an abstraction. Love is what God the Father *did* in shaping your every limb, lending you a mind to know and a heart to love. Love is what God the Son *did* in nailing your sins to a cross in his own bruised and battered flesh. Love is what the Holy Spirit *does* in transforming you into a living image of the risen Christ. And so love must be what *you* do: living all ten of the Commandments, not five or even nine; embracing the whole Christian gospel, not only the peace it brings but the struggles as well; following not only the appealing Christ of Bethlehem but the offensive Christ of Calvary.

III

This suggests my third point: Follow more nearly. If you want to follow our God more nearly, gaze closely on Christ. To "follow"

Christ is not quite the same thing as to "imitate" Christ. God does not expect you and me to copy Christ, to reproduce the life Jesus led in Palestine.[5] Not ours to be born in a feeding trough, to dress as he dressed, walk as he walked, raise the dead to fresh life. We live in different historical circumstances; we have our own unique call from God. And remember, you and I live our faith, hope, and love in ways Jesus in his restricted life could not experience. He was a man, not a woman; he was a teacher, but not a scholar; he did not experience old age or Alzheimer's disease.

To follow Jesus is to be his disciple. And to be a disciple, in Gospel terms, is to be called, as Peter and Matthew, James and John were called, to have a vocation that stems from Jesus. Called to what? To have one Master, ultimately one only Teacher. The basic, life-and-death question I have constantly to confront is this: Who or what rules my life? Someone rules it, something shapes it. Who or what is my master, my god?

Recent research highlights three contemporary gods: money, power, fame. But don't flinch: I shall not blast them. They are not evils in themselves. Without Catholic money Holy Trinity, Georgetown, the Society of Jesus would die. Power annihilated the Nazi hate machine, keeps the superpowers from nuking the earth. Fame enabled pop singer Bob Geldof to organize concerts that fed millions to starving Ethiopians, found him confessing: "Fame to me is not imprisoning—it expands what you are capable of doing."[6] The question is: Why money, why power, why fame? For me . . . or for the other? Who sits on top of the money, the power, the fame? You . . . or Christ?

In the last analysis, when push comes to shove, to follow Christ means that you are ready to carry a cross. "Whoever does not take his/her cross . . . is not worthy of me" (Mt 10:38). For to be Jesus' disciple is to pattern yourself after a crucified Master who came not to be served but to serve, warned his disciples against the perils of fame and first places, turned savagely on Peter when he rebelled against the passion of his Lord.

What cross will be yours? I have no idea. I know from my own experience that the cross is not limited to the close of our earthbound existence, to the terminal cancer, the cardiac arrest. Whatever makes for pain—pain of flesh or of spirit—should be part and parcel of discipleship: diverticula or disappointments, schizophrenia or the wrenching of my heart, dying hopes or the death of a dear one, the insecurities of youth and the trembling of the aging—whatever it is that pricks my pride, assails my lustiness, intimates my mortality, takes the very joy from my bones. This it is to follow Christ. But only if your agony is a ceaseless self-giving, in freedom, into the hands of our incomprehensible God.

Have we strayed from the Trinity? Not really. To follow Jesus is to enter into the life of our triune God. For, as Jesus promised, "If [you] love me, [you] will keep my word, and my Father will love [you], and we will come to [you] and make our home with [you]" (Jn 14:23). And more: "If you love me, you will keep my commandments. And I will pray the Father, and He will give you another Counselor, to be with you for ever, even the Spirit of truth, whom the world cannot receive, because it neither sees Him nor knows Him; you know Him, for He dwells with you, and will be in you" (Jn 14:15–17).

Good friends, this Sunday should be specially sacred to you. For today you celebrate a triune God not secreted in outer space but alive deep within you. If you're wondering what to pray for, pray with *Godspell* to see this your God more clearly, love more dearly, follow more nearly. It's worth doing in this life, because that's pretty much what you'll be doing in the next . . . for ever.

Dahlgren Chapel
Georgetown University
and
Holy Trinity Church
Washington, D.C.
May 21, 1989

13
NOT MY DISCIPLE UNLESS . . .
Twenty-third Sunday of the Year (C)

- Wisdom 9:13–18
- Philemon 9–10, 12–17
- Luke 14:25–33

I trust that today's Gospel had you "taking gas." If not, you weren't really listening. What does it take to be a disciple of Christ? Not one of the original Twelve—Peter, James, John; simply a follower of Christ, a Christian. Oh yes, you must be baptized, must believe in the Lord Jesus, must live all ten of the Commandments. But, if you can credit St. Luke's Christ, you must add three mind-boggling conditions. (1) You have to hate your father and mother, your wife or husband, your children, your brothers and sisters, even your own life. (2) You have to carry whatever cross Christ or life lays on you—preferably with a smile. (3) You have to give up every possession you own.

How does that grab you? Is it possible to make human and Christian sense out of the three conditions, without emasculating the mind of Christ? We have to try; at some point every Christian with the use of reason has to try. Your life depends on it—your life "in Christ."

I

First, you cannot be a follower of Jesus unless you hate—hate just about everybody you have good reason to love. If you take "hate" literally, there's a problem here. To hate means to have a great aversion to someone or something, often with ill will, to dislike intensely, to detest, to abhor. Elsewhere Jesus made it crystal-clear that his followers may not hate anyone that way—and that includes Iran's Ayatollah or Palestine's Arafat, Hitler or Stalin, drug dealers or Savings & Loan managers, Ku Kluxers or unrepentant rapists. He insisted that the second great commandment is to love your neighbor as you love yourself—no matter who the neighbor happens to be, whatever the color or class, the religion or sex. He declared solemnly: "You have heard that it was said, 'You shall love your neighbor and hate your enemy.' But I say to you, Love your enemies and pray for those who persecute you" (Mt 5:43–44). And the most difficult command of all: "Love one another as I have loved you" (Jn 15:12). Love unto crucifixion.

Obviously you cannot have it both ways: Love everybody and hate your family. What then?[1] Look at the context. Jesus is on his journey to Jerusalem, the road to death. Great crowds surround him, all sorts of people, many of them willing to join up with him but without appraising the cost. He wants them to think it over seriously. Remember the example he gave? What king before waging war doesn't sit down with his kitchen cabinet and ask, "Tell me, can our 10,000 rout their 20,000?" So, you who yearn to follow me, think it over. To be my disciple is extraordinarily difficult. Absolutely nobody, absolutely nothing, comes before me. I am your one Lord and Master. In case of conflict, your nearest and dearest take second place.

How do I know this is what Jesus meant? I turn to the corresponding text in Matthew. How does Jesus put it in Matthew? "Whoever loves father or mother more than me is not worthy of me; and whoever loves son or daughter more than me is not worthy of me" (Mt 10:37).

There you have, in simple language, without exaggeration, the first condition for a Christian: Jesus is number one in your life; no one, no matter how close to you in love, no one comes before him. What Jesus wants, Jesus gets. Forget the word "hate"; the simpler sentence is tough enough.[2] Putting Jesus at the top of one's love list has done over the centuries what Jesus predicted: It has all too often "set a man against his father, and a daughter against her mother, and a daughter-in-law against her mother-in-law; and a man's foes will be those of his own household" (Mt 10:35–36).

So then, question one in Christian hardball: Where does Christ rank in my day-to-day existence? Not only in general, but when the chips are down, when I have to choose between rival loves: Christ or money, Christ or power, Christ or fame, Christ or sex, Christ or pleasure.

II

But making Jesus *numero uno* is not enough. To be his disciple, to be a genuine Christian, calls for a second condition: You have to carry a cross. Here you touch the very core of Christianity: I mean the mystery of suffering, history's endless tale of tears. No human escapes it—believer or atheist, Christian or Jew, black or white, young or old. And the forms the human cross takes are legion: the acne on an adolescent's cheek, the heartbreak of a dear one's death, the schizophrenia that severs a personality, the AIDS that riddles the flesh, a world war that took 50 million lives, the war on the womb that takes 50 million more each year. It's all around you—on a flaming runway in Sioux City, on the drug-infested streets of D.C. It covers whole newspapers each day; it is part and parcel of human living. It's in your past—your family history; it's in your present—in your bones and marrow; it shadows your future—what will tomorrow bring?

So far, sheer fact: Like it or not, a cross is, or will be, intimate to your life. Your task and mine is to take sheer fact and transform it. Into what? Into Christian living. Keep suffering from degenerating into sheer waste. Integrate it into your life, keep your life from schizophrenia, manic today, depressive tomorrow. Take the pain that seems so useless, so senseless, so frustrating, and make it life-giving, even a source of profound joy.

But surely, Father, you jest. By what alchemy is such a transformation possible? I jest not, believe me. I jest not because here, if anywhere, what I preach has to be real, has to hit you where you live. I shall not unveil the mystery of suffering, explain to your satisfaction why you blew an exam or contracted cancer, why crib deaths take place and children are born with Down's syndrome, why sinners apparently have such a good time and you saints are all mucked up. I do not know why.

But this I do know: If God-in-flesh hung on a cross for three hours till his heart gave out, suffering has to have a profound place in the story of salvation—in your story. It has to make sense—even if you and I are too earth-bound to see it.

But there is a sliver of light. Central to Christian suffering is a crucial sentence of St. Paul: "I rejoice in my sufferings for your sake, and in my flesh I complete what is lacking in Christ's afflictions for the sake of his body, that is, the Church" (Col 1:24). Sheer pain is not a blessing; simply to take pleasure in pain makes you a candidate for a masochists' club. I don't race Georgetown's streets shouting the joys of chronic colitis. Behind Paul's gospel of suffering is a profound realization: To make human or Christian sense, pain must have a purpose.

You experience it on a human level every day. Soldiers give their lives courageously . . . for their country. Mothers endure torment . . .

for a child to be born. A fireman braves a burning building . . . to save an elderly woman. Archbishop Romero falls beneath a hail of bullets . . . to defend his Salvadoran people. It is purpose that transmutes sheer suffering into sacrifice. And the one purpose that overshadows all others is . . . love. Such was the driving force behind Jesus' journey to Jerusalem: "God so loved the world . . ." (Jn 3:16). And all this—Bethlehem to Calvary—out of love for men and women most of whom do not know him, or know him and pass him by, or give him grudgingly an hour a week, or never weep though he bleeds—who work and play, live and love, no differently than if he had never lived or died.

And so for you. Christ's sacrifice, the self-giving that saves a world, is not yet finished. Oh yes, his cross is the world's salvation. But in God's wisdom you and I have to take that cross to ourselves, carry it on our own shoulders. And that we do each time we murmur in the midst of any distress, "For you, Lord."

But that is not all. Suffering with and for Jesus is not a private pact, a neat deal between Jesus and me. It resonates, vibrates worldwide. Somewhere in Antoine de Saint Exupéry's *The Little Prince* you will find an insightful sentence: "There is no pain nor passion that does not radiate to the ends of the earth." In our theology, your sacrifice and mine, our suffering out of love, can bring God's grace to a suffering servant next door and to the farthest reaches of the earth, to Georgetown and Capetown. But only if we endure out of love. Whether it's a migraine headache or agony of spirit, whether it's a cancer-riddled body on a hospital bed or the age-old patience of the Polish people, no suffering need be wasted. What I endure out of love God touches to others—to give courage, to deepen faith, rekindle hope, enliven love. Quite concretely, how each of you lives the Christ-life rests in large measure on how all of you carry your cross. No suffering need be wasted—not if you love enough.

III

Ready for a third condition? To follow Jesus, to be his disciple, you have to give up all you have. All of you? Certainly sounds like it. But the problem with each Sunday Gospel is that you get an extract, a snippet, out of a larger whole; the passage you hear is not in context. I recall a Catholic priest quoted as preaching "To hell with the Catholic Church." What was not quoted was his next sentence, "So say the enemies of the Church."

It is only rarely that you can pluck a single sentence from the

Gospels and think you know the mind of Jesus. So here. Where riches, possessions, are at stake, even Scripture scholars shake their heads, especially over Luke.[3] On the one hand, you have a radical Jesus. I mean the Jesus who rails at riches: "Woe to you who are rich, for you have received your consolation" (Lk 6:24). God's kingdom belongs to the poor (v. 20). This is the Jesus who sees riches as simply evil. On the other hand, you have the moderate Jesus. I mean the Jesus who never tells his dear friends Lazarus, Martha, and Mary to give up all they have; the Jesus who proclaims salvation to little Zacchaeus because he promises *half* of his wealth to the poor (Lk 19:8). This is the Jesus who counsels prudent use of what you have to help the less fortunate; who advises you to share what you have; who knows from experience how generous his well-to-do friends can be, and loves them for it.

Which is the real Jesus? Only a semester in Scripture could do justice to the problem.[4] But a church is not a classroom, a liturgy not a lecture. Still, the very paradox that vexes the biblicist—radical Jesus or moderate Jesus—can speak eloquently to all of us who want to follow him.

The radical Jesus stands before us as a constant challenge. We know from sad experience that a peril lurks in possessions, in anything we humans own: a condo in Colorado or a Cabbage Patch doll, high intelligence or a high-C voice, a fabulous figure or a salary in six figures, computer wizardry or political power. The peril? Simply that it's mine, and it can dominate my existence, manipulate me. If it does, all else takes second place—including Christ. I no longer hear his voice, am deaf to his command or counsel: to give it all up or only half, to care and to share, to let go. The radical Jesus poses a perennial question: What rules my life?

The moderate Jesus turns our attention away from peril to opportunity: the potential in my possessions. In the last analysis, whatever is mine (save for sin) is a gift. Even if it stems from my brilliance, that brilliance itself owes its origin to God—to the God who gave me life. But a gift of God is best used if it is shared. Each of you is gifted—much as your modesty may demur. It matters not what your specific possessions are: millions or the widow's mite, intelligence or influence, wit or wisdom, compassion or competitiveness, personality or power, aggressiveness or gentleness, profound faith or buoyant hope or limitless love. Use them as Jesus invites or commands you. To a few he may say: Give all your worldly wealth to the poor and come, follow me in utter trust. To most: Share what you have; use it for your sisters and brothers. Employ your intelligence to free enslaved minds, your power to produce peace, your compassion to heal fragmented hearts, your hope to destroy another's despair, your love to make life livable for the unloved.

Good friends: Today's Gospel is "heavy metal." And still, it is the gospel—literally, "good news," "glad tidings." What's so good and glad about it? It answers a critical question: How shall I live? (1) Make sure that no person however deeply loved, no thing however precious, pre-empts the place Christ should occupy in your priorities. (2) Put every pain to profit, make it a saving grace for others, by linking your cross to Calvary. (3) Whatever your gifts, don't clutch them greedily, share them—as Christ asks it of you.

The result will surprise you, perhaps already has: You will experience a deep-seated joy not even Madonna or the Redskins can supply. For when you live the way Jesus lived, you will feel the way Jesus felt. Ain't anything like it.

Chapel of St. William
Georgetown University
and
Holy Trinity Church
Washington, D.C.
September 10, 1989

14
HE LIFTED UP HIS EYES AND SAW
Twenty-sixth Sunday of the Year (C)

- Amos 6:1, 4–7
- 1 Timothy 6:11–16
- Luke 16:19–31

This evening you seem to ask of me a mission impossible. For three reasonable reasons. (1) You ask me to preach within a convention on empowerment in the American Church—in laity and liturgy, in parish and prophecy, in woman and inner city.[1] (2) You ask me to preach on the heels of recognized experts like Hans Küng and Rosemary Haughton. (3) You ask me to preach in the context of three liturgical readings that pronounce woe on the self-indulgent, command you to keep the Christian way of life "unstained and free from reproach" (1 Tim 6:14), and condemn to hell those who receive good things in their lifetime. Where dare a homilist take off?

Fortunately, a homily is not a lecture. And so I would ask you to leave the lecture hall, come apart and rest a while, let the Lord speak to you—even if, as with Balaam's beast, the Lord speaks through the mouth of an ass (cf. Num 22:28). Ponder a parable on power and powerlessness—in three short acts. First, a retake of the parable. Second, a problem the parable poses for the powerful. Third, the Lord's solution.

I

First, the parable. On his journey to Jerusalem, in his movement to death, Jesus describes two contrasting life-styles, two types of Palestinian Jew. To make it contemporary, why not transfer it to the District of Columbia?

One of the two characters is "the man who has everything."[2] He

89

lives like a king, royally. He has his luxury condo overlooking the Potomac—no minority neighbors rocking and rolling round him. Money? Why, he lights his Havanas with five-dollar bills. His suits? From Saville of London. Shoes? Crafted by Gucci. Ties? Monogrammed by Cardin. Food? Catered by Lady Ashley. Transportation? A chauffeured Bentley, plus a Porshe for quick fun. In Luke's phrase, "daily he [makes] merry in splendid style" (Lk 16:19).

Outside the gatehouse, at a respectful distance, a pitifully poor man. No rich garments his; he is clothed from head to foot with ulcerated sores—and even these he must share with dogs. He is for ever hungry. Not for him reindeer with lingenberry sauce; his best hope is the rich man's leavings, scraps usually given to animals. His very name is appropriate: Lazarus, "God has helped"; no help in anyone human.

Even in death they differ. The rich man is buried with proper pomp and ceremony. After all, are not riches a sign of God's favor? Poor Lazarus is left unburied; not even a potter's field for him. It is left for angels to carry that shriveled, stinking body away.

But then a remarkable reversal. Where do we find the rich man? In Hades. Here no feasting, only tormenting thirst; no rustling silk, only painful flames. And Lazarus? In "Abraham's bosom" (v. 22), in a place of honor, a place of intimacy. No ulcers, no hunger; only endless rest, unfailing felicity. And a chasm separates the two, so broad as to be unbridgeable—there is no crossing over from either side to the other.

II

Now move to the problem the parable poses for the powerful. Why is the rich man condemned? Not primarily because he is wealthy, though one verse (25) seems to suggest it. He is condemned because he never actually *saw* Lazarus at his gate. The first time he sees Lazarus is from Hades—and so you have that revealing expression, "He lifted up his eyes and saw . . ." (v. 23).[3] One of the most unrecognized perils of wealth is that it can blind you. You do not see what you ought to see—whom you ought to see. Not bad will so much as blindness.

Now that peril threatens not simply riches; it overhangs all possessions. It is not only a plundering Marcos and his shoe-collecting Imelda who never really see the crucified other. A child clutching her Raggedy Ann doll; a top HUD official[4] who gives preferential treatment to a Puerto Rican developer because he seems close to the Vice

President;[5] an insider trader on Wall Street; a top-flight geneticist whose prime principle is "We can do it, therefore we should"; a scholar so locked in his books that people don't matter; a college student who has never learned to share her 4.0; a priest who prefers sacrifice to mercy; a Congressman so into perks for his constituents that no other U.S. districts exist; a whiz kid who implants a virus that infects thousands upon thousands of computers; a magisterial Roman official so protective of the marriage bond that he fears the bleeding hearts of women in chanceries; a wealthy televangelist who banks a $500,000 bonus the same month he fires 283 employees; drug dealers who refuse to look beyond the dollars to the addicted; a superathlete who will use any means to win—these and a host of others are not so much evil as blind. And what has blinded them is the possession they clutch.

"He lifted up his eyes and saw. . . ." Only if we lift up our eyes, lift them above our small selves, beyond what we own, will we really see the other, actually see the deprived and degraded, the drug-abased and the sexually abused, see the disaster to people in any domination, whether male or white, military or financial, clerical or lay. Only if we lift up our eyes will we be concerned for community.

III

This leads nicely into my third point: the Lord's solution to the power problem, to the peril in power. The crux of the matter is the gripping dialogue between the rich man and Abraham. What the rich man realizes—far too late—is that in neglecting poor Lazarus he was neglecting the law and the prophets.[6]

Follow the dialogue. "Father [Abraham], send [Lazarus] to my father's house, for I have five brothers, that he may warn them, lest they too come into this place of torment." Abraham's response? "They have Moses and the prophets; let them listen to them." Let them listen to Leviticus: "You shall love your neighbor as yourself" (Lev 19:18); to Isaiah: "Defend the fatherless, plead for the widow" (Isa 1:17); to Micah: "What does the Lord require of you but to do justice and to love kindness?" (Mic 6:8); to Yahweh's thundering threat that without love and justice your sacrifices are an abomination to heaven. "No," says the rich man (vv. 27–30). How tragic a monosyllable! No. Like me, my brothers will not listen to God's word in Scripture. Even if Lazarus appears in a vision or a dream and delivers a brilliant lecture on the Bible and social justice, they won't change their life-style. There's only one way to get through to them: if Lazarus alive, raised from the dead, drops in on my brothers as a living witness not only to life after death but to the flames that await the unjust, the bliss that envelops the despised of the earth. I promise you, that will grab them.

From Abraham, an equally emphatic no. "If they do not listen to [God's word in God's Book], they will not be convinced even if some-one rises from the dead" (v. 31). We might add 20 centuries of experi-ence testifying that even a resurrected Jesus, suggested in the closing clause, may not convert a well-heeled human who is blind to the grind-ing poverty that accuses our wealth, who does not see that it is Jesus who lies in rags at his gate.[7]

Good friends: This weekend you are immersed in profound con-versation on a critical issue: empowerment in the Church. As the years go on, the optimist in me says, more and more of you will share church power, will be empowered to determine decisions that shape Catholic existence—yours and others'. History trumpets a sobering thesis: Power corrupts. Not always, not everyone. But all too often—and not infrequently those whose motives are of the purest, whose very con-cern for the rights of God blinds them to the needs of God's people. All God's people—not only those whose needs you share.

May I be so brash as to commend today's parable to you for scotch-taping to your refrigerator door? Two thoughts therefrom in particular. (1) Whenever you must exercise power, cast your eye up and down: up to the God who alone *is* Power (Mt 26:64; Mk 14:62), the Power in whom you participate, the Power identical with Love; down to the Lazarus who should not have to beg for crumbs, whose servant you are. (2) Let your handbook of power be the Book of which today's saint, dear irascible Jerome,[8] wrote: When your head droops at night, let a page of Scripture pillow it.[9] Not only "Moses and the prophets" but the Christ who in his own words "came not to be served but to serve" (Mt 20:28).

Omni Shoreham Hotel
Washington, D.C.
September 30, 1989

15
GOD OF THE LIVING
Thirty-second Sunday of the Year (C)

- 2 Maccabees 7:1–2, 9–14
- 2 Thessalonians 2:16—3:5
- Luke 20:27–38

You know, so far in today's liturgy you've been criminally cheated. Yes, cheated. For the experts across the Atlantic who shaped this liturgy gave you a scissors-and-paste version of the first reading—one of the most celebrated stories in Hebrew literature. I mean the story of a mother and her seven sons. Not just any mother, and not just any sons. A mother who is forced to face all her seven boys as they die savage deaths on a single day for a dictator's delight—because they refused to eat pork. Let me (1) tell you the whole story swiftly, (2) touch the story to today's Gospel, and (3) suggest what the story and the Gospel might say to you and me in November 1989.

I

First, the story. For sheer drama, little rivals it till we stand with another mother beneath her only Son's cross on Calvary.

The context of today's story? It takes place about 175 years before Christ, in the Seleucidan kingdom of Syria. King Antiochus IV Epiphanes has decreed that all the peoples within his kingdom be one in law, one in custom, one in religion. The Jews in particular have provoked his wrath; he is determined to secularize them. Any Jew found with a copy of the Mosaic law is to be executed; Sabbath, circumcision, food laws—not to be tolerated.

In today's story, a Jewish mother and her seven sons are commanded by the king to eat the flesh of swine. By Hebrew law this is forbidden, and so all eight retort with the Hebrew equivalent of "No way, José." Antiochus orders them put to death slowly, agonizingly, in

93

ways that will amuse his cronies. Each suffers horribly. Tongues are cut out, hands and feet cut off, heads scalped, limbs mangled, bodies fried in pans and caldrons. Most amusing to the spectators, the mother has to look on as each son perishes in turn.

Courageously, each son faces up to the king—in language fashioned of profound faith, heartfelt hope. Son 1: "We will die rather than violate the law of our fathers" (2 Macc 7:2). Son 2: "Cursed king, you can indeed cast us from this life, but the King of the universe will raise us up to new life for ever" (v. 9). Son 3: "This tongue and these hands that you will cut off, I got these from God, and from God I hope to get them back again" (v. 11). Son 4: "I cherish the hope that God will raise me up, but as for you—you will never rise to life" (v. 14). Son 5: "Because you have power among men, you do what you please. But don't think God has forsaken our people. Keep acting like this, and God's mighty power will torture you and your descendants" (vv. 16–17). Son 6: "We are suffering for our sins, but don't kid yourself that in fighting against God you will go scot free" (vv. 18–19). And all the while their mother encourages each: "The God who shaped you will give life and breath back to you" (v. 23).

Then comes the seventh and youngest son. Antiochus tries just about everything to weaken his resolve. "I'll make you rich beyond your wildest dreams. You'll be my friend and buddy. I'll put you on my kitchen cabinet, give you political power" (cf. v. 24). It doesn't work, so the king appeals to the mother. "Look, lady, talk to him. Help him to save himself. Why die over a pork chop?" (cf. v. 25). She does talk to him—a great line: "Son, don't be afraid of this butcher. Take death, so that I may get you back again with your brothers" (v. 29). He does; he welcomes death, so that God may have mercy on their nation.

And then the final sentence in the story, surprisingly simple, so moving in its simplicity: "Last of all, the mother died, after her sons" (v. 41).

II

What has that amazing story of Hebrew faith in common with today's Gospel? One word: resurrection. You see, the persecution of the Jews under Antiochus had roused in the persecuted masses an unexpected hope: the first unwavering Hebrew hope for a resurrection of the dead. And what the mother in Maccabees and her seven sons announced to Antiochus, Jesus thundered to the Sadducees.

It wasn't easy. Remember who the Sadducees were: an aristocratic priestly class in Jerusalem, the highly conservative element among the Jews.[1] Conservative in that they stood rigidly by ancient Israelite belief; no room for development of doctrine, for change, for creativity. And so they denied that the soul is immortal, denied that the body will rise from the dead. Why? Because these were not clearly taught in the "five books of Moses"—in Genesis or Exodus, in Leviticus or Numbers or Deuteronomy. And that was the only law that mattered—the written law. All else—oral interpretations, later traditions, more moderate understandings—forget it!

This is the group that posed to Jesus the question in today's Gospel. A somewhat ridiculous "what if" question from Mosaic law.[2] A man dies, leaving a wife but no children. His brother must, by law, take the wife and raise up children for his brother. In the case at hand, seven brothers take the same wife and leave no children. The question? If, as you say, the dead rise, whose wife will the childless widow of seven husbands be? Or an apparent dilemma: Which do you choose, resurrection or the law of Moses?

Jesus' response, as so often, is a gem. He cuts through the legalism with a swift sentence: The Lord our God "is not God of the dead but of the living" (v. 38). Jesus brings the Sadducees back to Moses, whom they have quoted. In effect he says: "Remember how the Lord appeared to Moses 'in a flame of fire out of the midst of a bush' (Exod 3:2)? How God identified Himself: 'I am the God of Abraham, the God of Isaac, and the God of Jacob' (Exod 3:6)? Yahweh did not say, 'I was' their God; Yahweh said, 'I am' their God. This is God's very name, 'I AM.' This eternal 'I AM' brings your dead ancestors back to life."

The point is this: The God whose creative power can bring Abraham, Isaac, and Jacob to life at one swoop no longer needs the process of parenting. In the age to come, the widow of the seven brothers, like the seven sons and their mother, is no longer defined in terms of marriage or generation. She lives the risen life of a completed human person. Our God is "the God of Abraham and the God of Isaac and the God of Jacob" (Lk 20:37) not because they were *once* alive, but because they are *now* alive, are *always* alive. Our God is a God of the living.

III

So much for Old Testament and New. Now what of you? You see, I am not satisfied if at this point you agree noisily that patriarch

Abraham and apostle Peter, Ignatius Loyola and Elvis Presley are alive—are alive in soul and will one day arise in flesh. To be alive to God is not something that begins beyond the grave, a consolation prize for a life of misery in a vale of tears, a blue ribbon for being good and avoiding the fleshpots of 14th Street. A God of the living demands that you be alive *now*. Alive not only because you breathe deeply or race the Marine Marathon, wolf Domino's pizzas or sway to Springsteen, cut a cancer from a colon or argue a case in court, bring off a Ford-Jaguar deal. All well and good; here are slices of life. But you are more amazingly alive to God if you are living the life of God.

This is not souped-up rhetoric. God's only Son did not take your flesh and walk your earth, was not lashed with whips and pinned to twin beams of bloody wood, so that you might simply live till ninety. He lived and died so that you might share his life, his joy, now. What is this living in the concrete? Go back to the seven brothers and their mother. They were alive to God before they died, for three good reasons. (1) They believed tenaciously in a God ever faithful to His people. (2) Their hopes rested not in miracles of earth but in the power and love of God. (3) They loved God with all their heart and mind, soul and strength; loved others as much as they loved themselves. St. Paul put it pithily to the Christians of Corinth: "Faith, hope, love abide, these three; but the greatest of these is love" (1 Cor 13:13). These gifts you have; but I'm afraid they are often swept away, forgotten, neglected in the rat race strangely called "human living."

First, at this moment each of you possesses a power no person or computer on earth can give you. You can believe, on God's word, what passes proof. You confess a God at once One and Three. You believe that a Jew crucified like a common criminal in a cramped corner of the world almost 20 centuries ago was and is God's very Son divine. You believe that when water washed your brow a year ago or 50, you became a new creature, filled with the presence of your God. You believe that when your tongue cradles what looks like bread, what feels like bread, what tastes like bread, you are hosting not bread but the body of Christ. You believe that, when free of serious sin, you are as much a shrine of divinity as is the tabernacle here before you. And on this you live; for your faith is at its finest when you surrender to God all that you are—mind and heart, liberty and memory, passion and power. This it is to be alive to God.

Second, you have a gift we call hope. Not a wimpy "Maybe things will turn out o.k." Rather, a confident expectation that wherever you turn, whatever your problem, God will be there. Not always with an answer, but always with a presence, a strength, a courage out of this world. A confident expectation that your life will not end in six feet of dirt, will in fact never end, that you will always be alive to God, that the spiritual part of you will survive the corroding of your flesh, that one day the whole person that is "you" will come together again, but without the pain, without the tears. Unless such is your hope, there is no point in your presence here. And if I may quote one of my few deathless sentences, "If heaven is not for real, I shall be madder than hell."

Third, you can love. Most humans (present congregation excepted) toss the word "love" around with loose abandon. It covers everything from "together till death" to one-night stands, from the fidelity of the seven sons in Maccabees to the sleazy sex of "Miami Vice."[3] Through God's gracious giving, you harbor within you the power to love as Jesus loved—love a child, love a man or woman, love God. As Jesus loved—nothing held back, your whole person on fire, even unto crucifixion.

Genuine love may be difficult to define, but it's relatively easy to recognize. You sense it in Maccabees' mother of seven, in Mother Mary beneath her Son's cross, in Mother Teresa asking for every single one of the world's unwanted infants, in millions of mothers enraptured by a newborn child. You yourselves love that way when, in response to Jesus, you feed starved stomachs and cool parched tongues, welcome the homeless and clothe the naked, clasp the hands of the sick and burst the bars that imprison so many all around you.

Good friends: In recent weeks the world has been stunned by an unprecedented movement from slavery to freedom. It was startling enough when Poland compelled Communism to compromise. It is little short of miraculous when Hungary declares itself an independent state and the Berlin Wall crumbles. In hundreds of photos from overseas, eyes sparkle with fresh hope, laughter leaps from lips too long enslaved.

I do not think it outrageous to suggest that we Catholics could stand a similar eruption of freedom. I do not mean an insurrection against Rome—casting off all sorts of shackles we feel, rightly or wrongly, lessen our liberty. I mean something still more profound— the liberty that today's liturgy celebrates. I mean a living response to the German philosopher Nietzsche's caustic criticism: You Christians do not look redeemed. I mean a fresh realization that right now we are *risen* Christians, that our God is a God of the living, that we are alive to God only to the extent that faith, hope, and love power our everyday activity. I mean a feeling that faith, hope, and love are not shackles that repress, forbid, say no to human living, but rather, as Jesus promised, "the truth [that] will make you free" (Jn 8:32). I mean an incredible joy in being Catholic, in being faith-full and hope-full and love-full —a joy that is infectious, that attracts such as do not share our vision, forces them to wonder how the cross that is erected over our world and over our lives is not a summons to unrelieved tears but the source of new life—rich, deep, vibrant, thrilling.

I doubt that any of us will ever have to face the terrible choice that Antiochus put to the seven brothers and their mother: Give up your faith . . . or die. Our problem may be even more difficult: Live your faith . . . and feel gloriously free.

Dahlgren Chapel
Georgetown University
and
Holy Trinity Church
Washington, D.C.
November 12, 1989

Weddings

16
CASUAL COOKOUT, LASTING LOVE
Wedding Homily 1

- Genesis 2:18–24
- 1 Corinthians 12:31—13:13
- John 2:1–11

Melissa and Scott: I am not sure you can call this a sermon or a homily. I shall not really "preach" to you, nor shall I linger on the Scripture you have selected. Rather, with God's Word as my background, with over seven decades of wedding-watching behind me, let me speak out of my deep affection for you. Let me speak of yesterday, of today, and of tomorrow.

I

Yesterday. I recall a Memorial Day weekend, less than a year ago. A back-yard cookout. It remains in my memory because it was the first time I met you, *and* the first time you met each other. Skeptics may call it coincidence. Increasingly I doubt that. For all that my "thing" is theology, God-talk, I have no special insight into the mind of God. And yet I refuse to believe that God is not somehow there, somehow behind the minor miracle when scads of strangers come together from wherever, two sets of eyes meet, and a casual cookout leads to lasting love.

Only you two know intimately how your love has grown. For a Jesuit to invade that sacred space would be a sacrilege. But I dare to tell you how that love looks to us who are privileged to love you differently but no less dearly. These eleven months recall to many of us what St. Paul sang so lyrically to the Christians of Corinth: "Love is patient and kind . . . not jealous or boastful . . . not arrogant or rude. Love does not insist on its own way . . . is not irritable or resentful . . . does not rejoice at wrong, but rejoices in the right. Love bears all things, believes all things, hopes all things, endures all things" (1 Cor 13:4–7).

It has not been all heaven—how could it be and still be love on earth? *Love* may be all St. Paul describes, but *lovers* can be impossibly impatient, unbelievably unkind. Lovers can be juvenilely jealous, ridiculously rude. Lovers can resent most the one they love most, can want their own way like little children, can refuse to endure what earthly love imposes. If any of this has been your experience, it does not mean you were never in love. It only means that these eleven months were a beginning, not an end; a promise, not the consummation. And as we who love you looked on from near and far, the promise looked rich indeed. And the promise leads to my second point.

II

Today. Melissa and Scott, if that first meeting of your eyes was a gift of God, today's exchange of your words is a still more wondrous gift. For at least four reasons. First, this ceremony itself is a powerful public statement. You are declaring to the Christian community, declaring to the farthest reaches of the earth, declaring to heaven itself what is already a fact: your profound love for each other. Were you living on a desert island, such a statement would be needless; a private kiss could seal it all. But the world in which you live needs constantly to hear what you proclaim today. At a time when that awesome monosyllable "love" is used for everything from a one-night stand to the unbuttoned promiscuity of TV's "Dallas," you define love as self-giving, a gift of your whole person each to the other, a commitment of all you are and all you have. It's a courageous statement, a glorious declaration, and it helps us incurable romantics to hope again that actually it is not economics but love that makes the world go round.

Second, in a few short moments you will share a ceremony so sacred that within Catholicism we call it a sacrament—a sign so sacred that it brings God and God's grace to you. More striking still, of this sacred rite I shall not be the minister—as I would be if I were baptizing you. You are the ministers here. Not a small thing, I assure you. For it means that you two, Melissa and Scott, will be the channels through which God comes to you. In giving yourselves to each other, you will be channeling God to each other. God will come to you through each other. Through simple syllables ever ancient, ever new, you will give each other your two most priceless gifts: yourself and God.

Third, in the Christian vision your wedding is a breathtaking symbol. In your life together you represent an even more remarkable union: the union of Christ with our humanity, with the body of Christians. It's so deep, so awesome, that we could never have imagined it, had not God's inspired Word revealed it to us. The living, dynamic interplay that goes on between the risen Christ and his people, the invisible interplay of love that links Christ to all of us—this tells you the kind of love, the special oneness, our Lord expects of you in your wedded existence. Two, while remaining two, become wondrously one.

Fourth, in an era when few dare to say "for ever," when contracts and pledges are broken overnight by Wall Street traders and government officials, by coaches and quarterbacks, by the long-married and the short-, by politicians and priests, you make bold to murmur, "I take you . . . till death do us part." It sounds so brash, this plunge into a future hidden from your eyes, this pledge which recalls a sentence in an older marriage manual, where the priest says, "And so, not knowing what lies before you, you take each other for better for worse, for richer for poorer, in sickness and in health . . . until death." Not knowing what lies before you. This leads into my final point.

III

Tomorrow. Only two things, pundits proclaim, are sure about tomorrow: taxes and death. Let me suggest one other certainty—far more attractive, considerably more comforting, than the IRS and the undertaker. Let me explain.

Admit it, the future *is* in large measure mystery. You cannot promise yourself tomorrow. And if tomorrow does dawn, you cannot predict with assurance just what it will bring. Even weatherman Willard[1] sticks to jet streams, cold fronts, and high pressures. You do know what is part and parcel of human existence—highs and lows even for those who love lavishly. You will feel so full of vim and vigor that you can barely bear it, and you can grow sick in spirit or infirm of flesh. You can joy in a job that fulfils you, and you may rot away at a job too small for your spirit. Peace can flood your home and anxiety stress you out. In the eyes of your children you will be reborn, but children can choke you with their crack and coke. Life will be all around you, but death of dear ones is only a stone's throw away.

No need to dwell on this; you've at least seen it. The point I want to press, the promise this precious rite makes, is that whatever happens, unexpectedly or relentlessly, one thing is certain: God will be there. When with hands clasped you say "I take you," God's hand will clasp your own. It takes three to make a marriage.

You see, you cannot make it on your own. A 4.0 in mind or a 10 in flesh, a Brite smile on your lips or Brut in your armpits, an iron will or a gentle disposition, a baby carriage or a BMW, all the TV commercials wrapped into two people—it's not enough. If you remember naught else from this homily, remember this: If God is not the unseen guest, not only in your home but in your heart and head, your oneness is in peril. Marriage is much too difficult to entrust to two people, to a man and a woman.

This is not pious prattle, just what a priest is expected to preach. This is what the centuries cry, what the experience of ages announces, what the gospel of Christ trumpets. It is what St. Paul declared to the Christian community in Rome: ". . . hope does not disappoint us, because God's love has been poured into our hearts through the Holy Spirit who has been given to us" (Rom 5:5). God loves you, God lives in you. That is why you can dance out of this house of God with confidence—not arrogance, only confidence—because within you both is the one same divine Spirit of God, ready to flame within you, to spark a relationship that may dull but will never die, a love that may settle into routine but never into a rut, a oneness where there is indeed "I and thou" but never "mine and thine."

God will be there: God your Father, with His only Son. You have Jesus' own guarantee for that, his solemn pledge the night before he died: "If [you] love me, [you] will keep my word, and my Father will love [you], and we will come to [you] and make our home with [you]" (Jn 14:23). Can you really imagine that after Calvary's cross Christ forgot about you, left you on your own? No. Here Catholics and Protestants are at one: Our God is a "God with us," not a deity off in some blue yonder serenaded by a choir of angels. Here is your tomorrow—three sets of clasped hands: your hands, Melissa; your hands, Scott; and the hands of Christ pierced with nails for you.

But never forget that "if" of Jesus: "If you love me. . . ." You cannot take Christ for granted, pay him lip service on Sunday, beg him for rescue when pinned down in a foxhole. Today's sacred ceremony makes sense, human and divine, only if it is a promise. Not only God's promise that He will be with you, but your promise that you will be with Him—in good times and bad, with megabucks or a hole in your wallet, in sickness and in health . . . till death.

A final word—to all of you who have come together because you care, because you love this dear couple. I say to you what I say to each gathering such as this. Today's sacred scenario is not a spectator sport. You are not looking on from the outside. Today is your day too—all of you who have played some part, large or small, in the love that reaches new heights this morning. But tomorrow is yours as well; for without you this couple's tomorrow will be perilous indeed. They depend on you. Not only to keep Scott in hockey sticks and Melissa in chafing pans. Far more importantly, they need your constant caring. For, again, they will live their love not on a South Pacific isle but in a world where hate mingles with love, blood and guts with wine and roses, black-tie banquets with babies' bloated bellies, rock 'n' roll with AIDS and Alzheimer's. Melissa especially knows this beneath a nurse's cap. She experiences it day in and day out, dies a little with each AIDS victim, each heart that stops before her eyes. To survive, they need you . . . each of you.

And so, dear Melissa and Scott, I presume to speak for every man, woman, and child assembled here. Our most wondrous wedding gift to you is . . . ourselves. Whenever you look for us, we shall be there. Not so much our credit cards as our homes and our hearts. Quite likely, then, with God within you and us folk around you, you will experience together the joy of Jesus—the profound joy he promised to those who follow him, the genuine joy he gives even in the depths of desolation, the joy he guaranteed "no human being will take from you" (Jn 16:22). So be it, now and until death do you part.

Holy Trinity Church
Washington, D.C.
April 15, 1989

17
TO THE NETHERLANDS, WITH LOVE
Wedding Homily 2

- Genesis 2:18–24
- 1 Corinthians 12:31—13:8
- Matthew 5:1–12a

Good friends all: This is surely a day which the Lord has made! Without making light of Frans's executive expertise or the determination of the Beerkens clan, I suggest that only the Lord could have brought the Netherlands and the States together as we see it this afternoon.[1] If the Dutch have "discovered America" this week, I assure you that we late-comers to civilization have found profound delight in the friendly folk whom Julius Caesar dared to invade in 58 B.C.

Still, it is primarily for Cathleen and Frans that this day has been made by the Lord. If I were pope, I would decree that this homily be given by two of you long-wedded couples—one Dutch, the other American; but by the rules of the Catholic game you must listen to a confirmed bachelor. But it's just possible that a look at marriage from outer space, from God's view of things, might counter the concepts we Americans get, and export for Continental consumption, in TV's "Divorce Court" and "Dallas."

Now God's view of things has been focused for us by the three passages Frans and Cathleen have plucked from God's inspired Word. These texts have told us, in swift succession, (1) how a loving Lord made us in the beginning, (2) how our Lord God expects us to love right now, and (3) what sort of living makes us "blest" in God's eyes. A word on each.

I

How did God make us in the beginning? For starters, remember that God did not have to make us at all. God did not need us. Believe it

106

or not, Father, Son, and Holy Spirit could have been utterly happy without you and me. But profound love has a built-in bent to share. Even God's love is like that—the divine love shared for eternity among Three whose reality means they are turned totally to one another.

This thrilling Trinity, for some reason that only Love divine can explain, decided to share love, to spread their love around. And so God made sun and sky, earth and ocean, moon and stars, the fish of the sea, the birds of the air, the beasts of the field. But things—from the amoeba and the atom to the panther and the planet—could not respond to God's love; things could only receive love, could not return it. And so God shaped a creature we call human, attuned to God in its total being. Here divine imagination broke out in two incredible ways.

First, in shaping the human, God did not create what today we might call an alien—someone utterly foreign to the Creator. Here Genesis is brief and clear: "In the image of God He created [the human]" (Gen 1:27). There is something divine about you—literally. Theologians and Scripture scholars have spilt ink and sweated blood over what this "something divine" might be,[2] and we find ourselves submerged in mystery. But this we do know: Each of you, in your wholeness, stands in a relationship to God so unique, so intimate, that God's Word declares you "like God."

Second, God was not happy with one only kind of human like to its Lord. With a foresight for which we must for ever be grateful, God fashioned male and female. Not in some casual sort of way. With divine delight God shaped them in such wise that each would be drawn to the other, that from this attraction a self-giving called human love would spring, that from their love a miracle would be born: a child, the fruit of their oneness, a child like them, a child like God.

II

This power to love at the very dawn of creation takes us to the passage from Paul: how God expects us to love right now. St. Paul's outburst is a touching tribute to love, much favored by brides and grooms. But it raises problems.[3]

Of course "love is patient, love is kind"; but lovers can be impossibly impatient, outrageously unkind. I fret if you keep me waiting—for breakfast or the bathroom, for your make-up or my brunch. You fume because I put a stop watch on you, make you punch a time clock.

And if we're not careful, we can dissect each other as mercilessly as a critic cuts up a second-rate movie.

Of course "love is not jealous"; but lovers can grow green-eyed with jealousy. You grudge me my job, how fascinating I find it, the hours it tears me from you. I envy you your yuppie friends, or I can't stand their arrogance. I don't like the way you smile at so-and-so; that smile is my private property.

Of course "love is not rude"; but lovers can be boorish and churlish, sullen and surly. Familiarity, the aphorism has it, breeds contempt. With the years, I take you for granted. I say things I never dreamed of when I was courting your love. I neglect you in a crowd, forget anniversaries, kiss you the way I kiss my sister. And you—you can forget all too easily that I am thin-skinned, I too hurt when you treat me like part of the furniture, like an overstuffed chair.

Of course "love is not self-seeking"; but lovers get rigidly set in their ways. I'm for black and white, the spare and the stark; you're for pinks and the warm, what's cozy and cuddly. Monday nights are for TV football; you knew that when you married me. How can any human babble so long on the phone? Can't you see I'm busy? What's so important that it cannot wait? And stop rumpling my hair; I just combed it.

Of course "love rejoices in the truth"; but lovers can fly into fits over what is true. We forget that truth is a complex, sticky, tricky thing; that the way *I* see truth is burdened with a whole background going back to the womb; that my truth gets mixed with likes and dislikes; that stubborn I would rather die than admit to a woman, or before our children, that I'm wrong.

Of course "there is no limit to love's forbearance, to love's trust, to love's hope, to love's power to endure"; but lovers can grow intolerant, can doubt or despair, find one another difficult to endure. For the years take their toll of us. A dear one dies, in childhood or of Alzheimer's, and God can die as well. If the green years of promise fade, hope can wither as well. And how will you endure me when the firm lines turn to fat and I no longer remind you of Tom Selleck?

Perhaps "love never fails, never comes to an end"; but, dear St. Paul, ever since you penned that lovely line, countless lovers have fallen out of love.

III

Now that sobering contrast between love and lovers is not intended to discourage you; it is not a commercial for the single life. But it does raise a question. In the face of the foibles and frailties that threaten true love, is there not a counteragent, a way of living that could keep Cathleen and Frans "blest" in God's eyes, might help preserve their love in something of its youthful vigor? There is indeed. The answer lies in the third passage they have borrowed from the Bible. I mean what we call the Beatitudes: "Blest are. . . ."[4]

Frans and Cathleen will be blest, will be fortunate, if they are "poor in spirit." I mean, if they realize that, however rich they may get in this world's goods, they owe whatever they are, whatever they have, ultimately to the loving Lord who gave them life, who gives them breath, the God without whom they could not blink an eye, lift a hand, kiss each other in love. They will be blest if they look for their security and salvation not to other humans or to material things but to God. Oh yes, they will not live in splendid isolation; by their very nature they are social animals; their lives are already intertwined with social, economic, and political realities. And God wants it so. But what God does not want is self-deception: a conviction or a feeling that they can "make it" on their own, that they can live as images of God without God.

Frans and Cathleen will be blest, will be fortunate, if they "hunger and thirst for holiness." I do not mean hands piously folded, eyes lifted adoringly to heaven. I mean a strong oneness with God that colors every facet of their lives and their loves. I mean what a passionate North African Christian wrote almost 1700 years ago:

> How beautiful . . . the marriage of two Christians, two who are one in hope, one in desire, one in the way of life they follow, one in the religion they practice. . . . Nothing divides them, either in flesh or in spirit. . . . They pray together, they worship together, they fast together; instructing one another, encouraging one another, strengthening one another. Side by side they visit God's church and partake of God's Banquet; side by side they face difficulties and persecution, share their consolations. They have no secrets from one another; they never shun each other's company; they never bring sorrow to each other's hearts. Unembarrassed they visit the sick and assist the needy. They give alms without anxiety; they attend the Sacrifice without difficulty; they perform their daily exercises of piety without hindrance. They need not be furtive about making the Sign of the Cross, nor timorous in greeting the brethren, nor silent in asking a blessing of God. Psalms and hymns they sing to one another, striving to see which one of them will chant more beautifully the praises of their Lord. Hearing and seeing this, Christ rejoices. To such as these He gives His peace. . . .[5]

Frans and Cathleen will be blest, will be fortunate, if they "show mercy." I mean, they should reflect to others the generosity God has shown to them. Happily, compassion is connatural to them, part of their make-up. The new thing is that, from now on, when they go out to the less fortunate, the less gifted, to those who hunger for justice or a loaf of bread, for freedom or a simple smile, their hearts and at times their hands will go out *together*.

Frans and Cathleen will be blest, will be fortunate, if they are "peacemakers." The world in which they must live out their love is terribly wounded by violence—from the wars that ravage countries, through the hates that savage cities, to the naked viciousness that TV blasts into our parlors in prime time. We need the strong gentleness of this dear couple—to listen to the cries of the crucified, to speak words that reconcile, to touch with hands that heal. Remember, peace begins not in the councils of powerful nations; peace begins in the human heart—in your heart and mine. Most importantly for this day which the Lord has made, peace, like charity, begins at home. Peace begins with two persons, a man and a woman, who are at peace with each other, who are at peace with their God.

A final word—a word that ceaselessly needs retelling. Good friends from far and near, this day consecrated to a couple is *your* day too. Not simply because you joy in their joy. Not only because each of you has played a part, large or little, in the love that comes to ecstatic expression today. I have insisted that what Cathleen and Frans are engaging to be and to do is impossible without God. Now I insist that their partnership for life is perilous without *you*.

You see, to live together as images of God, to live the kind of love St. Paul sang, to be poor in spirit and rich in holiness, compassionate and creators of peace, Frans and Cathleen need what is peculiarly yours to give. Not so much Dutch curtains, Italian pasta, Irish linen. Rather, your example. The example of men and women who, for one year or 50, have taken each other for better for worse, for richer for poorer, in sickness and in health. Men and women who reverence one another because the other is like God. Men and women whose love has no limit in its self-giving, in its power to endure. Men and women who have not been seduced by the divine dollar or the golden guilder, but love above all else the God in whose likeness you have been shaped. Men and women who know that to love God is to love God's children, especially the homeless and the helpless, the unloved and the un-wanted, the drug-addicted and the AIDS-afflicted. Men and women prepared to pay a price for peace: I mean, forgive as Christ has for-given you, take the first step to reconciliation even when you are in the right, embrace enemies the way Pope John Paul II embraced his would-be assassin.

So generous a gift, good friends, has an awesome advantage over most gifts: It need never end. In fact, it can get better as the years move on—as your own love grows: your love for God, your love for one another, your love especially for this dear couple whose joy in each other brings such delight to our hearts. It need never end because what you are giving is your very self. May I, in your name, promise this wedding gift to Frans and Cathleen?

Holy Trinity Church
Washington, D.C.
April 22, 1989

18

SPACES IN YOUR TOGETHERNESS
Wedding Homily 3

- Tobit 8:4–9
- Colossians 3:12–17
- Gibran, *The Prophet*

Three intriguing texts have been proclaimed to you. Not indeed by chance. They were culled with care by Margot and Del from three unusual little works: one from Hebrew hands, another from the New Testament, the third from a modern mystic and rebel. Do they suggest another "war of religion"? Quite the contrary. They complement one another impressively—especially what each has to say about love. Since today's intense joy and the swift passage of those texts from tongue to ear may have lessened their impact on you, let me dwell a bit on each. Three texts, three movements. (1) Tobit: Love is from above. (2) Paul: This love from above has to be lived here below. (3) Gibran: This love, to last, demands at the same time togetherness and distance.

I

First, a Hebrew insight: Love is from above. The text of Tobit was fashioned probably two centuries before Christ. It has been called "A fascinating amalgam of *Arabian Nights* romance, kindly Jewish piety, and sound moral teaching."[1] And still the Roman Catholic Church regards it as inspired, part of Scripture. Much of this story about the wisdom of faith centers on Tobit's son, Tobias. Tobias goes off to a distant land and marries a Jewish maiden named Sarah. This he does on the advice of an angel. I suspect he needed a nudge from an angel, because Sarah's first seven husbands were killed by a demon on their wedding night.

At any rate, the prayer of Tobias on his wedding night, the prayer plucked for your hearing this day, takes us back to Genesis, to the beginning of creation. And Genesis tells us that love did not come about because in prehistoric times two evolving apes were chemically attracted to each other. Love, lifelong love, was born because a loving God, shaping the first humans out of nothing save love, shaped not one type of human but two. Two who would image God in different ways—male and female. Two who would be drawn to each other—in spirit as well as in flesh. Two humans whose love would bear fruit in a third person, a child, somewhat as the love of the first two persons in the Trinity *is* a third person—the Holy Spirit. Two whose love would be, till time is no more, the source of human society, the expression on earth of the love in heaven that is the secret life of God.

Yes, Margot and Del, your love was made in heaven millions of years before you were born. Your love was born in the loving mind of God; for even God's love, especially God's love, is so creative that it bursts the bonds of self, incarnates itself ceaselessly in images of itself —in such as you and me. Such, Del and Margot, is the source of your love, and its model. For the way God loves tells you that, if your love is genuine, it will at once unite you in unique love to each other *and* spin you out to others—in particular, to the despised and the desperate, to the feeble and the forlorn, to those who hunger for justice and peace, to such as yearn for the touch of your hand, who hope against hope that you care.

II

Second, a New Testament text. It stems from the early 60s of the Christian era, from an impassioned St. Paul, from his pen in prison. The Apostle to the Gentiles is telling believers in an insignificant town in Asia Minor what it means to *live* as a Christian. You have just heard it sung, and to comment on a song is a sort of sacrilege. But it might be intriguing to see how what Paul says of all who are baptized into Christ applies to those who wed in Christ. For if love is from above, it has to be lived here below.

Forgive each other, Paul demands. Not an easy command, if only because it collides with a contemporary conviction about love: "Love means never having to say you're sorry." Nonsense! Hogwash! Ever since the first man bit into forbidden fruit, "I'm sorry" has to fall as frequently from our lips as "I've sinned." It need not mean love has died. At its best, it echoes what Roman Catholics declare in their Act of Contrition: "O my God, I am heartily sorry for having offended thee, and I detest all my sins . . . most of all because they have offended thee, my God, who art all good and deserving of all my love." Within the Christian story, "I'm sorry" sums up a sad litany of sins against God and against God's human images; but the saving centerpiece is the prayer from the parched lips of a crucified Christ: "Father, forgive them; for they know not what they do" (Lk 23:34).

Is there an unforgivable sin within marriage—a sin a spouse might not forgive even if God does? A homily is not the place to argue that agonizing question. I do say that marriage is a bond, a covenant, not between a god and a goddess, but between a man and a woman, between two imperfect images of God, frail and forgetful for all their good will, self-willed for all their self-giving, amazingly unleashing their frustrations on those they love. Little wonder Paul counsels you, "Put on compassion, kindness, patience, putting up with one another." And then that compelling comparison, "As the Lord has forgiven you, so you also must forgive"—a glorious Greek verb that implies a free and gracious giving (Col 3:12–13). In a Christian context, forgiveness is not a weakness; it is a sharing in Christ's own reason for borrowing our flesh.

Then that pithy precept of Paul, "Be thankful" (Col 3:15). It says so much. The word has a rich history—found frequently on ancient inscriptions where cities and their people etch "thank you" to their benefactors. It is the Christian word for Eucharist, our supreme act of thanksgiving to God.

So too, Del and Margot, for you: Be thankful. You would not stand here in love, were it not for others. I mean especially those who bore you and fed you, changed your diapers and endured your adolescence, gave of their substance for your education and set you free to live and to love. I mean those who surround you this day, invited by you to celebrate your love because in varied ways unknown to me but vivid to you they have helped to shape you, in large measure or small have brought this day to pass. I mean so many, bound to you by blood or otherwise linked to you in love, who share this day in a singular way because they share what we call "the communion of saints," the faithful men and women who have died but are alive as they have never lived before, and in the Lord's presence are holding heavenly gossip, insatiably curious about whom each of you is marrying. Never cease to be thankful, for experience has already taught you that your acre of God's earth will never cease to be crowded with women and men without whom your life together would be less than human, less than godlike.

And then, Paul urges, "Whatever you do, in word or deed, do everything in the name of the Lord Jesus . . ." (Col. 3:17). Not easy, I assure you. It means that in the last analysis you have only one Master. Make megabucks if you must, but let not possessions possess you. Exercise power if you will, but propel your power to service. Enjoy fame if it comes, but mainly because fame makes you known to the millions who feel that no one cares, who beg for the touch of a human hand—your hand. Only one Master over your marriage, only one Lord of your love: a God-man who "came not to be served but to serve" (Mk 10:45).

III

Third, a text from a contemporary mystic, a modern prophet of Lebanon. For Kahlil[2] Gibran, "the key to all things is love."[3] Very much a rebel against all orthodoxies, he found in the Gospels "the deeper meaning of life expressed not in logic . . . but in terms of pure poetry."[4] The passage plucked by our couple from *The Prophet*[5] focuses on marriage and runs in part as follows:

> You were born together, and together you shall be forevermore.
> You shall be together when the white wings of death scatter your
> days.
> Ay, you shall be together even in the silent memory of God.
> But let there be spaces in your togetherness. . . .[6]

"Let there be spaces in your togetherness." Sounds at first hearing like a contradiction. Either you're together or you aren't. Why this mystical mumbo jumbo about spaces in our togetherness? For at least one overriding reason. If you're in love, it is a deadly mistake to try to "possess" the object of your delight—whether a divine person or a human, whether imprisoned marble or free-flowing rivulet. Critic Walter Kerr once phrased it in a paragraph riveted for ever in my memory:

> To regain some delight in ourselves and in our world, we are forced
> to abandon, or rather to reverse, an adage. A bird in the hand is *not*
> worth two in the bush—unless one is an ornithologist, the curator
> of the Museum of Natural History, or one of those Italian vendors
> who supply restaurants with larks. A bird in the hand is no longer a

bird at all: it is a specimen; it may be dinner. Birds are birds only
when they are in the bush or on the wing; their worth as birds can
be known only at a discreet and generous distance.[7]

The point, Margot and Del, is this: The very love that binds you
together demands that you give each other . . . space. Space to be
each your own self, not swallowed up in the other. Space to feel
genuinely free, not smothered by the other. Space to grow inside and
out, not shrink in mind and heart. Space to develop rich relationships,
not limited but expanded by your own unique love. Space simply to
be. It is not birds alone that "can be known only at a discreet and
generous distance." Lovers too. Paradoxically, it is precisely this respect for space that makes for a lifetime of togetherness.

Actually, on this level of your love I have no fear for you. You are
not teen-agers awash on the springtide of passion. You have already
lived the early summer of earthly existence, have experienced much of
what it means to be authentically alive, have learned to distinguish
genuine love from its counterfeits. I would say you are well positioned
to appreciate the profound depths of Gibran's counsel:

> Sing and dance together and be joyous, but let each of you be
> alone,
> Even as the strings of a lute are alone though they quiver with the
> same music.[8]

Dear Margot and Del: I suspect that you sense the love that
surrounds you this day in this sacred shrine. Take it as a foretaste, a
pledge, of the caring you can count on during the years that lie ahead.
For you, our love will always be there—in good times and in bad, in
poverty or wealth, in sickness and in health, until death do us part.
And still, though ever so close to you, we promise to keep "a discreet
and generous distance"!

St. Catherine's Church
Spring Lake, New Jersey
June 3, 1989

19
I HAVE A DREAM
Wedding Homily 4

- Tobit 8:5–7
- Colossians 3:12–17
- Matthew 5:13–16

Earlier in this century, historian-poet Carl Sandburg said, "Nothing happens unless first a dream." Many of us Americans experienced this most explosively in 1963, when in this our nation's capital, in the shadow of Abraham Lincoln, Martin Luther King Jr. proclaimed to a divided nation, "I have a dream . . . a dream that my four little children will one day live in a nation where they will not be judged by the color of their skin but by the content of their character." Ever since that dream, this country has never been quite the same—not simply "the home of the brave" but increasingly "the land of the free."

Today I want to tell you about another dream, a dream that began before time began, a dream that will end only when the earth as we know it shall be no more. It is a dream in three acts. The dream began with God; the dream was deepened by Jesus; the dream is echoed by Susan and Sean.

I

First, God's dream. Yes, before time began, God had a dream. A dream that one day the love that makes the Trinity the divinity it is would be shared with others. A dream that in God's good time, when the sun had lit the day and the moon the night, when birds were making music in the air and fish were cleaving the waters and panthers were prowling the forests, two unique images of God would adorn this planet. A dream that these two, unlike any other creature, would mirror God's intelligence and God's love. A dream that these two

117

would be strikingly similar but dramatically different, would image
God as male and female. A dream that male and female would be
drawn to each other, would seek and belong to each other, in such
fashion that their two-in-oneness would reflect God three-in-one:
There would always be "I and thou" but never "mine and thine." A
dream that from their singular oneness would be born another "I,"
image of these two and of God. A dream that in their love God would
walk with them, that these three would always walk together, in good
times and bad, in sickness and health, in poverty and wealth.

And so it came to be; God's dream was realized. Tobias summed
some of this up for you in the touching prayer you heard from his
wedding night:

> Blessed are you, O God of our fathers,
> and blessed be your holy and glorious name for ever.
> Let the heavens and all of your creatures bless you.
> You made Adam and gave him Eve his wife
> as a helper and support.
> From them the race of humankind has sprung.
> You said, "It is not good for the man to be alone;
> let us make a helper for him like himself."
>
> (Tob 8:5–6)

The history of that divine dream for human marriage is familiar
to you. God's chosen people lived it for centuries. Not perfectly; for
freedom and sin can limit a dream, even if they do not defeat it. Still,
the Jews of old gave us Abraham and Sarah: Abraham father of our
faith, Sarah "pushing ninety-one hard" and pregnant, both "laughing
at the idea of a baby being born in the geriatric ward and Medicare's
picking up the tab."[1] They gave us Isaac and Rebekah, to whom the
Lord gave Esau and Jacob as sons, even though she was barren. They
gave us Tobias and Sarah, so devoted to their parents, so determined
to "grow old together" (Tob 8:7). They gave us Zechariah and Elizabeth, parents of John the Baptist, both described by Luke as
"righteous before God, walking in all the commandments and ordi-
nances of the Lord blameless" (Lk 1:6). They gave us so many more,
millions lost in the mists of history, millions forgotten while Scripture
records Solomon's "700 wives and 300 concubines" (1 Kgs 11:3).
Wonder of wonders, God's dream of marriage gave us Mary of Nazareth, who gave us Jesus.

II

Now it was this Jesus who recaptured God's original dream of married love and deepened its meaning. He recaptured his Father's dream when the Pharisees asked him about divorce and he responded in three terribly strong sentences: "Have you not read that He who made them in the beginning made them male and female, and said, 'For this reason a man shall leave his father and mother and be joined to his wife, and the two shall become one'? So they are no longer two but one. What therefore God has joined together, let not man or woman put asunder" (Mt 19:4–6).

More than that: Jesus deepened God's original dream. Into God's eternal dream for all humankind Jesus inserted his own dream for the marriage of Christians. He raised the wedded life of Christians to a new dignity. He wanted the love of husband and wife to be an incredibly expressive symbol: It was to represent the intimate union that links Christ to his Church, to his people.

This is not just technical theology. Unless you grasp this, you may well miss the mystery of marriage. Not mystery simply as something hidden, but something hidden that God has revealed to us. You see, the risen Christ has saturated our life with what we call sacraments. I mean seven sacred ceremonies that guarantee God's grace to us from infancy to old age, from baptism to the anointing of the sick—promise God's presence to us throughout our lives, especially when crises occur, when dark clouds gather, when human hands and hearts are not enough, when to be faithfully Christian calls for heroism, courage beyond our native ability.

So it is with marriage. Today's ceremony is a sacred rite not simply because it takes place in a house of God, not only because it happens within the Eucharist, our central act of worship. Christian marriage is a sacred ceremony because it is a sacrament, because here our Lord's own dream is realized. When you marry in Christ, you know that Christ is for ever part of your life together. You are not simply two-in-one; you are three-in-one. Never again will you be completely on your own. At home or in an office, with friends or alone, in ecstasy or in depression, his love hovers over you, covers you over.

And, marvel of marvels, this is the one sacrament where the priest is not the minister of the sacred event. Susan and Sean, I may baptize you, confirm you, absolve you from sin, change bread and wine into Christ's body and blood for you; I do not marry you. You marry each other. A more profound reality than you realize. It means that, in giving yourselves to each other, you are each the channel of God's grace to the other. Very simply, in a few short moments you will give to each other the two most dear to you: You will give . . . yourself, and you will give . . . God.

III

This leads directly into my third point. The dream that began with God, the dream that was deepened for Christians by Christ, is echoed today by Susan and Sean. Echoed in a startling way. Echoed in the striking Gospel text they have personally plucked from Jesus' Sermon on the Mount: "You are the salt of the earth. You are the light of the world" (Mt 5:13a, 14a).

Now this is not just a lovely thought. What Jesus said to his first disciples, he says today to Susan and Sean. He told his first disciples that, like a pinch of salt that gives a special flavor to food and keeps it from corrupting, it is the task of his followers, small and insignificant though we seem, to transform what we touch, improve the quality of human living, add a rich relish to life, preserve our sin-scarred earth from moral corruption, from pollution, from destruction. He told his first disciples that, like the miracle of man-made light that enables us to see despite the darkness, we who believe in him dare not hide our gifts in a kind of flour bin, keep them selfishly to ourselves or for our groupies. What God has given us—life and liberty, truth and tenderness, beauty and bounty, goodness and grace—this we must cast out over our world like a fresh dawn, to give light to so many who sit in all sorts of shadows. Why? Not for our own sweet sakes. "Let your light so shine before men and women that they may see your good works and give glory to your Father who is in heaven" (Mt 5:16).

This is true of all of us. By our baptism we are summoned to be salt of the earth and light of the world. But why this Gospel today, at a wedding? Because, dear Sean and Susan, from this hour forward, from here to eternity, you will bear a fresh burden, a new blessing. You are to be salt and light in a manner impossible to you before: You are to be salt and light *together*. So will your dream echo the dream of God and his Christ.

How, concretely? First, you are summoned to salt and light *family* life. In a nation where 50 percent of marriages corrupt, you dare to dream the ideal. Today you proclaim to a culture fearful of final commitments, skeptical of the slender syllables "for ever," your conviction that with God you can accomplish the "mission impossible," that two fragile human beings can live and love till death do you part. Today you signal to your world that two can indeed be one, not because your personalities mesh, not because your SAT score is 1450 and your physique a seductive 10, not because you have megabucks to burn, but because with you there is "I and thou" but never "mine and thine," because the hands of God enclose your own and the same God-man rests within you both.

Second, you are summoned to salt and light the life *around you.* You don't need a homilist to tell you that you live in a broken world. At the moment I do not have in mind apartheid in South Africa, shriveled bellies in the sub-Sahara, Christ crucifying Christ in Belfast, hatred bitter as bile in the Middle East. I have in mind the Big Apple where you will work and worship, dance and dream. Upbeat ads bombard you: "I love [big heart here] New York." By all means love it—love the city that nurtured me and fed me to the Jesuits. There is much to love, from A to Z—from the Aquarium to the Bronx Zoo, from the Battery to Broadway, from cathedrals to museums. But I'm afraid the love in the ads is not the love that will salt the city and light it. For the love in the ads is not the love in the ruins.[2]

The ruins? Crack and coke, kings of the streets; the lonely on park benches; untold thousands ravaged by AIDS; war on the womb and on old age; hotels that are hovels for the homeless; Covenant House with its annual 12,000 runaway boys and girls pimped and prostituted; yes, insider trading, political corruption, rugged individualism—the list is almost endless. Precisely how your love will reach out to what ruins, this is not mine to conjecture. I only know you must reach out—together. Like thousands of the good and the gifted whose hands and hearts are already outstretched in the ruins. Without such as you today's Gospel is a mockery. Our salt will have "lost its taste" (v. 13) and the light that is Christ in us will no longer "shine before men and women" (v. 16). And the Big Apple, for all its outward sheen, may prove worm-eaten at its core.

Knowing you as I do, Susan and Sean, I have high hopes for you—high hopes for your life together, high hopes for the city of your adoption. I pray that the joy you take in each other may radiate to the ruins. If it does, it will return to you a hundredfold; your cup will run over; the joy Jesus promised you will be full.

"Nothing happens unless first a dream." Good friends all: You gather here not as curious spectators but because each of you has played a part, large or little, in the dream that Sean and Susan reveal this day. Still, your role in their dream is far from finished. As the dream unfolds, as they experience the lights and shadows many of you know to your joy and sorrow, they will need you in varied ways: your presence or your prayers, the clasp of your hand or the strength of your smile, your courage in crisis or your fidelity in faith—perhaps something as simple as a Bud Lite on a humid day. And the married among you might let your light shine before them a few short moments from now. As Susan and Sean join hands and promise their lifelong love, you might link your own hands and murmur once again to each other, "I take you to be my wife/I take you to be my husband. I promise to be true to you in good times and in bad, in sickness and in health. I will love you and honor you all the days of my life."

Can you imagine a wedding gift more welcome to Susan and Sean?

Holy Trinity Church
Washington, D.C.
June 10, 1989

20
LET YOUR LIGHT SHINE
Wedding Homily 5

- Song of Songs 2:8–10, 14, 16; 8:6–7
- 1 John 3:18–24
- Matthew 5:13–16

Good friends: Three powerful passages have been proclaimed to you. Passages from the world's best seller—a collection of books we are convinced contains God's mind in our regard. Passages Peter and Susan have carefully culled because therein they discover three facets of love that speak to their dream of life-together. Passages, therefore, that you and I should ponder if we are to share in their dream. Three passages that provoke three reflections: (1) the human face of love; (2) love in deeds rather than words; (3) wedded love and the world around you. A word on each.

I

First, the human face of love. You know, the Song of Songs makes many a Christian uncomfortable. The poetry is vividly sensuous, the imagery at times erotic. How can you read aloud in church, or alone in the silence of your study, a book that begins, "O that you would kiss me with the kisses of your mouth! For your love is better than wine" (Cant 1:2)? Passionate kisses in the Bible? "Dallas"[1] is bad enough. Why read in the Bible what we deplore on the tube?

For one good reason: Human love stems from God—from the God who shaped man and woman in the beginning, made them such that they would be drawn to each other in soul and body, fashioned them to "become one flesh" (Gen 2:24), told them to "multiply and fill the earth" (1:28). The Song of Songs sings of love and fidelity[2]—of the love and fidelity that were God's dream before time began. But the love God created is not an abstract, outer-space intellectualism. It is

123

the closest, most intimate, most passionate, absorbing, all-embracing union this side of heaven. Without it the human race would have died in the Garden of Eden.

By dignifying the Song of Songs as God's Word, the Synagogue and the Church strike a resounding blow against a heresy that refuses to die: a popular misconception among Christians that the human body is nothing but an instrument, a tool of the soul; that the body is but a burden from which the soul cries for release; even that the soul has been imprisoned in matter because it sinned in an earlier existence. Such an attitude, inside marriage or outside, pays slender homage to God. It fails to recognize that the body is an essential part of us, that without the body we are creatures incomplete, that, whether in heaven or purgatory or hell, a separated soul, as a famous Frenchman phrased it. "still longs for its body with a purely natural impulse of love."[3]

What the Song of Songs suggests to us is that marriage—the marriage of Susan and Peter—is a wedding not sheerly of souls, not only of bodies; it is a wedding of persons, complete persons, spirit and flesh in one. Persons whose self-giving at its best is many-sided: thoughtful and emotional, tender and passionate, quiet today and restless tomorrow, at times desolate in the other's absence, ecstatic in the other's presence. Such is the love that was read to you, the love that "is strong as death," the love that "many waters cannot quench, neither can floods drown it" (Cant 8:6–7).

You know, some disenchanted evening when prime-time TV leaves you cold, you might pick up the Song of Songs. Read it through (seven pages), see how an imaginative God can inspire a man and a maid to sing of their passion in the lyrical language of love.

II

So much for love in words. Not that words are always adequate or regularly required. But most of us humans need to be told we are loved—even when we know it! All too many marriages have foundered because all too many machos have forgotten how to murmur "I love you." Still, words can come cheap. Even when sincere, the poetry of the Song of Songs, "You are all fair, my love" (Cant 4:7), must play second fiddle to the First Letter of John: "Little children, let us not love in word or speech but in deed and in truth" (2 Jn 3:18).

It may seem paradoxical for a confirmed bachelor to instruct a bride and groom on how to "love in deed and in truth." And yet, seven decades of wedding-watching, seven decades wherein I have watched the words "for ever" all but disappear from contracts and covenants, seven decades in which I have seen uncounted husbands and wives love and honor each other "all the days of [their] life"— perhaps these experiences may speak realistically to Susan and Peter. If they make little sense, nothing is lost. The best of Burghardt, I keep insisting, is not necessarily the cream of Catholicism.

First, your love is likely to last if your love is laced with laughter. It means that you take yourself and your spouse, your work and your world seriously, but not too seriously. (1) Aware of your gifts, you are aware also of the absurdities in your make-up, "get a kick" out of this strange creature who believes and doubts, gets manic and depressive, sweats off a pound of fat at noon and Bud Lites it back at dinner. (2) You can smile at the face across from you for life—the quirks and mannerisms, the habits and characteristics that delighted or amused you when you were courting but for some strange reason irritate after the honeymoon. (3) You put your job, however prestigious, in similar perspective. Whether courthouse or countinghouse, Congress or commerce, you still regard it not with an all-consuming grimness but with the humor the novelist Thackeray defined as "a mixture of love and wit." Your job should be your servant, not you its slave. Here you might remember that Speaker of the House John McCormack dined with his wife every night for 42 years. (4) Together you look out at your world with a mix of concern and light laughter. For if a sense of humor means the ability to appreciate what is comical or incongruous, absurd or ridiculous, it's all out there in spades.

Second, your love is likely to last if your love is graced with wonder. On a superlative note, wonder at each other. Not "I wonder how you could ever be so stupid." Rather, grateful surprise, amazement, awe that you could ever have met, that this first meeting could have flowered into love, that this love could lead to "I take you . . . till death do us part." A wonder that shows in your eyes.

Third, your love is likely to last if you never take each other for granted. Diamonds may be for ever, but they will never replace the touch that cannot lie, the unexpected orchid, the fulness with which you care and share—share with each other your inmost self.

Fourth, your love is likely to last if, as the Letter of John insists, you "keep [God's] commandments and do what pleases Him" (1 Jn 3:22). This is not pious prattle, exhortation you expect from the pulpit. Without this, wedded life sits on a time bomb. This you know. You know that before all else, prior even to your profound love for each other, God commands you to love Him with all your heart and mind, the whole of your soul and strength. This, I know, you want desperately to do—to grow in the love that St. Paul says "has been poured into [your] hearts through the Holy Spirit who has been given to [you]" (Rom 5:5).

Here what matters most is that you grow *together*. Not on private paths; hand in hand. Help each other to know your loving Lord more intimately—through study and contemplation, at your desk and on your knees. Share with each other your experiences of Christ and his caring; your love of God should not be top secret. Above all, let your hands and tongues reach out together for the food that will nourish your love as naught else can: the body and blood of Christ. As today, so always, it is in the Sacrifice of the Mass that your own sacrifice, your own self-giving, must find its fulfilment.

III

So far, Susan and Peter, your love for each other—how splendidly human it is, and how you can live your love so that it lasts. One important point remains—the passage you have picked from Matthew, from Jesus' Sermon on the Mount, a text at once felicitous and formidable: "You are the light of the world. Let your light so shine before men and women that they may see your good works and give glory to your Father who is in heaven" (Mt 5:14, 16). Those words take your love for each other and thrust it out to a small world. Let me explain.

In Greek mythology there is a touching story of a handsome young man named Narcissus. Proud of his own beauty, he was coldly indifferent to the swarms of young ladies who loved him. Angered by this indifference, the gods punished Narcissus by forcing him to fall in love with his own reflection in a fountain. Captivated by his own image, Narcissus could not leave the pool, pined away in desperate desire for his own beauty, was changed into the flower that bears his name.

A legend, yes; but it can speak eloquently to today's sacred event. You are not joined into "one flesh" (Gen 2:24) merely to fall in love with your own beauty, your gifts of nature and grace—your intelligence and freedom, your faith and hope and love. Not merely to fall in love with the images of yourselves to be fashioned from your flesh. The recessional that closes this liturgy is expressive: You will move from church to world, from sanctuary to city, from sacred music to screams of anguish.

Your task, from here to eternity, is to cast your light over your city, to suffuse your city with what Jesus called "your good works." If that sounds dismally dull to you, paint it in its true colors. You do not need a visitor from Washington to tell you that your Eden is enveloped by Gethsemane, your life-style by ways of living and dying that cry out for compassion or conversion. TV bombards your living room not only with terrorism in Tripoli and starvation in Sudan, but with nearby streets where crack is king and murder is a "Saturday night special," where human beings "live" amid cockroaches and filth and grown men and women rummage for leftovers in garbage cans, where teen-agers gang-rape and teen-agers are sold for sex, where fetuses beg mutely for life and the elderly for love, where computerized cheating is an art form and ethics is for wimps, where AIDS is our Black Death.

This is not a tirade against contemporary culture. I am simply suggesting that, for God's sake and our country's sake, the intelligence and love of countless couples such as Susan and Peter must turn outward. Only if their light is not hidden beneath a bushel but shines resplendently upon our social, economic, and political life can Christ's own dream for married love be realized. "Let your light shine. . . ."

Peter and Susan: Only you know intimately how graced and gifted you are, how much has been given you by a loving Lord and loving parents, by the hundreds remembered or forgotten who have brought you to this day. Forget not that gifts, divine and human, are most richly used when they are shared. I dare not predict just where on earth our Lord Christ will summon you to live and love. I do know that, wherever he calls you, the deep love you already share with each other will increase and multiply to the extent that you turn together to others—especially the dear folk who have been redeemed with the same blood that purchased you but whose lives are less human, less divine, than they ought to be.

Put another way, dear Susan and Peter, what I am saying is simply this: The sacrament you will soon receive, the sacrament that will unite you uniquely in Christ, fleshes out the mission you received in the sacrament of baptism. Back then, utterly unaware of it, you were commissioned in water and the Spirit to let the light of Christ within you shed its redeeming rays over others. Today, in fuller awareness of your Christian commission, you resolve to "let your light shine" *together*. That resolution you will seal with a third sacrament; for when the body of Christ nestles in your palms and on your tongues, you may well whisper with Christ the words of his consecration and yours to the world around you: "This is my body, [given] for you" (Lk 22:19; 1 Cor 11:24).

Can you possibly doubt that this is a day that *the Lord* has made?

Holy Cross Church
Rumson, New Jersey
June 17, 1989

21
THROUGH LOVE BE SERVANTS
Wedding Homily 6

- Ruth 1:16–17
- Colossians 3:12–17
- John 13:3–5, 12–15

This afternoon is an extraordinary moment for me. You see, I am not a parish priest; I operate out of a university context. In consequence, I "perform" at weddings only a handful of times each year—only when someone dear to me asks me (1) to receive his or her lifelong commitment in the name of Christ's Church and/or (2) to speak a word of wisdom congruous to the occasion. To receive the vows is easy enough: A priest is simply the Church's official witness; he really doesn't *do* anything; this man and this woman are the ministers of this sacrament. But to speak unwed to two about to wed raises problems in wisdom.

Fortunately, Mary and Louis have eased my task. How? By the readings they have selected from God's Book, the readings you have just heard. No couple in my experience has looked more closely into God's Word for the meaning of their marriage. No couple has chosen the texts with greater care, deeper thought, finer sensitivity. Why? Because what they want you to hear is what they want their lives to reflect. And so these passages are worth your prayerful pondering—and mine. A word on each.

I

First, the swift segment—two verses—from the book of Ruth. Now those of you who are ultrasmart about Scripture may be a bit amused. Those lovely lines promising deathless love were spoken by Ruth not to her husband (her husband was dead) but to her mother-

129

in-law! Louis and Mary know this. As Mary wrote to me, "We realize this is addressed by a daughter-in-law to her mother-in-law, but it so well conveys a sense of profound union between two people that we could not resist it." In that context listen again, this time not to Ruth but to Mary speaking to Louis, Louis to Mary:

> . . . where you go I will go, and where you lodge I will lodge; your people shall be my people, and your God my God; where you die I will die, and there will I be buried. May the Lord do so to me and more also if even death parts me from you.
>
> (Ruth 1:16–17)

Five promises—each to the other—that spell some of the unique oneness that is marriage. (1) Wherever life takes you, I shall be there. Not every single moment; that way madness lies. Not always physically; that way suffocation lies. But you will always know that wherever you are, there I am—I, my deepest self—even should an ocean at times wash between us. (2) Where you lodge I will lodge. Marriage is not two condos with visiting privileges. Art Buchwald once wrote a column titled "Latchkey Husbands"—a husband wondering, childlike, what to do with himself, how to pass the time, till his wife comes home from *her* job. Marriage is the most intimate relationship this side of heaven —so intimate that Scripture speaks of it as "one flesh" (Gen 2:24). (3) Your people—those you love, those who brought you to life, your close friends, those to whom you have given part of your heart—your people shall be my people, even if at times I do not see them with your eyes. I shall try to love them as you do, even if at times it takes some doing. (4) Your God shall be my God. Not in some abstract, philosophical fashion. No, we shall worship as one, pray together, talk about God together, get to know God together, love God with a single heart and soul, all our combined mind and might. (5) Where you die I will die. Not *when* you die I will die. Rather, even death will not part you from me; death for us is the promise of life for ever, together.

II

Second, the profound passage from St. Paul's letter to Christians in an insignificant town of Asia Minor. Again, a word from Mary: "We chose this reading for two main reasons: one, it emphasizes that our lives are lived in Christ; and two, it focuses on love as forgiveness."

Their lives will be lived in Christ. A remarkable expression, "in

Christ," terribly important for Christian living. It must be, if only because St. Paul in a handful of letters uses it 165 times. What does it mean? Most often it expresses the incredibly close union between Christ and the Christian, so close that Paul can write, "If anyone is in Christ, one is a new creature" (2 Cor 5:17), can exclaim, "It is no longer I who live, but Christ who lives in me; and the life I now live in the flesh I live by faith in the Son of God, who loved me and gave himself for me" (Gal 2:20).[1]

What will it mean for Louis and Mary? Before all else, the profound realization that their oneness with each other is cemented beyond telling by their oneness with Christ. These are not mere words. Marriage "in Christ" means their conviction that if they succeed in loving for life, in loving unto death and beyond, it will not be because they have high I.Q.s and sparkling personalities, are naturally nice folk and "laid back," but because they have the mind of Christ, because they do the will of Christ, because together they try to "see [Christ] more clearly, love [him] more dearly, follow [him] more nearly."[2] It will be because their life together is centered on this Eucharist which recaptures the most amazing love in human history, the love that led God's Son to borrow our flesh and transform it in blood to his own likeness.

In a special way Paul stresses forgiveness. For years all too many Americans were seduced by a Hollywood version of love: "Love means never having to say you're sorry." To our temporary embarrassment, we bought this romantic rubbish. Christianity itself is a ceaseless cry for forgiveness. The cross is God's supreme act of forgiveness—on all who murmur sincerely, "I'm sorry." Whom did Jesus love most? Sinners who showed they were sorry: the tax collector beating his breast in the temple, the woman washing his feet with her tears, the crucified robber asking only to be remembered, Peter weeping bitterly for his triple denial. Wherever there is neither sorrow nor forgiveness, there you have a jungle—whether it's Northern Ireland or the Middle East or South Africa, whether it's a drug-infested street or the bitterness of a hostile home. It is precisely because I love God that an act of sorrow bursts from my lips. Our Catholic Act of Contrition is a splendid example: "O my God, I am heartily sorry for having offended thee. I detest all my sins . . . most of all because they have offended thee, my God, who art all good and deserving of all my love."

Marriages rot because a macho male hasn't the guts to say "I'm sorry." Marriages crumble because a stubborn wife will not take the first step to restore love: "He's in the wrong; let him beg." Believe it or not, I officiated at a wedding where days earlier the two sets of parents had a disagreement. Result? Two wedding receptions. All good Catholics, of course. St. Paul was so wise: "Do not let the sun go down on your anger" (Eph 4:26). Paul was so right: "As the Lord has forgiven you, so you also must forgive" (Col 4:13). There is your model. Not just forgive because you're a good guy, a real doll. Forgive because a God of compassion has forgiven you, forgiven you more than you can possibly forgive another. Say the Our Father and mean it: "Forgive us our trespasses, *as we forgive* those who trespass against us." As we forgive. . . .

III

Our third text comes from the Last Supper. The Gospel you heard was preceded by an introductory sentence you did not hear: ". . . when Jesus knew that his hour had come to depart out of this world to the Father, having loved his own who were in the world, he loved them to the end" (Jn 13:1). And what did he do to show his endless love? Yes, he gave us his flesh as food, his blood as drink. But what else? He got down on his knees and washed the feet of the Twelve—including Judas who was about to sell him for silver. Why?

> Do you know what I have done to you? You call me Teacher and Lord; and you are right, for so I am. If I then, your Lord and Teacher, have washed your feet, you also ought to wash one another's feet. For I have given you an example, that you also should do as I have done to you.
>
> (Jn 13:12–15)

How do Mary and Louis touch this scene to their life to come? I quote my favorite bride again: "Love entails more than easy romance. Love means mutual service." Marriage as service? Are you out of your cotton-pickin' mind? Not at all. I admit, not many Americans think of marriage in terms of service. For many, service has an unsavory history. It recalls southern slavery and northern discrimination, jobs in toilets and menial kowtowing to the affluent and the powerful. But for the Christian, "servant" is an honorable term. It goes back to Christ himself, to the God-man who, in his own words, "came not to be served but to serve, and to give his life as a ransom for many" (Mt 20:28). Every moment of his life, from his birth in a feeding trough to his death on twin beams of bloody wood, was for others, for you and me, for every human from Adam to Antichrist.

And so for Christians, men and women who profess to follow Christ. To follow him is to serve, to live for others. It is St. Paul's trumpet call: "You were called to freedom, my brothers and sisters; only do not use your freedom as an opportunity for the flesh, but through love be servants of one another" (Gal 5:13). Service does not destroy equality; the President of the United States is, at his best, our servant; the pope has for centuries gloried in the title "servant of the servants of God."

And so for marriage. My hopes for Mary and Louis are unusually high, because they recognize that wedded life is a struggle—not which of the two will dominate but which one will outdo the other in generosity, in self-giving, in service. Not piling up brownie points; simply playing Christ each to the other.

But playing Christ each to the other will move them out to an even broader service—together. As they leave here with Christ newly alive within them, they return to a world of stark contradictions. A world where most of us live in reasonable comfort, but up to 800 million are chronically undernourished, every 60 seconds 28 people die from hunger-related causes, one child in ten dies before its first birthday—and in our own land every third black child is born into poverty. A world where most of us take a gracious home for granted, while 14.4 million refugees water the roads of exile with their tears. A country where thousands of our college graduates "make it big" each year, while thousands of runaway kids are bought and sold, pimped and prostituted. A land where most Americans profess our motto, "In God We Trust," but untold millions have for their living god money or power or fame. A land where Catholics and Protestants now talk to one another like Christians, but we Catholics are dreadfully divided, from contraception to Communion in the hand.

Just how God is calling Mary and Louis to serve, precisely where, is not mine to say. Still, I have a dream. Knowing their interests, I see their service as opening minds and eyes. Minds that are stunted, closed minds, eyes that have only tunnel vision, eyes that see only what they want to see. Opening minds to the things of God, to the people of God, to God's very self.[3] Opening eyes to see that "The world is charged with the grandeur of God,"[4] that every life is infinitely precious no matter how fragile or wrinkled, that the sin-scarred can by God's grace be better than they are. They are so wonderfully alive, Mary and Louis—alive with the hope that springs from being young, from being in love, from being "in Christ." In the final analysis, he it is who will let these two servants know how he wants them to serve, whose feet he would have them wash. They have only to obey the Lord

God thundering from the hill of transfiguration, "This is my beloved Son . . . ; listen to him" (Mt 17:5).

Good friends, a final word. You have been invited here because, for a year or a quarter century, you have helped bring this day to be. By all means, take deep satisfaction in what you have done. But your task is not finished. Today a fresh challenge confronts you. For all God's promise of grace over their lives, Louis and Mary cannot live without you—without the grace that is you. Surprised? Don't be. No one of us can live a human life alone, no one of us creates anything absolutely alone, no one gets to heaven all by his or her lonesome. And no bride and groom "live happily ever after" in splendid isolation.

This marriage, like every marriage, is earth-bound. It is lived on this earth, on this street, in this culture, among these people. It is subject to Shakespeare's "slings and arrows of outrageous fortune": a Black Monday on Wall Street, an air disaster in Sioux City, a gunshot in the night, illness of flesh or spirit, love grown cold, you name it. What Mary and Louis need more than Waterford crystal is simply you—just knowing you are there with your care, with your love, in good times and bad, amid joy and woe, in ecstasy and desperation. Especially the wedded among you, the example of men and women who, for one year or 50, are living proof that, despite the tough odds, God's own dream for life-together-for-life is not fantasy, can be captured and lived by a man and a woman.

So then, let your presence here turn into a promise. Actually three promises, in harmony with the three scriptural passages we have pondered together. May I promise Louis and Mary that where they are, you will always be, because distance will never lessen your love? May I promise them that if anything divides the wedded among you, you will not hesitate to murmur "I'm sorry" or to forgive "as the Lord has forgiven you"? May I promise them that you too will serve the broken world about you, reach out to the hungry and the heartbroken, the lonely and the loveless, someone whose flesh or spirit is wasting away? No more acceptable gift can you give, for in these promises you will be giving . . . yourself.

Holy Trinity Church
Washington, D.C.
August 12, 1989

22
FAITH, HOPE, LOVE ABIDE, THESE THREE
Wedding Homily 7

- Isaiah 40:25–31
- 1 Corinthians 13:1–13
- Matthew 17:14–20

Gentry and Roger: Your choice of a preacher is something of a paradox. For three reasons. About to wed, you turn to a celibate. Episcopalians, you call on a Roman Catholic. After Gentry's four years at Georgetown, you can still listen to a Jesuit. Fortunately, we three seem agreed that a wedding is not a counseling session, not a cram course in successful marriage, not sex instruction from Dr. Ruth. My task is somewhat more simple, definitely more delightful. I want to put this hour into a Christian context, set your words to each other into the framework of God's word to you. I shall do this by focusing on the Word of the Lord we have just been privileged to hear proclaimed, the three segments of Scripture you have yourselves selected. They reveal, in successive stages, three gifts that make for a marriage "in Christ," gifts St. Paul trumpeted to the Christians of Corinth: "So faith, hope, love abide, these three; but the greatest of these is love" (1 Cor 13:13). Three momentous monosyllables—momentous for marriage; a word on each.

I

First, a striking scene in Matthew's Gospel. A loving father begs the apostles to heal his epileptic son; they try but fail. The father kneels before Jesus, implores his help; one word from Jesus and the boy is "cured instantly" (Mt 17:18). The disciples are puzzled; they ask Jesus, "Why couldn't we heal the boy?" His answer: "Because of your little faith. For truly, I say to you, if you have faith as a grain of

135

mustard seed, you will say to this mountain, 'Move from here to there,' and it will move; and nothing will be impossible to you" (v. 20).

Why this Gospel today? What can epileptics and mountains say to Gentry and Roger? Far more than you might suspect. The first momentous monosyllable is faith. Not faith in the sense of some irrational backup you appeal to when logical argument fails. Not even faith as a fixed formula you repeat on Sundays: "I believe in one God, the Father almighty; I believe in Jesus Christ, His only Son, our Lord; I believe in the Holy Spirit, the Giver of life." I mean faith in its fulness: the gift of your whole self to God, without reservation, without condition. "Whatever you want, Lord."

Such is the faith that moves mountains. But Jesus is not interested in your ability to move Stone Mountain onto Peachtree Street. He is telling you that, if you surrender to him your life and liberty, your mind and memory, all you are and have, let him literally do with you as he wills, you will do marvels that naked human nature could never effect.

Such is the faith Roger and Gentry need from this day forward. In a culture where the words "for ever" have disappeared from our vocabulary, where contracts in your Omni[1] or on Wall Street are hardly worth the paper that spells them out, where roughly 50 percent of marriages break up, where "till death" means "till the deal is dead," to covenant for life is to move mountains. It is close to impossible unless your covenant this day is a gift not only of each to the other but of both together to God.

That is why All Saints is so significant this evening. It is indeed a gorgeous setting for a social gathering; it is even more impressive as a sacred symbol. Here is where God's people celebrate history's supreme act of self-giving, the saving movement from the Last Supper to Calvary, from Eucharist to cross. Here, fittingly, is where Roger and Gentry murmur to each other, murmur together to God, the words of Jesus that crystallize his gift and theirs, "This is my body, given for you" (Lk 22:19–20). Given . . . for ever.

II

Such faith leads to a second momentous monosyllable. It stems from a passage of Isaiah, a long-time favorite of Gentry's, from the section called the Book of the Consolation of Israel. Listen to part of it again, and touch it to this couple we love:

[The Lord] gives strength to the fainting:
  for the weak He makes vigor abound.
Though young men faint and grow weary,
  and youths stagger and fall,
They that hope in the Lord will renew their strength,
  they will soar as with eagles' wings;
They will run and not grow weary,
  walk and not grow faint.

(Isa 40:29–31 NAB)

Central to that passage is a simple monosyllable: hope. By "hope"
I do not mean a wishy-washy "Gee! Wouldn't it be nice if . . . ?" I
mean a confident expectation that what I yearn for will take place.
Isaiah[2] is addressing Jews who have experienced a major disaster:
banishment to Babylon, political impotence, the destruction of their
temple. Some of them are near despair, doubt Yahweh's power, cannot see the Lord's hand in history and their own experience. These he
assures that God will soon deliver them from captivity, return them to
the land they love, restore their sacred temple. Hope in the Lord!
Trust Yahweh—utterly!

And what of today? No similar disaster here in All Saints; and still
a critical moment, a covenant for life. And this text is not a historic
relic, buried in the year 550 before Christ. Through this passage
which Gentry loves so dearly our good Lord is speaking once again—
speaking to this dear couple, promising that if they "hope in the
Lord," they too "will renew their strength, will soar as with eagles'
wings" (Isa 40:31). Let your experience and your imagination take
wing, and listen to the Lord speaking to Roger and Gentry:

In your two-in-oneness you and your children will shape a small
community beloved of me. You too shall be my people, and I shall
be your God. As the years move on, you can expect the profound
joy that your deep love already provides. And yet, you can hardly
escape totally the cross which human and Christian living lays on
flesh and spirit, the ills that torment all my children. The future is
indeed hidden from your eyes. But the very vows you exchange
suggest some possibilities: "for better for worse, for richer for
poorer, in sickness and in health." Some of your crosses may prove
so heavy, so long-lived, that you will doubt my power to rescue you,
doubt that I care for you, doubt that I love you—perhaps doubt my
very existence.

But always remember this: If your hope for happiness rests not
on humans but on me, if your love for each other is cradled in my

hands, I will always pour into you the power to endure. If you are
weak, let me be your strength. If you are faint, let me renew your
vigor. Put your hope in my hands and you will soar as with eagles'
wings. I do not say that every cross will be lifted from your
shoulders; I do say that every cross will be bearable. And not only
bearable; in your cross will be the joy I promised the night before I
died for you: the joy "no one will take from you" (Jn 16:22).

Dear Gentry and Roger, if your wedded oneness is to survive, if it
is to soar as with eagles' wings, one bottom line is hope. And for all the
hope that you must place from day to day in men and machines, in
computers and competition, in intelligence and influence, beyond
and above all these you must rest your confidence in the Lord—the
Lord who fashioned you like God, who brought you together in love,
who led you to this hour, who alone will always be there, with you,
near you, in you.

III

The third momentous monosyllable? Love. The passage you
heard from St. Paul tops the 40 biblical hits for brides and grooms.
And why not? "If I speak in the tongues of men and of angels, but
have not love, I am a noisy gong or a clanging cymbal. And if I have
prophetic powers, and understand all mysteries and all knowledge,
and if I have all faith, so as to move mountains, but have not love, I am
nothing. If I give away all I have, and if I deliver my body to be burned,
but have not love, I gain nothing" (1 Cor 13:1–3). Put that to music,
give it a Springsteen or a Madonna beat, raise the decibels to ear-split-
ting levels, keep repeating "noisy gong, noisy gong," and it will go
gold, if not triple platinum.

The trouble is, the love St. Paul has in mind is not a one-night
stand, not what you find on TV's "Love Boat." What Paul is proclaiming is what singer Amy Grant would call "Love of Another Kind."
Basically, it is what he wrote to the Christians of Rome: "God's
love . . . poured into [your] hearts through the Holy Spirit who has
been given to [you]" (Rom 5:5). Now God's own love for you is not
some ethereal, gossamer, outer-space, intangible feeling. It is incredibly concrete. God's love for you means that the Holy Spirit lives within
you; and because the Holy Spirit is alive and active in you, you are
gifted with what Paul calls "the fruit of the Spirit." And what is that?
Listen to him as he lists nine gifts you have: "love, joy, peace, pa-

tience, kindness, goodness, faithfulness, gentleness, self-control" (Gal 5:22–23).

You begin your life together not simply with a chemistry that draws you to each other, a quickening of your whole being when brown eyes meet green, personalities that mesh, similar ideals and interests, high IQs and high boiling points. Thank God for these gifts, but thank God even more that the wonderfully human traits you have are caught up and raised to the nth power because God loves you and you love God, because God lives in you, because "in everything God works for good with those who love Him" (Rom 8:28).

"With those who love Him." You see, for wedded love to last, for wedded love to grow, you must make one all-important change in St. Paul's rhapsody. He sings of *love:* "Love is patient and kind" and so on and so forth. Of course! But how do you move from abstract love to concrete lovers? How can you possibly promise each other "*We lovers* will be patient and kind, not jealous or boastful, not arrogant or rude; *we lovers* will not insist on our own way, will not be irritable or resentful, will rejoice not at wrong but only in the right; *we lovers* will bear all things, believe all things, hope all things, endure all things" (cf. 1 Cor 13:4–7)? Only if you live the two commandments that sum up Jewish law and Christian living: "You shall love the Lord your God with all your heart and soul, all your mind and strength; and your neighbor as yourself" (Mt 22:34–40; Mk 12:28–31; Lk 10:25–28; cf. Deut 6:5; Lev 19:18).

The startling, thrilling, breath-taking reality is this: God is alive within you, and, as Jesus told you, "with God all things are possible" (Mt 19:26). Roger and Gentry, you are doubly blessed: Not only is your love touchingly human; your love is movingly divine. A few moments from now, when you clasp hands as symbol of undying oneness, you can be confident that those hands are enfolded in God's hands.

Good friends: You gather here this evening as an uncommon community of love. You gather here because, in God's precious providence, each of you has played some part in the complex of events that has led to this sacred moment. I hesitate to tell you this, but . . . your task is not yet done, will never be done. To live faithfully, day after day, year after year, the love that is their ecstasy today, within a culture so devastated by doubt, by despair, by deadly hate—this Roger and Gentry cannot do without you, especially the wedded among you. They need for support men and women whose lives sparkle with St. Paul's triad. (1) In a culture where commitment is rare and ridiculed, continue to give yourselves totally to God and one other. (2) In a culture where all too many rest their hopes for happiness on the triumphs of technology, sing ceaselessly with the Psalmist, "You, O Lord, are my hope,/ my trust, O Lord, from my youth" (Ps 71:5). (3) In a culture where love TV-style covers a multitude of sins, let your love bear all things, believe all things, hope all things, endure all things.

An unusual wedding gift, I know. The twin miracle of it is, the gift is you, and the gift will only grow with the years.

All Saints' Episcopal Church
Atlanta, Georgia
September 16, 1989

23
FAITHFUL FRIEND, ELIXIR OF LIFE
Wedding Homily 8

- Sirach 6:5–6, 14–17
- 1 John 4:11–17
- Luke 10:25–28

Sara and Matt: Almost from the day I agreed to your gracious request that I witness your wedding, I have been intrigued by the passages you selected from Scripture. These three texts obviously were not chosen in haste, at random; they have meaning for your marriage. And each text says something unusual, strikingly pertinent to your life together. This you sense; let me expand a bit on each.

I

Begin with the selection from Sirach—a book of distilled wisdom written almost 2200 years ago. No couple in my limited experience has plucked it for a wedding. Why not? Because it speaks of . . . friendship.

> A faithful friend is a sturdy shelter:
>   he that has found one has found a treasure.
> There is nothing so precious as a faithful friend,
>   and no scales can measure his excellence.
> A faithful friend is an elixir of life. . . .
> (Sir 6:14–16a)

Of course you can be friends without being married. What makes this text pertinent is that you can be married without being friends. It reminds me of a film a couple of decades ago; it was titled *Lovers and Other Strangers.* Yes, marriage can be a contract between a man and a woman who are and remain strangers.

What is it that makes for friendship?[1] First, attraction: Two people are drawn to each other, seek each other out, are happy when they are together. Second, affection: Two people like each other—yes, genuinely love each other; a love that shows itself at times in laughter, at times in tears. Third, it is a mutual thing: Each responds to the other. That is why only persons can be friends. I can love a good Bordeaux, but I cannot be its friend—except perhaps in my cups. Fourth, friendship is a spiritual thing. Brute animals cannot be friends. Peculiar to friends is concern with not only flesh and matter, but with the life of the spirit—intelligence, will, emotion. Fifth, a friend is unselfish, is a friend because of qualities in the other, will do things without thought of personal gain, will sacrifice for the other, sacrifice even life itself. Sixth, at the height of friendship friends are fused in soul—what St. Augustine called "one soul in two bodies."[2]

Is it any wonder that so brilliant a theologian as St. Thomas Aquinas saw the love of friendship as the supreme form of love?[3] And is it now any wonder that Matt and Sara have vowed to be married friends?

II

So far, Sara and Matt, genuine friendship. But friendship takes on a fresh dimension when you who like and love marry—and marry in Christ. For now another love enfolds your own. Here God enters the picture in a singular way.[4] Not to destroy friendship, but to perfect it. Not to transmute friendship into something else, but to impregnate what is splendidly human with what is peculiarly divine.

How does today's sacred ceremony affect your friendship? The Jesus who told his apostles at the Last Supper, "No longer do I call you servants . . . I have called you friends" (Jn 15:15), graces your friendship this day in a startling way. God has already been a friend to you—but to each of you individually. Today Jesus, with his Father and his Holy Spirit, becomes friend to both together, to both of you as one. How? (1) It is the Lord God—not I—who presides over your union, who confirms your commitment. (2) This same Lord God promises you that through all the years that lie ahead, through the bittersweet of wedded living, in good times and bad, in poverty or wealth, in sickness and health, God will always be there, will always be with you, always within you, your strength and solace, your joy and ecstasy, your very Love.

But a covenant, whether of Israel with Yahweh or Sara and Matt with the same God of Jesus, is not a one-sided affair. This is why your choice of a Gospel is particularly pertinent, a happy selection. A lawyer asks Jesus, "Teacher, what shall I do to inherit eternal life?" Jesus responds, "What is written in the law? How do you read?" The lawyer knows his law: "You shall love the Lord your God with all your heart, and with all your soul, and with all your strength, and with all your mind; and your neighbor as yourself." Jesus is pleased: "You have answered right; do this, and you will live" (Lk 10:25–28). Such is the return of love Sara and Matt are commanded to make—not requested, commanded. Only if your love for each other is turned to God, only if you respond with your whole being to the love that shaped you out of nothing, to the love that purchased life for you on a gory cross, to the love that brought you together against all the odds —only with such love dare you look ahead with heady hope to married friendship rather than "spouses and other strangers."

Very simply, give yourselves together totally to God, somewhat as Jesus has given himself unreservedly to you. Do this and, in those three slender monosyllables of Jesus, "you will live." Not simply eat and sleep, work and play, dance and dream, laugh and cry. In all of that, you will live "in Christ," live together as you have never lived before, live what St. Paul trumpeted to the Christians of Galatia: "It is no longer I who live, but Christ who lives in me; and the life I now live in the flesh I live by faith in the Son of God, who loved me and gave himself for me" (Gal 2:20).

III

Friends to each other, friends to each other in Christ. Wondrous indeed! One question remains: How, in down-to-earth concreteness, can you perfect your nuptial friendship, perfect God's love in you? Your selection from the First Letter of John is splendidly suggestive: "If we love one another, God abides in us and His love is perfected in us" (1 Jn 4:12).

"If we love one another. . . ." How frightening . . . and how encouraging! Frightening because, unless our love goes out to others, God does not live in us. Frightening because, if we believe Jesus, the other is not simply someone we like, feel comfortable with, toast with "This Bud's for you." The other includes the bore I can't abide and the cousin who consistently cuts me down, the neo-Nazi and the ayatollah, the drug-addicted and the AIDS-afflicted, the rapist and the insider trader, the hundred and one types of the human that turn me off. Encouraging because, if you credit the Letter of John, your love for the other is proof beyond question that you love God.

I do not doubt your love for the other, especially those who experience more of Good Friday than of Easter Sunday. The new thing, from this hour on, is that in your love for each other you go out to the other . . . together. It is not the task of a homilist to tell you precisely how your love will take you to the other; the God you love so intensely will clue you in as time goes on. Let me simply suggest what your self-giving should mean.

This past Tuesday I was privileged to speak at Calvary Hospital in New York's Bronx.[5] Calvary is a 200-bed acute-care facility for persons in the final stages of cancer: 20 percent of the patients die within a week of entering; 50 percent are dead within three weeks; 96 percent are dead or discharged to a more appropriate setting within four months. And still, the place is alive with life. The lobby is airy, sunfilled; posters proclaim in colorful calligraphy respect for life; just about everyone greets you with a smile; the staff exude a sense of caring—from medical director through pastoral caregivers to 200 volunteers. You want lox and bagels for breakfast, eggs over easy? You've got it. Progresso tomato sauce, not Ronzoni? They'll go to the store and buy it. You want a martini with dinner? No sweat. You need someone to listen, really listen, to your pain, to talk about dying unto resurrection? No problem. Birthday parties, exhibits, concerts, arts and crafts, ceramics—it's all there for you. Listening to patients, singing to patients, praying with patients, crying with patients—that's what Calvary is all about. The nursing director tells of a patient who learned that his daughter was fatally ill and would die before him: "He wanted to be so macho, but he just cried and cried. I held his hands in mine and prayed silently. I didn't know what to say."[6]

Why such a story about dying this day when you are coming alive? One basic Christian reason. In loving your "neighbor" as Jesus has loved you, in going out together to others less fortunate, less loved, in pain of flesh or spirit, you will not be just doing "something nice." You will be sharing life—your life and God's life. You have so much of life, almost to bursting. Share it! Give it away! This is your Christian vocation, yours as well as mine. The paradox is, the more of life you give, the more you have. You will experience it when you give life to your first child. You can experience it day after day if you let our Lord lead you to those friends of his who are gasping or grasping desperately for a share in his life and yours. Etch indelibly on your minds and hearts the text you selected from Sirach: "A faithful friend is an elixir of *life*" (Sir 6:16a).

Sara and Matt: This is not a "canned" homily; it has not come off the shelf. Fortunately, you have forced me to speak of friendship, forced me to stress what all too many forget or never knew: Unless husband and wife are friends, marriage turns sour or dies on the vine—"Saturday Night Live,"[7] the rest of the week deadly. You have reminded all of us forcefully that, for wedded friendship to grow and deepen, wife and husband had best be friends with the Lord who lived and died to transform us from slaves to his dear friends. And you have inspired me to link your living love to the incurably dying, not to sadden this day, but simply to reveal vividly that from this day forward your life is to give life—not only to each other, but together to the little acre of our world on which you dance so lightly. Share your life and God's life. No greater joy can I pray for you—together.

Holy Trinity Church
Washington, D.C.
September 23, 1989

24
TWO IN ONE: THREE PARADOXES
Wedding Homily 9

- Tobit 8:4–9
- Colossians 3:12–17
- Matthew 22:35–40

Lisa and Fern: When God shaped you—fashioned you individually and for each other—He was fashioning what we call a paradox. A paradox, you know, is a seeming contradiction. Something I say doesn't seem to make sense, the two parts do not appear to fit, and yet it turns out that they really do. On this day of singular love, I want to stress three paradoxes that enter intimately into your life together.

I

Paradox number 1: You are amazingly alike, and yet you are distinctly different. You are alike. After all, you are both human— reasonably human. To begin with, each of you is a creature of intelligence. You can shape an idea—from a simple sentence like "I am" to the formula for an atomic bomb. You not only see a flower the way a honeybee does; you can analyze it, appreciate it. You not only hear the sounds of Bach's *Jesu, Joy of Man's Desiring* the way a kitten might; it makes sense to you, delights you. When you touch each other, it is not simply animal pleasure; it has meaning for you. And this mind of yours can reach to the heavens and grasp something of God. As St. Paul put it, "Ever since the creation of the world [God's] invisible nature, [God's] eternal power and deity, has been clearly perceived in the things that have been made" (Rom 1:20).

But you are more than mind. Each of you is a creature capable of love. Not "Miami Vice"[1] style, not a one-night stand. Rather, God has so gifted each of you that you can go out totally to another, mind and heart, flesh and spirit. Unlike the beast, your love is not blind, it blossoms from knowledge; your love is not simply getting, it is giving, without counting the cost, even unto crucifixion; your love is free, you can give it or withhold it as you will. And in such loving you can, as St. Paul phrased it, forgive "as the Lord has forgiven you" (Col 3:13).

Yes, you are incredibly alike. And yet you are so different. In a vivacious bit of verse entitled "In Praise of Diversity," Phyllis McGinley sang vividly of our dreadful tendency to reduce the human orchestra to "one shrill, monotonous, level note": black or white, yes or no, for or against, no nuances. And she went on:

> Or so it seems. Yet who would dare
>   Deny that nature planned it other,
> When every freckled thrush can wear
>   A dapple various from his brother,
> When each pale snowflake in the storm
> Is false to some imagined norm?
>
> Recalling then what surely was
>   The earliest bounty of Creation:
> That not a blade among the grass
>   But flaunts its difference with elation,
> Let us devoutly take no blame
> If similar does not mean the same.[2]

Why did God make you similar but not the same? Listen to the opening act of Scripture: "God created the human in [God's] own image; male and female [God] created them" (Gen 1:27). Why? So that each of you could praise God by mirroring divinity in your own unique fashion, reflecting God's infinite beauty in distinct ways. So that, when male and female come together for life, the union of the similar but not the same will praise God more wondrously than either can alone.

So then, dear Lisa and Fern, delight in your difference. Don't try to shape the other in your own image; help shape each other more perfectly in God's likeness—a God whom no single one of us, not all of us together, can image to the full. It takes male and female to image our God, and even then we fall short.

II

Paradox number 2: Wedded oneness demands "I and thou," forbids "mine and thine." "I and thou," of course. Love is not love if one is absorbed, swallowed up, in the other. Whether I love the Lord my God or another human being, I never cease to be myself. Oh yes, it makes for high poetry to lose myself in your eyes, especially over twin glasses of ruddy Burgundy; but even then, for all my drowning in your luminous orbs, I am always I, and you are ever you. Even when St. Paul cried, "It is no longer I who live, but Christ who lives in me" (Gal 2:20), he was not yielding up his personality, ceasing to be Paul. He was simply becoming more Christ*like*.

And so for Fern and Lisa. Their singular oneness, this "two in one flesh" which Genesis and Jesus glorify, is not a takeover; it is more like a merger in which only love "takes over," the kind of love where paradoxically each can give all to the other without ceasing to be Fern and Lisa. Each will help the other to grow—but to grow as Fern, as Lisa, not as a clone of each other. To love in truth is to love as Jesus loved: not possession, only self-giving without ceasing to be one's self.

"I and thou" indeed, but nowhere "mine and thine," what St. Augustine somewhere called "those ice-cold words." I am not outlawing separate checking accounts, two cars and two computers, personal toothbrushes, "his" bath towel and "hers." These are practicalities a celibate gladly leaves to the married. I find altogether acceptable, I resonate to, that insightful sentence in Gibran's *Prophet,* "let there be spaces in your togetherness."[3] I am referring rather to a perilous way all too many think about marriage, where the stress is on my turf and yours, my life and yours, my sacred likes and dislikes. Monday night is pro football, come hell or high water, and your contribution to wedded bliss is to bring me my Miller Lite at half time. Or that timeless gem of stupidity, "This is the way I feel, and I don't care what anybody says"—including the other half of my soul. What frightens me is what centuries of wedded life witness: spouses who live in the same house but not together, for whom sharing means only dividing.

Fortunately, dear Lisa and Fern, such is not my experience of you, such is not really my fear for you. The way you hold hands and the way your eyes hold, the years you have grown together and the vows you will shortly exchange—these promise "I and thou" without "mine and thine." The problem is, the years threaten to take their toll. Lovers take each other for granted, romance turns to routine, "real" life takes over. It is a peril that compels my third paradox.

III

Paradox number 3: Your wedded life is at once human and divine. Touchingly human. For, despite your angelic qualities, this is not a marriage of angels. You are not only intelligence and love, you are flesh and blood, a fascinating blend of spirit and matter, what you can see and what is invisible to the naked eye. And so you are heir to the whole range of human experience. Saints sin, and the sinner turns saint. Wisdom grows, hair and stomach fall. Married love ripens, deepens, and married love must contend with neuroses and psychoses, with indifference and infidelity. You will joy in the birth of a child, and sorrow in the death of your dearest. And so experience proclaims poignantly that marriage "till death do us part" is not something we produce on our own. Each day the media announce the death of love, despite good will and a gentle spirit, despite a 4.0 and a Colgate smile, despite firm friendship and firm necklines, despite a prime credit rating and a wicked tennis serve, despite money and power and fame. A good start, but not enough.

What else is demanded? The human in you must be wedded to the divine. Not to some strange God in outer space, cold and unapproachable, who made you and left you to your own devices, your natural gifts. What you need for deathless love is what you have: a God who not only gave you life but gave his life for you, not only "dwells in unapproachable light" (1 Tim 6:16) but lives within you, not only fosters you with general care but feeds you with his body and blood, not only blesses this day but actually binds you together. "What God has joined together," Jesus warned, "let no human put asunder" (Mt 19:6). What *God* has joined together. . . .

Now God's love for you and in you lifts your human living to a share in divine life. But oneness with God dares not be one-sided. If your wedded life is to last, Lisa and Fern, it is not enough that *God* loves *you*. You know how tragic love is when only one of the two is in love. Imagine (if you can), my friends, Fern loving Lisa as lavishly as he does, but Lisa not particularly interested. Then imagine (and you can) Christ our Lord loving you enough to die for you, enough to live in you, and you giving him one hour a week out of 168. Such benign neglect makes little sense—that the Redskins and Orioles get, say, ten times more of our time than does God.

Not that you must be thinking of God half the day, stop the Dow Jones board with a prayer, preach Christ at each coffee break. Rather that our Lord God should always "be there"—like breathing—as much part of your life as mother or father, as your children, as your job.

If you want a splendidly concrete way to respond to God's love in your life together, let your wedded oneness go out to the pain that surrounds you, to the fears and tears on the road you travel. I mean those who hunger for bread or thirst for attention; those whose home is street or shelter, whose robe is rags; those who rot spiritually behind iron bars or physically on hospital beds. For it is only when your love for each other turns outward that it mirrors the love in the Trinity, the love that links God the Father and God the Son, totally happy in their love for each other but moved to share that love by giving life to others, men and women who are like God.

And so for you, Lisa and Fern. You are pre-eminently privileged. You share so much of the joy Christ promised whoever tries to follow him. Not by your own deserving—by God's free gift, beyond our understanding. I am suggesting strongly that, somewhat like God, you share that joy, share your love, with those who find it so difficult to smile from their cross. You see, if you do not find Christ *there*, crucified indeed but still there—you are less likely to find him *here*. God's word in the New Testament is sobering: If you do not love your brother or sister whom you see, you cannot love God whom you do not see (cf. 1 Jn 4:20).

A final word to all of you, especially the married among you. The three paradoxes I have preached to Lisa and Fern are your paradoxes too. If you want to present to our precious couple a wedding gift especially personalized, promise them a profound look into your own love. (1) How ready have you been to allow the other half of your life to be similar but not the same, to be himself or herself, even if *you* happen to be the ideal human? (2) How large a role does "mine and thine" play in your life—your rights and delights, your likes and dislikes, your comfort and convenience? (3) Where do God and His Christ rank in your Top Ten, in the list of your loves? Is it really God you love with all your heart and soul, all your mind and strength? Or does God take second place when the chips are down?

The love of Fern and Lisa—exuberant and ecstatic, thoughtful and tender, selfless and supportive—is not only a "nice" thing to see. It is a challenge to the rest of us: a challenge to recapture the love that sparked our younger days. I mean a renewed sense of wonder: wonder at, delight in, the other whom you have come to take for granted; wonder at, delight in, the Lord who brought you together, the Lord who keeps you together, the Lord without whose love you would be terribly loveless.

Today, dear friends, if only for a swift hour, we experience love in its rich freshness. For this gift, dear Lisa and Fern, we are deeply in your debt. Keep smiling on us. You'll never quite realize, and only we know, the difference you make in our lives, in our loves.

Church of St. Joseph
Herndon, Virginia
October 7, 1989

25
WHAT YOUR LOVE SAYS
Wedding Homily 10

- Genesis 1:26–28, 31
- Romans 8:31–35, 37–39
- John 15:9–17

Tracey and Tim: It is an awesome thing you ask of this homilist today. To phrase in fragile human syllables what is not only human but divine; to compress into 15 fleeting minutes of time a lifetime of living; to invade a love that is intimate to two and only two—this stretches the imagination. Especially if the words to come are tinted with non-Grecian gray, and the experience behind them is masculine and celibate.

Perhaps I can do best by suggesting not what your love means to you but what your love says to us. Better still, what your love says (1) to God, (2) to the world around you, and (3) to us who are privileged to know and love you.

I

First, your love says something to God. It has to, even if you cannot put it into words. It has to because your love for each other is not of your own making, something you two created all by yourselves; your love is born of God. You see, your love did not begin yesterday, did not even begin on a hilltop called Georgetown. It has an incredibly richer history. It goes back before time began—Father, Son, and Holy Spirit loving one another so intensely that they wanted to share that love with others. They decided to shape human images of themselves, two creatures strikingly similar but startlingly different, a man and a woman who would in their distinctive ways mirror what God is like, what love in God is like. Your love finds its origin in the first chapter of

God's own Book: "God created the human in God's own image . . . ; male and female God created them" (Gen 1:27).

That first human love—our tradition speaks of the first lovers as Adam and Eve—has come down to you through uncounted millions of years. No computer will ever reveal to you the centuries of love, the lineage of loving, the genealogy of lovers that in God's providence have come to term in you, in your love for each other. What the Lord God said to Israel through the prophet Jeremiah, the Lord God says to you: "I have loved you with an everlasting love" (Jer 31:3). God knew you before time ever was, knew that one day your eyes would meet, knew it would *not* be "love at first sight," knew that loving would flower from knowing and growing. And today God crowns your love in what we call a sacrament—a sacred ceremony that Christ conse-crated from a cross, a sacred ceremony of which not a priest but you two are the ministers, because when you say "yes" to each other you will be channeling God to each other.

Indeed your love says something to God. Your very presence in God's house tells God: "Our love we owe to you. And so today we rest this love in your hands. With your gracious grace, we shall try to love each other as your Son has loved us: without reservation, in good times and bad, in joy and sorrow. As your apostle Paul commanded us, we shall 'put on compassion and patience, forgiving each other as [you have] forgiven [us].' We shall 'let the peace of Christ rule in [our] hearts . . . let the word of Christ dwell in [us] richly, as [we] teach one another in all wisdom. And whatever [we do], in word or deed, [we shall] do everything in the name of the Lord Jesus, giving thanks to [you] through him' (Col 3:12–13, 15–17)."

II

Second, your love says something to the world around you. You don't need a Jesuit to tell you that wedded life is not "tea for two," a private party, a fantasy island, trespassers prosecuted to the full ex-tent of the law. You will live your love in the midst of . . . people—all sorts of people. When you exit this chapel, your love is not migrating to paradise. You take your love into a world riddled with contradic-tions—where love mingles with hate, tenderness with terrorism; lands like Lebanon, where a president is bombed dead after 17 days; cities like San Salvador, where six Jesuits have their brains blown out. What does your love say to such a world?

Basically, a message of hope. For all the hate that surrounds you, you proclaim with the Song of Solomon that "love is strong as death" (Cant 8:6). You tell a world riven by hate, from Belfast to Pretoria, that love is stronger than hate, that only love such as yours can make for peace. You know from recent history that Berlin Walls can crumble, Brandenburg Gates swing open, Solidarity rise from the ashes, apartheid give way to community, not by force of arms but by courage and compassion, by patience and perseverance, by faith in a God of love to whom nothing is impossible. Knowing that, you take your love for each other not to Eastern Europe or the Middle East, not to Central America or South Africa, but to your acre of God's world. I mean streets where cocaine is king and death never takes a holiday. I mean cities where grown men and women rummage for food in garbage cans, commerce is a jungle, and governments too often rule by corruption. I mean a "land of the free" where most blacks are still second-class citizens, 1.5 million innocents are aborted each year, and half of all wedded love ends in lovelessness.

How do you take your love there, how proclaim your message of hope? Not in the first instance by words but by the way you live your love. The burning question: Will you hide your love at home or be a couple "for others"? Wherever you turn, you will hear the cries of the poor. By the "poor" I do not mean only those who live below the poverty level. I mean the hundreds of thousands for whom life is a burden: from the children sexually abused or burned on hot stoves, through the adult eyes dulled with despair or aflame with anger, to the loneliness in the hearts of the aging. Don't throw up your hands at the enormity, the immensity, the hopelessness of it all: What can one husband and wife do? No. Reach out together to just one of God's suffering servants. Remember dear Mother Teresa. In Washington to touch her mercy to the capital city of our country, she was asked how she could possibly expect to alleviate the hurt and hunger of untold thousands. Her answer? "One at a time."

I cannot tell you just how to heal the hurts and hungers that surround you. I can only tell you that you must. Not only for the message of hope you send to the hopeless, the message of love you send to the loveless, but for your own love as well. The paradox of love is this: Your love for each other will deepen to the extent that your love wings outward, that love takes you out of your selves, gives you to a little world that must be your world as well.

It means you will have to experience some of the pain you want to soften. Some years ago, in Tacoma in the State of Washington, a priest returned to his parish after several months' absence for back surgery. An elderly woman he had never met before came to see him at the rectory. Leaning heavily on her cane and breathing with difficulty, she made her way slowly into his office and lowered herself into a chair. Looking at the priest, she said, "You've been quite sick, haven't you?" He said yes, he had been ill. She responded, "Good. Now you'll be able to understand what I need to share with you."[1]

<h1 style="text-align:center">III</h1>

Third, your love says something to us who are privileged to know and love you. One problem with aging—one problem among many—is that we oldsters tend to forget what it's like to be young. You puzzle us because in so many ways you are different: the thoughts you think, the words you use, the songs you sing, the dreams you dream. But to ask you to be more like us is only a little less idiotic than Henry Higgins in *My Fair Lady* singing "Why can't a woman be more like a man?"

The wonderful gift you give us is the way you look at us in love. The way you look today forces us to ponder more profoundly, helps us to grasp more vividly, what richer hopes lie with the young and the new. You remind us without words how Christian it is to risk: that to be genuinely alive you have to risk; to marry is to launch out with courage into a future unknown; to say "for ever" is to trust God for what is humanly impossible. You tell us without words that we do well to place our future in your hands—hands gentle yet so strong, so enthusiastic, so open to sharing. You urge us without words to recapture a lost laughter, to smile even through our tears. You challenge the long-wedded among us to look with renewed love into each other's eyes, to clasp again hands worn with age and caring, to repeat with you words to which the years have given fresh meaning: "I take you for better for worse, for richer for poorer, in sickness and in health, until death." In sum, you ask us to grow *young* along with you.

Such is your wedding gift to us—and, good God, how we need it! In return, we promise you a gift you cannot buy or measure. Whenever you need us, any of us, we shall be there. Perhaps not with Limoges porcelain or fondue forks, but always with hands outstretched, hearts warm, ears open. Wherever you go, you will never be far from us. However lonely, you need never be alone. You now have an "extended family" you never anticipated.

In this setting—a God who shaped your love, a world waiting for your love, friends sharing your love—in this setting, Tracey and Tim, give yourselves now to each other, confident that nothing "will be able to separate [you] from the love of God that comes to [you] in Christ Jesus" (Rom 8:39), nothing separate you from your love for each other.

Dahlgren Chapel
Georgetown University
Washington, D.C.
December 9, 1989

26
A PAIR OF EXPERIENCED HANDS
Wedding Homily 11

- Song of Songs 2:10–12
- 1 Corinthians 12:31—13:8
- Matthew 5:1–12

Pat and Jim: You do not make a homilist's task easy.[1] What does a celibate say to a man and a woman who have been in love as long as you have? The last thing you need is a love potion secretly concocted by Jesuit chemists. You share a single love, have come to share the same faith, will soon share in the same supper of Christ. What is there left to preach? Three remarkable realities: a sacrament, a promise, and a challenge.

I

First, a sacrament. The community we call Catholic is shaped around seven sacred signs, seven "events" we call sacraments. Community events. Baptism welcomes a child or an adult into the community; penance reconciles a sinner not only with God but with the community; the Eucharist is the community gathered for worship. In that context Christ our Lord touches you today in a special way. You see, your marriage, your life together for almost a decade, has always been a *holy* reality. Love such as yours could not be anything but holy. And so God has loved you, blessed you, throughout these ten years. What happens today? Today your love becomes part and parcel of a community. It is as if our Lord were saying:

Pat and Jim: At this point in your love, as you have grown in your love for each other, grown in your love for me, grown in your love for my Church, I want to express my special delight in your new covenant. Your love has always been a delight to me; you have always been gifted with my grace. But today I want you to share in a sacred rite I dreamed up for a remarkable reason: to let you live your love even more intimately within a community, with the support of a community of love, to live your love *for* the community.

Your coming together in this sacred shrine, the words you will shortly speak to each other, the renewal of your ten-year-old commitment—this tells the Christian world what you already know: God will be with you all the days of your love; God guarantees you His grace, His help, as long as your lives shall last. What too many good Christians do not realize is that, if baptism set you individually within the Christian community, today's celebration sets you there together. Together you are intimately part of a people, of a community wherein, as St. Paul put it, no one can say to any other, "I have no need of you" (1 Cor 12:21). Here is your sacrament: graced love, together, within one and the same Christian community.

II

Second, a promise. You see, most marriages at which I am the Church's official witness, at which I "perform," involve young people in their twenties. Invariably they are heart-warming spiritual experiences for me: the exciting, ecstatic love of the young. But in the context of our culture, with its 50% breakup rate, I send them forth with a prayer and a hope—a fervent prayer and a tremulous hope.

Not so today. If I may quote from Jim's delightful letter of December 28: "Would there be a time in your schedule when you could marry a pair of experienced hands? It may very well be an uplifting experience for you too—no acned groom, no tittering bride; just two happy people with fear of nothing nor anyone save God, going about life as prescribed."

The promise stems from your past: not a sweep-you-off-your-feet courtship, but a decade of devotion. For you, St. Paul's lyric outburst on love is not a lovely piece of literature you have read on some enchanted evening; it is something you have experienced. Ideal love may well be everything Paul claims for it—patient and kind and all the rest—but you know from trying to live it that lovers can be impatient and unkind, arrogant and rude, often insist on their own way, get irritable and resentful, do not invariably rejoice in the right, do not always bear all things, believe all things, hope all things, endure all things. You two have experience of the cross in your years of oneness. You know, not from books but from life, what divides and what unites, what hurts and what delights. Knowing this, you still want to murmur those syllables our culture no longer acknowledges: "for ever."

In consequence, your love gives promise of simply getting better all the time. Valleys, of course, for the cross is not swallowed up in the sacrament; it is simply integrated with it, makes sense in the sacrament. And still, not knowing what lies before you, simply trusting your love and God's, you take each other for better for worse, for richer for poorer, in sickness and in health. Do you wonder that my hopes for you are not tremulous but uncommonly confident?

III

Third, a challenge. The challenge springs from the Gospel you have chosen, from the Beatitudes that accuse our culture. Today I pick but one: "Blessed are the merciful" (Mt 5:7), the compassionate. The sacrament that sets you squarely within this Christian community declares with wordless eloquence that your love is genuinely Christian only if it does not hide within your four walls but moves out to "the other."

You have been generously graced by God. Graced indeed with new-found faith, but also with intelligence and love, with purpose and passion, with artistic feel and delightful humor. These gifts you must now bring with open hands and heart to your community and beyond —to so many who surround you and mutely beg for compassion. Not pity. Pity has overtones of condescension, bending down to another from a situation of superiority. Compassion is another word for love —love for an equal in distress.

It is not within a Jesuit's competence to circumscribe the area of your compassion, tell you where you are to reach out and to whom. Here it is the Christ you love who must point the way—Christ and your own gifts; Christ and your awareness of the world that surrounds you; Christ and the countless less fortunate who call out to you, stripped, beaten down, only half alive; Christ and the walking wounded we "pass by on the other side" (Lk 10:31). I simply presume to recall what for you needs no recalling, what an insightful woman psychologist has stressed so strongly:

> A love that is not for more than itself will die—the wisdom of Christian tradition and the best we know from psychology both assure us of this truth. It is often very appropriate at the early

stages of a relationship that the energy of romance and infatuation exclude the larger world from our vision. But over the long haul an intimate relationship . . . which doesn't reach outward will stagnate.[2]

"Over the long haul." The long haul, Pat and Jim, is already part of your experience. And the long haul has only deepened your love for each other; no stagnation there! I can only conclude that your love has been "for more than itself," does "reach outward." On this blessed day, freshly empowered with the strength of this community of love, take your clasped hands from this sacred spot, hold them out together even more expansively. Let your little acre of God's world see ever more clearly in you the Christ you were created to image, the Christ who from Bethlehem to Calvary and for ever is a Christ for others.[3]

St. Rita's Church
Alexandria, Virginia
March 17, 1990

Medley

27
AS ONE WHO SERVES
Homily for a Conference on Authority

- Galatians 5:1, 13–15
- Luke 22:24–27

We gather for worship within a conference, a conference on authority, on authority in Catholic intellectual life.[1] But it is not only on the level of scholarship, in "head trips," that the tension between authority and freedom rears its head. The tension begins on a prereflective level when the newborn utters its first wail of protest. It continues through the acne that is adolescence, under parents who won't feed you unless you obey. It finds a special focus when the young Catholic is obliged to attend Mass, faces up to Sinai's restrictions on sex. It touches new depths of despair if a man or woman is forced to forgo marital love when a marriage dies.

A homily is not the forum for definitive resolutions of a pervasive Catholic tension. It *is* the place for pacific, prayerful musing on a Catholic way of confronting the tension. Not so much for the scholar as scholar, but for all of us as believers. From our liturgical readings three words are all-important, three words that shape my three points: (1) freedom, (2) authority, (3) service.

I

First, freedom. "For freedom," Paul trumpets, "Christ has set us free. . . . You were called to freedom, my sisters and brothers" (Gal 5:1, 13). Paul's freedom, however, is not lawless license. It is a four-fold deliverance, freedom from four enslavements: from sin, from the law, from the self, from death.[2]

Freedom from sin: not from single acts—murder or lust, theft or false witness—but from Sin with a capital S, that malignant, malicious, malefic power, almost a personal force, a power hostile to God, a power that estranges from God. Freedom from the law: not from civil law but from the Mosaic law, good in itself, telling Paul what he must do, unable to empower him to do it. Freedom from the self: what Paul calls "flesh," my native existence left to itself, tyrannized by earth-bound leanings, man and woman in our contrast to God, subject to so much that severs from God. Freedom from death: not from physical death, but from all that stands against resurrectional life, life with God days without end.

From this fourfold slavery, Paul preaches, Christ has set us free. How? By dying and rising for us. Slavery to sin is now bondage to Christ. The law that was so onerous is now fulfilled by love. The self is no longer schizophrenic; the Spirit within us harmonizes flesh and spirit, my spirit and God's Spirit. We die indeed, but unto life, unto God, unto joy unconfined.

II

Remarkably free, aren't we? But when we flip the coin over, what do we uncover? What seems for all the world like a Christian enslavement: the New Testament *exousia*, which means not only freedom of choice but authority and absolute power.[3] Not only the authority of Jesus: "All authority in heaven and on earth has been given to me" (Mt 28:18). That makes obvious sense to a Christian. What Paul describes as bondage to Christ does indeed fence us in. The Sermon on the Mount is not a charter of license, of libertinism. Not only is murder still forbidden, but the anger within; not only adultery, but the lust in the look; not only hatred of neighbor, but hatred of enemy. Still, knowing that the same Christ who fences us in is the Son of God who borrowed our flesh to experience what we experience, who was pinned to a cross to set us free from our damnable slavery to sin and self, who rose triumphant from the rock to raise us to a share in his own life—knowing this, we yearn to see him more clearly, love him more dearly, follow him more nearly.

But the same authority in a self-perpetuating group of males? Christ's power handed on by "apostolic succession"? Concretely, 1752 canons that outstrip the 613 prescriptions the Pharisees followed so faithfully. Concretely, authority over the classroom and the bedroom, the printed page and the unspoken thought, the biological lab and the hospital O.R. Concretely, power to censor a John Courtney Murray and silence a Leonardo Boff. Concretely, power not only to declare definitively "This is what the Lord God has revealed," but to assert with binding authority "In vitro fertilization is a no-no."

It is not terribly difficult to say yes when we spy the finger and face of Christ in church authority: when Vatican II declares that "Christ summons the Church . . . to that continual reformation of which she always has need";[4] when John Paul II charges Third World powers with rape of the poor; when the U.S. bishops involve our people in discussion of nuclear weaponry; when Cardinal Bernardin calls for a "seamless garment" in dealing with death and injustice, and Cardinal Hickey calls for compassion for a priest with AIDS. The pinch comes when Christ's face is not too clear on the face of authority.

III

What then? My third point, the two texts proclaimed to you. I mean Paul's counsel to the Christians of Galatia: "Do not use your freedom as an opportunity for the flesh [for earthly, material conduct], but through love be servants of one another" (Gal 5:13). And I mean Jesus' directive to his disciples: "The kings of the nations lord it over them; and those in authority over them let themselves be called 'Benefactors.' But not so for you. No, the greatest among you must become like the youngest, the one who leads like the one who serves" (Lk 22:25–26).

In harmony with those two texts, John Courtney Murray noted a year after Vatican II two new signs of the times recognized at the council: (1) a growing consciousness of our dignity as persons, which demands that we act on our own responsibility; (2) our growing consciousness of community, that we are each with the others and for the others.[5] In this context the classical vertical relationship of command-obedience must be balanced by the horizontal relationship of dialogue between authority and the free Christian community. Authority no longer stands *over* the community, as a power to decide and command; authority stands *within* the community, as a ministry to be performed in the service of the community.

In this vision Christian authority exists primarily to unite. I mean, to establish communion, by initiating and sustaining Paul VI's "dialogue of salvation," eliciting the community's insights and stirring its love—with as much freedom as possible and only as much restriction as necessary. In this vision Christian freedom responds to the unitive function of authority by participating freely and lovingly in the dialogue of salvation, recognizing what must be done that the community may come together in a new way, refusing to be enslaved to self, to act against community.

No homily can dissolve the tension between freedom and authority; the tension will not away. But it may well be that "by situating this perennial polarity within the living context of community"[6] we can help make the tension healthy, reveal it as potentially creative rather than inevitably destructive. Fortunately, we have a model who not only lived unto crucifixion the conflict between authority and freedom but can empower us to live the tension creatively, imaginatively. I mean, of course, the Christ who said so simply this morning, "I am among you as one who serves" (Lk 22:27).

St. William's Chapel
Georgetown University
March 10, 1990

28
THAT THEY MAY ALL BE ONE
Homily for a Cathedral Centennial

- Acts 7:55–60
- Revelation 22:12–14, 16–17, 20
- John 17:20–26

The chronicles of your captivating cathedral, authored by your gracious rector, have faced me with a fair warning. When this edifice was dedicated a century ago, the preacher was a prelate, the bishop of Dubuque. His sermon, described as "argumentative and forcible," lasted two hours. It proved beyond doubt the real presence of our Lord in the Eucharist, but "made no reference whatsoever to the new cathedral nor to any related topic."[1]

Not so today. The Gospel proclaimed to you from the pen of the Beloved Disciple points unwaveringly to the purpose of Peoria's cathedral. Six slender syllables: "that they may all be one" (Jn 17:21). Let's muse on what these monosyllables may tell us about your parish's past, its present, its future: St. Mary's yesterday, St. Mary's today, St. Mary's tomorrow.

I

First, St. Mary's yesterday.[2] It is a fascinating story, for it is the ageless Catholic story of struggle and frustration, of success and failure, of sanctity and sin, of life and death. You have so much in your past of which you can justly be proud. I mean your tireless pastors from Benedict Spalding[3] and Charles O'Neill and Martin O'Connor —all three dead within eight years, each in his thirties, each of lung disease. I mean your first bishop, the gigantic John Lancaster Spalding, theologian and poet, author and lecturer, who preached persuasively to Catholics and non-Catholics with standing room only, devel-

167

oped parochial schools and advocated Catholic higher learning, fought successfully for the Catholic University of America, promoted improved education for the clergy, advocated education for women, even encouraged Irish immigrants to settle this far west of New York.

I read with admiration how your forebears slaved and scraped to pay off a devastating cathedral debt; how they struggled against discouraging odds for a parish school, for a new building to replace what had been in part condemned, to lift the level of learning at St. Mary's. I read with delight that Prohibition may have put distilling and brewing on the back burner but paled before surprising growth—religious growth as well. I read with edification what Bishop Joseph Schlarman said in his installation sermon in 1930: "I should like to see Peoria a place where 'unity and brotherly love build themselves a house,' a house in which the spirit of the Divine Master pervades and those who dwell therein are of one heart and one soul."[4] I read with regret how in the 50s many parishioners moved away, small businesses replaced homes, government projects made for a sharp decline in the parish population, and even a new highway took away 30 or 40 families.

I am amazed when I read about the religious imagination that went into your stained-glass windows, from the dark days of the Depression into the light of the late 30s. These windows are familiar to you, familiar to your faith; as for me, they take my breath away. For in the sanctuary Bishop Schlarman and the accomplished architect Ralph Adams Cram placed Mary, virgin mother holding her divine Child, surrounded by the prophet Isaiah ("Behold, a virgin shall conceive and bear a son, and shall call his name 'God is with us' " [Isa 7:14]) and St. Cyril of Alexandria, famed defender of Mary's divine motherhood in the fifth century. And along the sides they revealed in 12 remarkably beautiful windows the preaching of the gospel, evangelization, the spread of the faith to all nations from Palestine to Peoria. Here, in enduring glass, is symbolized the story of your ancestors.

What no history can adequately tell is the faith of your forebears, their trust in God, their love for one another—in good times and bad, in sickness and health, in poverty and wealth. Priests and people have labored for a century to make our Lord's high-priestly prayer extend to this garden that weds Eden to Gethsemane, joy in the Lord and a share in the passion of Christ: "that they may all be one; even as you, Father, are in me, and I in you, that they also may be in us, so that the world may believe that you have sent me" (Jn 17:21). Such was the faith, the hope, the love of those who worshiped here before you. Without them your lives would be quite different—perhaps even less Catholic. All of which brings me to my second point, the second phase of our story—St. Mary's today, the parish you know, the church you cherish.

II

A hundred years have passed. Peoria has changed, and with it St. Mary's. This is no longer a neighborhood parish; many of you stream here from distant streets, not because you are compelled by boundaries but because you are drawn by love. And that is all to the good. But it means that your parish is not the community it once was, not as cohesive as when you lived cheek by jowl, next door to one another, like one big family. In a sense, the family has scattered. And that is not the ideal family.

But, as so often in the Church's history, the good Lord who delights in making all things new has blessed you with fresh hope for community. Age-old Anglos have been enriched with the yeast, the ferment, of Hispanics.

It is at once a peril and a promise. The peril is not unique in Catholic existence. All through our story, when culture meets culture, sparks fly. Each culture has its cherished traditions, is profoundly afraid of losing what it holds dear, of being submerged in the other. Asians and Africans have looked with suspicion at missionaries from the West: Must we become Westerners if we turn Christian? Immigrants from Ireland and Poland, from Italy and Germany, have fought, at times savagely, to preserve their precious inheritance in this New World, their language and their way of living the faith, have understandably not wanted to go the way of Sitting Bull and the Sioux Indians. And the older, settled inhabitants have feared the influx of the new, the alien, the stranger. This is our turf; for generations we have labored to build what we have, and here come the young Turks to smash what we have erected with such care and love.

The peril is real, but richer still is the promise. You see, since the Second Vatican Council this Church of Christ we love so dearly, this community of Christ that began as a Jewish sect in Palestine and then spread into Gentile Europe, has given extraordinary signs of becoming genuinely a world church, a church at home in every clime, a church that can worship in the language of every race, a church whose liturgy can embrace an African dance as well as Handel's *Messiah*.[5]

And so must it be with you. St. Mary's today is the Catholic Church in miniature. Two cultures different in so many ways—in substance and style, in your story and your speech, in your art and your music—gather at the same altar, listen to the same Scripture, receive the same Christ in hand or on tongue, pray to the same Blessed Mother. When our one God sees this, He smiles; for He sees that, like His first creation, this too is "very good" indeed (Gen 1:31).

But always remember, our Lord's prayer "that they may all be one" is not simply a prayer that you be one in faith, in what you profess in one and the same Creed; not simply a prayer that you be one in hope, in your common confidence that God will give all of you all you need to live with Him now and for ever. You are to be one in love, in the way you share with one another who you are and what you have—the special gifts and graces God has showered on your precious cultures.

What St. Paul preached to the Christians of Galatia in central Asia Minor he proclaims to you in north-central Illinois: "You are all one in Christ Jesus" (Gal 3:28). But that basic oneness which is yours by one and the same baptism must not remain sterile, abstract, a matter of words. You are not two communities that use the same church. The Christ who hung on a cross for all of you wanted that cross to break down all barriers, destroy whatever divides, bring Jew and Greek, black and white, Anglo and Hispanic into a loving oneness that would prove to the world that God sent him and that God loves us even as He loves His Son (Jn 17:23).

And so I rejoice in St. Mary's today. By the law of averages, there will always be some who deplore the new, who yearn for "the good ol' days," who remember with affection the community-that-was. No harm in that . . . unless—unless you try to *live* in the past. No, good friends, today, right here, you live. Yesterday is a warm memory; today is life, God's life—God "alive and well" in a new St. Mary's that challenges you to respond to God and to one another in faith, in hope, but especially through the love that St. Paul said "has been poured into [your] hearts through the Holy Spirit who has been given to [you]" (Rom 5:5).

III

This leads directly into my third point: St. Mary's tomorrow. This cathedral is not simply the most magnificent monument in the diocese. A cathedral is a powerful symbol: What you see here stands for something not as easy to see, much more burdensome to build. I mean unity. On four widening levels: the unity of your parish within itself, the unity of this parish with the diocese, the unity of the whole diocese with the world-wide Church, and the unity of Catholics with all God's children, with the men and women who do not share our faith. I have sketched for you one aspect of this fourfold unity: the unity within your parish, the oneness between the rich cultures that make up St. Mary's. A final word on how you, how this parish, might feed into the diocese, into the universal Church, into the general human scene. Three suggestions.

First, you must reach out to the needs of your neighborhood. Here is a concrete contemporary challenge: to take the oneness that is yours within this cathedral and touch it to the suffering world you enter each day, the world outside these wondrous windows. The New Testament Letter of James chiseled the challenge into your stone: "If a brother or sister is ill-clad and in lack of daily food, and one of you says to them, 'Go in peace, be warmed and filled,' without giving them the things needed for the body, what does it profit? So faith by itself, if it has no works, is dead" (Jas 2:15–16).

Here, like Christ washing the feet of his disciples, your bishop[6] has "given you an example" (Jn 13:15). The love of his heart? In his own words, "the poor and the heartbroken." That is why he lives in gospel simplicity, why he gives away just about all that is his. The poor of Peoria are as precious to him as the poor of Palestine were precious to Jesus. Without words, his life is a lasting challenge to you. Touch your love to the loveless, your laughter to such as weep, feed the hungry and slake the thirsty, welcome the stranger and clothe the naked, visit the sick and the shackled. Without this you take the "Christ" out of "Christian." For "faith by itself, if it has no works, is dead."

Second, you have the means to make your cathedral a cultural and intellectual center for the tricounty[7] area and the diocese. Here your twin cultures are rich in promise. You can reveal to non-Catholics that Catholic is catholic: open to all that is human. Nothing that is human is alien to you: politics or poetry, Mozart or mariachi, historical tours or cathedral museums. Yours too to proclaim is not only the freedom of the children of God, your freedom from slavery to sin and self, but also the historic hour 145 years ago when in this very city Abraham Lincoln publicly denounced slavery. Show the world around you that your cathedral is not just a proud museum piece that preserves the past; from this sacred spot the arts can radiate to the far ends of the state. Make it a privilege once again not only to pray in Peoria but to "play in Peoria."

Third, make doubly sure that this cathedral continues to serve as a center of hospitality to the whole of the diocese. Whether it's catechumens or Boy Scouts, ordinations or golden wedding anniversaries, chrism Mass or cursillo movement, K. of C. or Daughters of Isabella, new Catholics or renewed Catholics, devotion to Our Lady of Guadalupe or simply to the mother of Jesus—welcome all with outstretched arms and open heart. See to it that all who enter here feel at home here, sense not only the presence of God but your presence as well. Why? So as to respond as disciples of Christ to his prayer to the Father: "that they may all be one."

When the cornerstone of this cathedral was laid, Bishop John Lancaster Spalding told an immense crowd:

> [This cathedral] is a building far too great in magnitude and cost for the simple needs of St. Mary's parish, but as a temple raised to the honor of the Most High God, it has a wider use and meaning. . . . It is the very center of a powerful community, the heart of the diocese of Peoria. . . . This cathedral is to be built strong, founded on rock hewn out of stone, a fitting symbol of the eternal truth of the religion of Christ to point all to a higher life. It is to be a great school of the truth of God, a great chair from whence divine wisdom is taught, a great voice to teach us that the earthy is not best, but that the spirit of man is the seat of all the divinest hopes and yearnings toward that which is nobler. . . . Only as we live for others do we rise proportionately in the scale of civilized beings whose nature it is to elevate and ennoble the best interests of all about us. There is no happiness except . . . we work for others. . . .[8]

Live for others . . . work for others. The challenge is as urgent today as it was when Archbishop Spalding sounded those syllables, as contemporary as when Jesus proclaimed the second great commandment of the law and the gospel: "You shall love your neighbor as [you love] yourself" (Mt 22:39). Only thus can we hope with our Lord Jesus "that they may all be one," that the faith we cherish will quicken the pulses of Peorians, strike a responsive chord in the heart of each woman or man whose life you touch.

Good friends in Christ: For your impressive past, I joy with you. On your present so rich in promise, I compliment you. For the future God holds in store for you, I pray that your oneness with one another will be a striking proof to Peoria that this cathedral is not lifeless stone but alive with love . . . God's love and your love.

St. Mary's Cathedral
Peoria, Illinois
May 7, 1989

29
DARE TO BE CHRIST
Homily for a Parish Sesquicentennial

- Deuteronomy 26:4–10
- Romans 10:8–13
- Luke 4:1–13

Today you confront me with a "mission impossible": 150 years of history, three temptations of Christ, three catechumens—all in 20 minutes. Happily, a homily is not a history, not a lecture on Scripture, not a class in catechetics. And still, today the three should somehow come together. I believe they do—and the link, as you might suspect, is . . . Christ. So, let me begin with your century and a half, move on to Jesus' wilderness experience, and end with three hearts athirst. Happily, these three stages correspond to your past, your present, and your future.[1]

I

First, your century and a half. It fascinates me. For several reasons. For starters, I see not only a parish but a community. I mean that singular miracle when Irish and Polish, German and Italian, Spanish and French, African and Ukrainian retain their identity—color, blood, accents—but are transformed into the one Christ. Through 150 years uncounted thousands have been baptized into the same Christ, have nestled the same Christ on hand or tongue, have confessed in their own varied ways "We adore thee, O Christ, and we bless thee, because by thy holy cross thou hast redeemed the world." You do not forget whence you came, but you remember even more gratefully who it is you have become. For all your fantastic and fearful differences, you and your forebears in faith have lived what St. Paul proclaimed to his fellow Christians: "You are all one in Christ Jesus"

173

(Gal 3:28). Even your priests—call them Barber or Barbelin, Romano or Ardia, Jerge or Gaché, Casey or Rey, Curry or Vespré, Havermans or Blox—scores have spoken with many tongues and still with one only tongue, "Jesus Christ is Lord!" (Phil 2:11).

Your century and a half fascinates me because this one faith of yours has not been sterile. Not only has it fashioned a well-known "refuge for sinners," confessionals famous throughout Philadelphia as an incredible haven for reconciliation with God and the Catholic community. Your faith has been a faith that does justice, a faith that serves not self but society, is aware of the other, the countless kinds of "Lazarus" who beg at your door for the crumbs from your table, who need you if they are to become genuinely human or Christian.

Early on, your ancestors in faith fought against the evils of alcoholic intemperance. They organized to relieve the distress of Irish immigrants and the straits of sailors. They started a home for working girls, formed a society to serve the spiritual needs of businesswomen. They helped open parochial schools throughout the city, took care of firemen and postal employees. They served those suffering from the "white plague" of tuberculosis, slaved to integrate blackness and whiteness into the one parish. They have supported Bread for the World and given hope to Boys' Hope, opened their hearts and their purses to needy sister parishes in Philadelphia and Camden.

In a word, what I read in your history is a parish, a people, that has struggled to live the two great commandments of the law and the gospel: "You shall love the Lord your God with all your heart, and with all your soul, and with all your mind. . . . You shall love your neighbor as yourself" (Mt 22:37, 39). A perfect people? I doubt it. Perfection comes only with resurrection. And still this century and a half is a success story, for it reveals what miracles of grace are possible if a people opens itself in love to God and God's images.

II

So much for the past—a past of which you may well be proud. To prod us into the present, today's liturgy focuses on the temptations of Christ. You see, those three temptations are not to be imprisoned in a Judean desert; they must speak to Old St. Joseph's as well.

What were those temptations all about?[2] Very simply, Jesus was tempted to use his power, his authority, as Son of God in his own interest, for his own purposes, apart from the mission given him by his Father.

Temptation 1: You're hungry, aren't you? Then don't be a fool. You've got power; the Son of God surely can work miracles. So, "tell this stone to become bread" (Lk 4:3). Satan's challenge? Forget your Father's design for you; the problem right now is bread; so, manufacture it. Jesus' response? "It is written in Scripture, 'Not on bread alone is man/woman to live, but on every word that proceeds from the mouth of God' " (Mt 4:4; Lk 4:4). Not like the Israelites in the desert sighing for the fleshpots of Egypt will Jesus seek his food apart from Yahweh. His Father will feed him. "My food is to do the will of Him who sent me" (Jn 4:34).

Temptation 2: You want to rule the world, don't you? Isn't that why you're here? Well, there you are: "Authority over all the kingdoms of the world, and the glory that goes with it, has been delivered to me. If you fall down and worship me, it will all be yours" (Lk 4:5–7). Satan's challenge? Accept world dominion from someone other than God; acknowledge as your master and lord someone other than your Father. Jesus' response? "It is written in Scripture, 'The Lord your God shall you worship, and Him only shall you serve' " (v. 8). Unlike ancient Israel, Jesus refuses to worship anyone save Yahweh, insists that his single mission is to see to it that his Father's kingship is established over each and all.

Temptation 3: You want to make a name for yourself, don't you? Well then, here's your chance, at the tip of the temple. Play Superman: ". . . throw yourself down from here; for it is written in Scripture, '. . . On their hands [angels] will bear you up, lest you strike your foot against a stone' " (Lk 4:9–11). Jesus' response? "It is written in Scripture, 'You shall not put the Lord your God to the test' " (v. 12). In contrast to the Israelites fed with water struck by Moses from a rock, Jesus refuses to demand miraculous protection for himself and his mission.

Good friends, you too have a mission from God, a charge laid on you by your baptism. Like your forebears, your Christian commission is to transform your acre of God's world, to shape it into a city of justice, of peace, of love. Your mission territory is wherever you are— where you work and play, order and obey, sweat and relax, laugh and weep, live and die. And this world you transform most effectively by your lives: attractive to the world because so human, a challenge to the world because so different.

Precisely here you confront today's temptations. Not exactly the temptations that assailed God-in-flesh, but similar enough. For you too are tempted to use your powers, your gifts, your possessions for your own sweet selves. Concretely, experts and experience, colleges and corporations tell us that three dangers threaten our human and Christian values: money, power, and fame. Not that these are evils in themselves; they are not. Where does the temptation lie? In amassing money to pack only your own pockets, piling up power principally to lord it over the powerless, entering halls of fame for the applause that pours over you. Run that route and you betray your God-given mission.

That is why I rejoice with exceeding joy when I see that in daylight the street people find here food for empty bellies, health for broken bodies, counsel for hearts unloved; when I hear that as evening falls your Care Walk takes you with soup and sandwiches to the homeless on the streets that surround us; when I find that you have a mercy-filled ministry to the sick, to such as lie helpless and sometimes hopeless on beds of pain. God's children can come here off the streets as well as from Society Hill and know that they are loved. I rejoice because it means that your liturgy is not an isolated hour each week; the Eucharist moves you from church to world, transforms you into eucharists for the life of the earth, the life especially of those who experience more of Christ's crucifixion than of his resurrection. Here, as an ancient Latin poet put it, "naught that is human is a stranger to [you]."

III

So much for the present—a present of which you may well be proud. To prod us into the future, Old St. Joseph's highlights today three catechumens. I do not know you; I have never met you. But you are terribly important in today's celebration; for you symbolize tomorrow. Let me explain.

Within Catholicism tradition is an honorable term. Not tradition in a musty, moldy sense—all that ever went before. Authentic tradition gathers up the best of the past, infuses it with the insights of the present, with a view to an even more Christian and human future. This parish is not called *Old* St. Joseph's because you reproduce every jot and tittle that Father Ryder introduced in 1839. In a profound sense, this parish is ever old and ever new: old because its deepest roots trace back to the apostles, back to Jesus; new because each age brings with it new people, unexpected crises, fresh solutions. Like your own body, your church remains the same and it grows.

Where, concretely, do I suggest that you might grow? First, be thrillingly aware that you are living members of a single body—the body of Christ. Recapture, etch on your minds and hearts, St. Paul's remarkable remark to the Christians of Corinth: No member of Christ's body can say to any other, "I have no need of you" (1 Cor 12:14–27). A wild idea, off the wall. I want you to look up from your personal navels, look past your nose, past your home, past your parish, past the City of Brotherly and Sisterly Love, cast your mind's eye over a billion Christians on your planet—millions of them hungry across the globe, hundreds bloodied in Belfast, thousands more battling for life in Beyrouth, millions persecuted behind an Iron Curtain. I am not asking you initially to do something about these tragedies. I am asking you to grasp the wild idea that not only do these members of Christ's body need you; you need them. Through their anguish you and I are graced. I know not how God does it; I simply know from the gospel that it is so. If the ancient saying is true, "The blood of martyrs is the seed of the Church," it is likewise true that the sufferings inflicted on Christ's body anywhere touch your lives without your even sensing it. We are a single body, the body of Christ, and through the passion of Christ the passion of Christians makes us more passionate Christians, makes us better than we are. This parish is linked through Calvary to the world Church—from Poland to Pretoria, from Armenia to Nigeria. Grasp that raw reality and your Christian existence will never be small, petty, self-centered.

A second stage in your growing: Let not problems sour you, turn you off, lessen your love. Problems will indeed plague you—from your culture, from your church, from your conscience. Old problems that refuse to go away—from the person of Christ through "one true church" to artificial contraception, broken marriage, and the kiss of peace. New problems that a new age provokes—from fetal experimentation through women-in-the-Church to removing the respirator from a loved one in coma. And problems I myself shall never see, cannot even conceive.

In consequence, you can expect factions in the Church of tomorrow, divisions dreadful enough to crucify Christ again. I have no instant cure, no miracle bromide, that will dissolve your dissensions, bring Right and Left into a harmonious Center. In fact, I fear it will always be thus in a human body—and the body of Christ is wonderfully and fearfully human. What we need badly in tomorrow's Church are peacemakers, reconcilers, those who will go the extra mile to link, if not heads, at least hearts. If the theme of your celebration is evangelization—reaching out to others with the gospel of God—never forget that gospel's second commandment: Love even those you dislike; let your love leap out to Sandinistas and *contras* alike; love even Catholics with whom you disagree. Above all, leave excommunication to God. Literally, to hell with hatred.

A third stage in your growing pervades the New Testament. Listen to the First Letter of Peter: "As He who called you is holy, be holy yourselves in your whole way of life, since Scripture says 'You shall be holy, for I [your Lord and God] am holy' " (1 Pet 1:15; Lev 11:14–15). Sanctity is not simply for a Katherine Drexel, a Mother Cabrini, a John Neumann. *You* shall be holy. Each one of you. Not a syrupy, hands-clasped, eyes-to-heaven sanctity. Rather, that tough virtue called Christian courage—where day after day, in fair weather and foul, in agony and ecstasy, you struggle to be better than you are, to love God above all else that attracts, love especially the crucified, the drug-addicted and the AIDS-afflicted, the unutterably lonely and the utterly unloved. Such is what the Church will need in the 90s, in the 21st century—not Sunday or Christmas Christians, but everyday, Good Friday Christians whose daily dying with Christ is a rising with him to new life. Dare to be saints!

With that word, good friends, I leave you: Dare to be saints. Dare to be . . . Christ.

Old St. Joseph's Church
Philadelphia, Pa.
February 12, 1989

30
MY BODY . . . FOR YOU
Baccalaureate Homily for a University

- Genesis 14:18–20
- 1 Corinthians 11:23–26
- Luke 9:11–17

For weeks you graduates had me groping, grasping at straws. What is the tie-in that could possibly link Corpus Christi, today's celebration of Christ's body and blood, with your graduation? Should I urge you to attend Mass regularly, so that insider trading will not corrupt your countinghouse, ambulance-chasing subvert your legal ethics, danger distance doctors-to-be from contact with the AIDS-afflicted? Not a bad idea, but it would not touch a more profound link between whatever you do and the body of Christ. So I dare to confront you with a daring thesis: Today's liturgy is the touchstone, the test, the criterion by which you should measure your life, appraise it as success or failure. The crucial text is a remarkably brief sentence from the second reading, Paul's first letter to the Christians of Corinth: "This is my body, [given] for you" (1 Cor 11:24; cf. Lk 22:19). My song and dance has three movements: (1) the body of Christ, (2) the body that is the Church, (3) the body that is yours.

I

First, the body of Christ. Not simply his flesh and blood, his bones and sinews, his veins and arteries. After all, the Son of God, in taking our flesh, did not become sheer matter, six feet of chemicals. He became a person, like us in all we are except for our sin. When Jesus walked the ways of Palestine, he was not a Middle East robot, triggered by button control from heaven. He learned by experience how to shape an idea and talk in Aramaic; learned by living to get angry at

179

hypocrites and weep over his city Jerusalem and his friend Lazarus; knew what it feels like to be hungry and tired, to be called a madman by his relatives, to have no place whereon to rest his head. And when he died, he did not "pass away" serenely, with dear friends saying the rosary around his bed, a priest murmuring "May the angels receive you into paradise." He died in far greater agony than most of us, even feeling for a bitter hour that his own Father was not there.

Very simply, when I say "the body of Christ," I mean a human being—intelligent, sensitive, emotional, loving. I mean someone so like us that for at least 30 years his own townspeople saw nothing special about him. Now that "body" came out of a mother's body, "grew in wisdom and years" (Lk 2:52), preached his Father's word and sweated a bloody death, for one reason. Never in over three decades was there a moment when he could not have declared, "This is my body, [given] for you." That is what the Incarnation is all about: "for you," for me.

But why? The answer comes from an astonished St. Paul: He "loved me and gave himself for me" (Gal 2:20). God's Son-in-flesh loved you—loved you enough to be born as you are, grow as you grow, die as none of you will ever die. Loved you so much that when he left you, he left his risen body with you under the appearance of bread, of wine. This is the body we celebrate this evening: the sacramental Christ, hidden indeed but remarkably real, because what is hidden is, as our age-old catechisms declare, "body and blood, soul and divinity." And, once again, "given for you." Christ did not leave himself in a consecrated host primarily to be worshiped. He is there, will be there till time is no more, for the reason he gave at the Last Supper: "Take, eat; this is my body" (Mt 26:26). Why? Because, in the inspired insight of Pius XII, if you have received worthily, you are what you have received. You are transformed into Christ.

It's a fact—this love we cannot fathom. We theologians have spilled centuries of ink and blood over it, have debated it unto frustration and heresy. And after mind is wearied and laser printer runs dry, we do best to lay aside our passions and our computers, kneel in adoration, and murmur to our hidden Lord with theologian Aquinas (in the rapturous translation of Gerard Manley Hopkins):

> Godhead here in hiding, whom I do adore
> Masked by these bare shadows, shape and nothing more.
> See, Lord, at thy service low lies here a heart
> Lost, all lost in wonder at the God thou art.[1]

His body . . . for you. From Bethlehem to Calvary, from a stable to a cross, his body . . . for you. Even now, in high heaven and in a helpless host, his body . . . for you.

II

Move now from the body of Christ to the body that is the Church.[2] In that same letter where Paul told the Corinthian Christians about the body of Christ given for them, he told them about another body that should shape their living. "By one Spirit we were all baptized into one body—Jews or Greeks, slaves or free . . ." (1 Cor 12:13). He compared it to the human body, to your body and mine. Look, he suggested, at your physical body. It's made up of myriad members. Happily, you're not all heart or hands, all stomach or spleen, all brain or buttocks. Why? Because it takes all sorts of parts working in harmony if the body is to be a body, if it is to be human, if you are to build ideas or cities, grow red with wrath or shame, frame words or run a marathon, waltz or break-dance, eye a sunset or hear a symphony, caress a child or taste a Big Mac, bake biscuits or make love. "The eye cannot say to the hand, 'I have no need of you,' nor again the head to the feet, 'I have no need of you' " (v. 21).

And so, Paul insisted, so it is with you: "You are the body of Christ and individually members of it" (v. 27). You play different parts indeed. Not everybody is pope or priest; not all are John Carrolls or Mother Teresas; not all are miracle-working Xaviers or exploring Marquettes; not everyone, thank God, is a Jesuit! But every single Christian is important if the Church is to be one. John Paul II cannot say to this class of '89, "I have no need of you." Not preacher to the pew, not white Christian to black, riches to rags, literate to illiterate, professor to pupil, lusty youth to doddering old. In Paul's words, "God has so adjusted the body . . . that the members may have the same care for one another. If one member suffers, all suffer together; if one member is honored, all rejoice together" (vv. 24–26).

"You are all one," Paul proclaimed, "all one in Christ Jesus" (Gal 3:28). But are we? In his time Paul had to flay fractious factions in Christian Corinth: "I belong to Paul," "I belong to Apollos," "I belong to Peter" (1 Cor 1:12). "Is Christ divided?" he asked. "Was Paul crucified for you? Were you baptized in the name of Paul?" (v. 13). In our time Catholics claw one another like cats in a sack: Prolife or prochoice? Mass with Bach or the St. Louis Jesuits? Women where I stand or males incorporated? Bedroom privacy or *Humanae vitae?* A pulpit is not the place to argue perplexing problems, passionately held convictions. In a church of humans, we shall always disagree. From Paul standing up to Peter in the first Christian century, through Thomas Aquinas condemned by the bishop of Paris in the 13th, to Marcel Lefebvre assailing the Second Vatican Council today, the body of Christ has never passed a perfect physical. I am neither damning discussion nor being permissive on heresy. Here I simply assert: If disagreement destroys our love, we are no longer the single body of Christ.

Oneness in mind and heart—an ideal, of course; but only if you and I slave towards that ideal will the Church ever come close to it, will Christ our Lord be able to proclaim proudly to the world outside our Christian gates, "This [this Catholic community] is my body, [given] for you."

III

Finally, good friends, let me move from the body that is the whole Church to the body that is you individually. How can you carry over into your concrete day-to-day existence the Christ of Bethlehem and Calvary, the Christ that is the Church, the Christ of the Eucharist? How can you murmur honestly, "This is my body, [given] for you"?

To be frank, you must. Not because Rome lays on you another burden, an eleventh commandment. Rather because Christ himself commanded it. If "the great and first commandment" is "Love the Lord your God with all your heart, soul, and mind," the second commandment "is like it: You shall love your neighbor as [you love] yourself" (Mt 22:37–39). And your "neighbor" is not just the friend next door who shares your Bud Light. If the parable of the Good Samaritan is part of your gospel, "neighbor" is anyone and everyone who needs you (cf. Lk 10:25–37).

There is a problem here: a for-me culture. Sociologists claim we are witnessing a resurgence of late-19th-century rugged individualism: Look out for number one; get to the well first before it dries up; the race is to the swift, the shrewd, the savage, and the devil take the hindmost.[3] A prestigious university celebrating its 350th birthday reports the three top goals declared by the class of 1990: (1) money, (2) power, (3) reputation.[4] A survey of 290,000 freshpersons in more than 500 colleges and universities reveals that "Being 'very well off financially' now tops the list of 'essential or very important' reasons

for going to college. To 'develop a meaningful philosophy of life' . . .
is now the lowest it has been in the 20-year history of the annual
survey. . . ."[5] A documentary in *Esquire* recalls "what everyone is saying these days": "money is the new sex."[6]

No, good friends. This Baccalaureate Mass makes complete sense
only if the body of Christ you receive and the body of Christ of which
you are a member thrust you from church to world murmuring, "This
is my body, [given] for you."

Given for whom? Not for an abstract mass called humanity.
Rather for two very visible sets of people: those you meet each day,
and those you don't. Those you will meet each day: I mean wife or
husband, your children, people at General Motors or General Elec-
tric, Bank One or Bristol-Myers, Aetna or Wang, Ohio Edison or Ohio
Bell, the *Plain Dealer,* CBS or the C.I.A., Harvard or Wharton, IBM or
the Jesuit Volunteer Corps. Here it is that you must discover God,
celebrate God, proclaim God. Here it is that the vocation built into
you at your baptism must come to life: to bring Christ where you live
and move and have your being, to help transform your acre of God's
world into a city of justice, of peace, of love. Not primarily by preaching; basically by being. Being what? Simply the Christ into whom this
Eucharist transmutes you. I mean a man or woman who attracts that
world and challenges it. Attracts it because you are so splendidly human, challenges it because you are more than human, alive with a faith
that triumphs over doubt, with a hope that overrides discouragement
and despair, with a joy that leaps like John the Baptist from the barren
womb of sorrow.

Your body given, second, for those millions most of you may
rarely meet. I mean the dark side of our culture: the homeless and the
helpless, the lonely and the loveless, the drug-infested and the AIDS-
infected, the thousand and one young runaways pimped and prostituted and angel-dusted—yes, those who sustain "the pain of being
black."[7] They will surround you, invade you, but you won't see them,
may indeed see them but, like the priest in the Gospel parable, pass
them by "on the other side" (Lk 10:31), unless. . . . Unless your eyes
have been opened by John Carroll and Jesus Christ.

"My body, [given] for you." A powerful Presbyterian preacher
once said: The religious man or woman is "a queer mixture" of three
persons, "the poet, the lunatic, the lover."[8] Such is my provocative
prayer for you as you descend this day from university "heights,"[9] as
you come down to earth. I pray that the poet may always find a place in
you; for the poet is a person of profound faith, seeing beneath the
appearances of things, seeing with new eyes—in your case, with the

eyes of Christ. I pray that there may ever be a fair measure of lunacy in you: the wild idea, the foolishness of the cross, the mad exchange of all else for God; for herein lies your Christian hope. And I pray that, however radical the risk, even on your cross you will always be Christ the lover, arms flung wide, your body given to your little world for its redemption—its redemption and yours.

God feed you . . . God lead you . . . God speed you.

John Carroll University
Cleveland, Ohio
May 27, 1989

31
MEDICINE AS MISSION
Feast of St. Luke

- 2 Timothy 4:9–17
- Luke 10:1–9

Thirty years ago today I preached to your ancestors of the Medical School.[1] That day I focused on three ways of practicing medicine: Medicine can be slavery, an art, a vocation. I do not retract what I preached before (I rarely do); but during these intervening three decades I have grown, have come to know three pertinent realities more profoundly: God, myself, and your profession. And so I believe I can speak more intelligently on one of those three ways of being a doctor: not on the slavery, not on the art, only on your vocation. In that context I shall ask three questions. (1) Is there anything particularly Christian about being a doctor? (2) Granted that there is, what demands does it lay on a Catholic institution like Georgetown? (3) That much settled, what do I see Jesus the healer asking of you individually?

I

First, is there anything particularly Christian about being a doctor? I could answer with something quite obvious. Jesus healed people right and left: epileptics and paralytics, a possessed boy and Peter's fevered mother-in-law. In his footsteps, therefore, many a Christian lays healing hands upon the sick—and sometimes with miraculous effects. Faith can heal; it's a fact.

But I am not talking about miracles, what *God* can do if we have faith. I am talking about healing as a profession shaped of skill, where cures come from scalpels, my inflamed ileum yields to Prednisone, a new heart beats not from my preaching but from a generous donor. I am talking about a profession that has limitations, that does not always heal, that deals daily with death. Why call this a Christian vocation? The response rests with a prior question: What has the Church's Christ-given mission to do with sickness?

Here two ways of looking at man and woman are inadequate for the Christian. On the one hand, believe it or not, the Church is *not* here to "save souls." Such a conviction pays slender homage to God, fails to recognize that the body is an essential part of me, that without my body I am a creature incomplete, that the body too yearns for redemption, to come alive through the Spirit of God, to be transfigured like the body of Christ through all eternity.

On the other hand, if the Church's mission is not simply to save the soul, neither is its mission to save soul *and* body. What the Church is all about is the human person, and the human person is an incredible oneness. Oh yes, you can *think* of me as body and soul, as flesh and spirit; for I am a fascinating wedding of material and immaterial, of what we can see-hear-touch-taste-smell and what escapes the most sensitive of senses and instruments. And still, the real, pulsating life I actually live is never one or the other. It is always and inescapably a man or a woman who is born and dies, loves or hates, gives life or takes it, laughs or cries, dances in sheer delight or winces in unbearable pain. With this in mind, you are not touching a man *with* melanoma, a woman *with* scarred uterus. *He* is sick, not his chest; and *she* is sick, not her womb. You are touching a living human person.

But even this is not enough—not enough for the Church's mission to the sick, not enough for a vocation. Where your service is distinctively Christian, where Georgetown's Medical Center should differ from the finest of secular institutions, is in your realization that in health care you are touching a human person *working out his or her redemption, his or her salvation*. Every listing in the massive encyclopedia of sickness—from AIDS and schizophrenia, through the cardiac insufficiencies and the intestinal diverticula, down to the acne on an adolescent's cheek—all this is intimate to a person in process.

A disease is not something objective, outside of me. It is I, for a time or terminally, as really and existentially part of me as is my hand or my hearing, my faith and my fears, my loves and my deepest yearnings. No matter what my explicit belief or unbelief, in illness I work out my destiny as a person: I grow or I diminish, I spend myself selflessly for others or selfishly for myself. And if I am a Christian, sickness (like gladness) should be my share in the life of Christ, my role in the story of salvation, my way of realizing a relationship of love with

God and with God's images on earth; and I simply cannot divorce this religious movement from what disease does to me as a human being. If disease diminishes *me*, it diminishes my Christianness. If sickness strengthens *me*, I take a giant step (or many small steps) toward my salvation, toward God. The equation is as simple as it is profound. Sickness = I, and I am a person in process—in process of salvation, of life with God now and for ever.

In summary, sickness calls out to the Church, to Christians, not simply or primarily for an anointing by a priest. Individually and as a family, you are privileged to touch a child of God at a specially crucial moment in his or her earthly existence—when the once-proud flesh is coming apart or the once-strong spirit has been broken, when fear clutches the heart and I am alone with my naked self. Here is Gethsemane; here is another Christ sweating blood, making his or her tortured way to Calvary, perhaps crying to heaven, "Don't let me die!" Your task, as a Christian community, is to work together, each with your God-given gift, to help that singular, unrepeatable person trudge with Christ to Jerusalem. When I don that dismaying hospital gown, you become my Christ; you are intimately involved in my redemption; you are my life, more profoundly than you imagine.

II

Second, what demands does all this lay on a Catholic institution like Georgetown? Let me get uncommonly personal, almost autobiographical. Medically speaking, I'm a fortunate man. Hospital beds have cradled me only twice in my life: an appendectomy in '32, a deviated septum-cum-tonsillectomy in '46. But the next time I change my black suit for your backless day-and-night dress, I suspect it will be quite serious. If so, I shall prefer Georgetown to Sloan Kettering. Not because it is more highly rated by accreditors; I know nothing of that. Rather because my illness will cry for more than scientific competence. It will not be an isolated episode in my life, divorced from who I am and what I am about and where I am going. I shall be working out my salvation. Through suffering and, ultimately, in dying.

I shall not be asking Georgetown for an "explanation" of suffering that satisfies my mind. Suffering enmeshes us in the problem of evil, and no philosopher has yet unmasked the mystery, cracked the code. Old Testament Job, wrestling with God over innocent suffering, was not favored with an explanation: God stressed divine mystery, simply showed Job His face. Even in the Christian vision the mystery does not disappear. Yes, St. Paul assures me that through suffering "I complete in my flesh what is lacking in Christ's afflictions for the sake of" God's people (Col 1:24). But I cannot *prove* that. Suffering will only make sense to me if Christ has shown his face to me.

Precisely here is where I shall need you. Of course, Christ can show his face to me without you, in Bellevue as well as G.U. But it will be easier for me to see his face if I see his face in you. It will be easier if I am not merely brought Communion by a minister making the rounds, but am surrounded by doctors and nurses, administrators and housekeepers, most of whom share some or all of my vision. If the people around me, the men and women whose flesh still glows with health, whose eyes sparkle and spirits soar, are clearly alive with the life of Christ. If to them I am not a room number, a disease, a blood type, a wrist tag. If the front office is as much concerned over *my* cross as over Blue Cross. If a nurse may discuss life and death with me without getting hell from a supervisor. If I feel there is a family around me, a family that senses what I am about to experience: a movement from life to, yes, life—but through a darkness I cannot even imagine. If among my life supports there hangs a cross above my bed to remind me that my agony, like Christ's, need not be a waste, that I too can murmur, "This is my body given for you" (Lk 22:19).

III

Third, what do I see Jesus the healer asking of you individually? I assume your competence. A scalpel in the hands of a devout but incompetent Christian is not my ideal of "the way to go." Given competence, I submit that your vocation as a healer calls for two further gifts. One is fairly obvious; the other may surprise you.

The obvious gift: competence wed to compassion. Compassion is a strong word that dots the pages of Jesus' life. Literally, it means "suffer with." You share my agony, my anguish, my pain. Not that it immobilizes your hand in the O.R. Simply that I sense in you someone who cares, for whom medicine is more than a computer, a patient more than a medical chart. You feel my fears as well as my pulse; you resonate to the loneliness that makes each hospital bed an island; you realize how that seamless hospital gown strips me naked, deprives me of all dignity—like the loincloth on our crucified Jesus. I know, you can *be* compassionate within, without being able to show it. That makes you a good man, a good woman; but it leaves me terribly alone, no matter how close you stand. A remarkably articulate surgeon, Richard Selzer, saw deeply into the problem from personal experience:

> A surgeon does not slip from his mother's womb with compassion smeared upon him like the drippings of his birth. It is much later that it comes. No easy shaft of grace this, but the cumulative murmuring of the numberless wounds he has dressed, the incisions he has made, all the sores and ulcers and cavities he has touched in order to heal. In the beginning it is barely audible, a whisper, as from many mouths. Slowly it gathers, rises from the streaming flesh until, at last, it is a pure *calling*—an exclusive sound, like the cry of certain solitary birds—telling that out of the resonance between the sick man and the one who tends him there may spring that profound courtesy that the religious call Love.[2]

My second demand may surprise you—though it should not. Last month I was privileged to lecture at Calvary Hospital in the Bronx. It's a 200-bed facility for men and women incurably cancerous, soon to die. Against all the odds, the place is alive with . . . life. Sunshine streams through the lobby; bright posters bedeck the walls; 200 volunteers serve with a smile, strum guitars, teach ceramics, celebrate birthdays, run to the store for Progresso tomato sauce. You want lox and bagels for breakfast? Coming up! A martini before dinner? Yes, sir![3]

Beneath the externals lies a Christian conviction: These patients are people, beloved of God and in need of human loving. So, administrator and doctor, nurse and linens-dropper, all without exception help these precious persons to live this day as if it were their first day, as if it were their last day, as if it were their only day.

What do I ask of you? That you bring to those you serve not only your life-giving technology, not only your Christian compassion, but a certain measure of joy. Not belly laughter; not a false "My, aren't we looking better today?" I want your face and your eyes, your lips and your hands to tell me that *my* life is precious to you, that I am not an object, that I am now genuinely part of your life. I want you to help me feel that, if this is my last day, it is worth living—if only because you have touched it with your love.

I wonder: Is that why St. Paul called Luke "the beloved physician" (Col 4:14)?

Dahlgren Chapel
Georgetown University
October 18, 1989

32
SING A NEW SONG TO THE LORD
Homily for the Blessing of a Pipe Organ

- Colossians 3:12–17

In almost a half century of priesthood, I have never preached on music. I have preached on all sorts of subjects, from God to money, from sin to social justice, from love of law to the law of love. But never on music. Why? Perhaps because I personally murder music; probably because music seemed a subject more suited to the professional platform than to the pastoral pulpit. But in the weeks since your persuasive pastor seduced me into accepting his invitation, I have grown immeasurably in my appreciation of the intimate link between music and the Mass, between song and the Sacrifice, between lyrics and liturgy. And so I dare this afternoon to tell you, simply and artlessly, what I have discovered. Three movements make up my song and dance: (1) music as power, (2) music as worship, (3) music as community.

I

First, music is power. You know as well as I that not only love and economics make the world go round; music runs them a close third. Through the centuries music has stirred the gamut of human emotions. Mozart's *Figaro* has for two centuries evoked our laughter and our sadness. Beethoven's "Ode to Joy" lifts hearts from Maine to Mexico. Pop concerts have relaxed and pleasured Bostonians by the millions. Sousa's "The Stars and Stripes Forever" sends patriotic shivers down our spine. Tchaikovsky's *Swan Lake* gives me time and again a feeling of rapture, of flying; his *Nutcracker* charms children out of their Christmas shoes.

Nor is music's power confined to leisure time, to the concert hall, to Washington's Mall on a summery evening. A recent article in *Pastoral Music* claims that

> America is a country awash in music. I recall the three young black men who passed me on the street last week doing a rap song: first one intoned, then the other two in flawless unison joined in, all in fluid union with a complex movement of their bodies that conveyed them down the block. Incredible! Rock concerts, stereo sets, and CD sales are all booming. Students seem to have headsets permanently attached to their temples as they crank out term papers. Even more incredible! Commuters play George Winston in the car on the way home from a day of stressful work to get their head or emotions back together.[1]

Your own teen-agers who yawn at sermons on sex pack JFK Stadium when Michael Jackson comes to town, howl in ecstasy, weep tears of joy, twist their bodies like pretzels. Barbara Cook holds Kennedy Center's Terrace Theater entranced as she sings with soft anguish an AIDS victim's

> Love is all we have for now,
> what we don't have is time.[2]

With our befouled environment threatening to throttle us, we old-timers are powerfully moved by Joni Mitchell musing in the 60s, "Take paradise and turn it into a parking lot." And do you know how many musical dollars were plunked down in the U.S. in 1987? 5.6 billion.[3]

Yes, music is power. The word I speak to you may well drift away with the hour; the jazz Ella Fitzgerald booms out at you clings to your bones.

II

Second, music is worship. Pervading the Catholic community is something close to heresy. I mean the feeling, the conviction, that music at Mass is at best part of the decoration—like an Advent wreath, the purple cloth around the Lenten cross, Easter lilies on the altar, the stained-glass windows. If the parish council had to choose between the collection and the music, it would surely get rid of the music. Music at Mass is all right for African Americans. They are born singing; for them, to sway is to pray. But spare us white folk "Kum Ba Yah," "We Shall Overcome," "Michael, Row the Boat Ashore."

I have news for you: Music at Mass is not something "up for grabs"; music is liturgy. If you won't believe a visiting Jesuit, credit the Second Vatican Council: "Sacred melody united to words . . . forms a necessary or integral part of the solemn liturgy."[4] This is not a sudden discovery. It goes back to the first century, when readings from Scripture were followed by singing of psalms.[5] It goes back to St. Paul urging the Christians of Colossae and Ephesus to "sing psalms and hymns and spiritual songs" (Col 3:16; Eph 5:19).[6] It goes back to Gregorian chant, so austere to our ears but strikingly emotional and expressive to the monks of the Middle Ages and to the faithful chanting the Lamentations on Good Friday.

Why music in the liturgy? Because music keeps our worship from being merely a matter of the mind, naked words that raise only the intellect to God. If you really sing, the whole man, the whole woman, comes to life. Not only your voice box but your diaphragm, your stomach muscles, yes your emotions. I mean the anxious Advent pleading in "O come, O come, Emmanuel"; Christmas joy in "Angels we have heard on high"; penitential sadness in the "Kyrie"; the agonizing "Were you there when they crucified my Lord?"; Easter ecstasy in "Christ the Lord is risen today"; elation in each "Gloria"; hope in the St. Louis Jesuits' "Be not afraid"; profound Eucharistic piety in that solemn "Ave verum"; every heart-stirring "Ave Maria"; Christian lightheartedness in "I danced in the morning"; thunderous gratitude in "Now thank we all our God." And you may possibly recall 17th-century poet John Milton equating the pleasure from music in church with religious experience:

> There let the pealing Organ blow,
> To the full voic'd Quire below,
> In Service high, and Anthems cleer,
> As may with sweetnes, through mine ear
> Dissolve me into extasies,
> And bring all Heav'n before mine eyes.[7]

But what should music be like to be worship? Remember, liturgical music, in and of itself, is like chewing gum: It is neither good nor bad. All depends on what is done, why it is done, how it is done. To make music the prayer of the faithful, our prayer, we must avoid two extremes: making our music *only* the Palestrina concert in which "we the people" cannot share, to which we can only listen; and the sickly,

sentimental garbage that may make us feel good but doesn't say anything to God. Oh yes, as you will shortly sense, "to experience beautiful music in performance is to experience the wonder of creation."[8]
But for the most part our worship in song is liturgical worship when it
is not passive listening but the song of the assembly, the participation
of the community in song to God.

III

This ushers in my third point: Music is community. You see, liturgy, Eucharist, the Mass is not a private party, a me-and-Jesus duet.
Good liturgy is done by community, in community, for community. It
is not only in social action but in the supreme act of our worship that
we can take to heart the classic reminder of St. Paul about the Church
of Christ: "There are many parts, yet one body. The eye cannot say to
the hand, 'I have no need of you,' nor again the head to the feet, 'I
have no need of you.' On the contrary, the parts of the body which
seem to be weaker are indispensable" (1 Cor 12:20–22).

Precisely here music plays a superlative part; for liturgical music
is done by community, in community, for community. Basic to this
point is a famous "oldie" that Coca-Cola popularized: "I'd like to
teach the world to sing in perfect harmony." To sing in harmony, we
need one another. No one can sing all four notes at the same time.
Also, to harmonize you have to listen—listen to what the others are
singing. Watch a barbershop quartet in action and you will see what I
mean. Each of the four needs every other.

But even apart from harmony, singing in unison makes for community. For each of you contributes. Within the same notes there are
overtones and undertones. You have to follow a beat, the pulse or
throb of measured music—up and down, loud and soft. Note how
different it is when you simply say the Our Father and when you sing
it. Speak the Lord's Prayer and it really doesn't matter how you say it.
Sing the Lord's Prayer and you're part of a distinctive whole:
hundreds of voices, now light as silk, now heavy as metal, now praising
God's kingdom, now bending to God's will, now pleading for bread
and forgiveness and escape from the Evil One.

Very importantly, to sing with others is not like singing in the
shower; you must be humble. You have to overcome self-conscious-
ness, become as simple as a child, accept your musical limitations, let
others supply for your lacks. You are not in competition with your
neighbor; you are worshiping together. The ultrasensitive around you

may be annoyed, the Pavarottis bristle; but the Christians among the Catholics will smile and just . . . sing. And you? You take a deep breath and with the Psalmist "sing to the Lord a new song, His praise in the assembly of the faithful" (Ps 149:1).

Good friends, after this impressive new organ is blessed, a priest will stretch out his hands over you and bless you in words you should etch deep within you:

> The Lord is worthy of all praise.
> May He give you the gift
> of striving to sing a new song to Him
> with your voices, your hearts, and your lives,
> so that one day you may sing that song for ever in heaven.

That prayer has more depth to it than meets the eye. For it tells us that the song which emerges from our mouth is not an end in itself. The vocal song should be a symbol—symbol of the song in my heart, the song that is my life. And so it compels an examination of conscience: Does my life sing to others the songs that burst from my lips? Does the way I live actually "sing the mighty power of God,/ the wisdom that ordained the sun to rule the day,/ the goodness that filled the earth with food"?[9] Does my Christian joy hymn to those around me that "Christ the Lord is risen today"? Does my sorrow sing the "faith of our fathers, living still/ in spite of dungeon, fire, and sword"? Does my catholicity, my love for all God's children, sing that "In Christ there is no East or West,/ in him no South or North,/ but one great fellowship of love/ throughout the whole wide earth"? Does my living hope sing that "the Lord is my shepherd,/ there is nothing I shall want"? Does my penance proclaim "There is a balm in Gilead to make the wounded whole, to heal the sin-sick soul"? Does my church life sing that "the Church's one foundation is Jesus Christ her Lord"? Does the Eucharistic Christ on my lips trumpet "Godhead here in hiding whom I do adore. . . . See, Lord, at thy service low lies here a heart lost, all lost in wonder at the God thou art"?

Today is indeed a day the Lord has made—has made memorable with music. So then, open not only your ears but your hearts to organ masters Bach and Pachelbel,[10] then rise to sing as one to the God to whom the sound of music is the voice of love:

> Holy Father, Holy Son,
>   Holy Spirit, Three we name thee,
> While in essence only One,

Undivided God we claim thee,
And adoring bend the knee,
While we own the mystery.

Yes, let your song today be your communal adoration, your whole selves bent low before mystery, bent low before Love.

St. Rita's Church
Alexandria, Va.
April 29, 1990

33
A TALE OF THREE MOTHERS
Homily for Mother's Day

- Acts 6:1–7
- 1 Peter 2:4–9
- John 14:1–12

Today I shall *not* preach on the liturgical readings. They are indeed worth a preacher's prime preparation: the intriguing selection of "the Seven" to free up the apostles for "prayer and the ministry of the word" (Acts 6:4);[1] you as "a chosen race, a royal priesthood, a holy nation, God's own people" (1 Pet 2:9); Jesus as "the way, the truth, and the life" (Jn 14:6). But this blessed day[2] compels me to focus on a theme as ancient as Eve. I mean . . . mother. I shall organize my approach around three absorbing persons: (1) God, (2) Mary, (3) today's mother.

I

First, God. I begin with a provocative sentence that stems from 1978: God is not only Father but "even more so Mother, who . . . wants only to be good to us," wants only to love us, especially if we are bad.[3] Even more than Father, God is Mother. The man who uttered those astonishing words was not your humble homilist; it was Pope John Paul I, who reigned for 34 short days before he was taken by sudden death—and not, I assure you, by an angry Father!

The point is, God does not have a sex; God is neither male nor female. An elderly gentleman with a long white beard should not exhaust the capacity of our imagination to image God. To spark your imagining, go back to the Scriptures. How do these inspired writings describe God's unbreakable love for the people of God's predilection, the people who have covenanted with God? As you might expect from a patriarchal culture, largely in metaphors taken from male experi-

196

ence: God is father, warrior, jealous husband, king. But not only thus; impressively in images of maternal birthing and caring. "[A]s mother, with all that this entails: pregnant with a child in her womb, crying out in labor, giving birth, nursing, carrying and cradling her child, comforting and having womb love (tender mercy and compassion) for her child."[4] Take simply that anguished cry of Israel exiled in Egypt and the Lord's maternal response:

> But Zion said, "The Lord has forsaken me,
>   my Lord has forgotten me."
> "Can a woman forget her sucking child,
>   that she should have no compassion
>   on the son of her womb?
> Even these may forget,
>   yet I will not forget you.
> Behold, I have graven you on the palms of my hands. . . ."
>   (Isa 49:14–15)

Further, you will find God pictured in roles taken from other female experience: "midwife, nurse, seamstress, mistress of a household, and owner of money who searches for a lost coin that is very important to her, rejoicing with neighbors when it is found"—this last a homey yet powerful image Jesus uses for God the Redeemer.[5]

All this, and much more, tells us something highly important for the way we think of God, image God, deal with God, pray to God. The divine Mystery that envelops our lives—we cannot possibly grasp it with a single image, or even with all the images rolled together. And for all the reverence we rightly give to the Our Father, we shall do ourselves a dreadful disservice if that remarkable prayer puts only a male face on our God, keeps us from sensing John Paul I's "even more so Mother, who wants only to be good to us." It could also damage a genuinely Christian vision of the human person, perpetuate the long-standing macho conviction that only the male is created directly and fully in God's image, that woman images God through man, that therefore only males are made to lead, females to obey.

II

Let's move from a mothering God to one woman mothering. Mary of Nazareth lights up the Gospels at a number of crucial moments. Still, two moments have special significance for Mary as mother: Bethlehem and Calvary, Christmas and Good Friday, a stable and a cross, birth and death.

The mother Luke pictures in Bethlehem delights us, but no longer surprises us. A teen-age girl becomes mother of a unique child, gives her blood and bones, her breath and beauty, to God's only Son. The focus is on the single child, the one only child, that blossoms from her body. We have celebrated that miracle of miracles for centuries—celebrated it in tireless carols about a "silent night, holy night," a "joy to the world" without compare; in masterpieces on canvas and in the art of the catacombs; in solemn liturgies that transform cathedrals and grass huts from Alaska to Zaire. Before this mystery all Christians, whatever their differences, bow down in adoration. The two, Madonna and Child, will always be together as long as there is a December in our world—a mother holding her child, a mother holding God-in-flesh out to the world, out to us.

But Mary's motherhood did not cease with Jesus. For Mary is *our* mother too. This is not pious pap, pretty poetry for the elderly as they murmur their beads; it is strong meat for strong Christians. It goes back to the last hours of Jesus' life, to a scene on Calvary that moves our emotions but rarely our minds. Recall those spare syllables in John's Gospel: "When Jesus saw his mother there with the disciple whom he loved, he said to his mother: 'Woman, here is your son.' In turn he said to the disciple: 'Here is your mother' " (Jn 19:26–27).

> . . . if Mary was refused a role during the ministry of Jesus as it began at Cana, she finally received her role in the hour of Jesus' passion, death, and resurrection. In this climactic hour men [and women] are to be recreated as God's children when the Spirit is breathed forth. . . . In becoming the mother of the Beloved Disciple (the Christian), Mary is symbolically evocative of Lady Zion who, after the birth pangs, brings forth a new people in joy. . . . Her natural son is the firstborn of the dead . . . , the one who has the keys of death; and those who believe in him are born anew in his image. As his brothers [and sisters], they have her as mother.[6]

Little wonder that Jesuit poet Gerard Manley Hopkins could compare the Blessed Virgin to the air we breathe:

> . . . men are meant to share
> Her life as life does air.
>   If I have understood,
> She holds high motherhood
> Towards all our ghostly good

And plays in grace her part
About man's beating heart,
Laying, like air's fine flood,
The deathdance in his blood;
Yet no part but what will
Be Christ our Saviour still.[7]

III

Third, today's mother. She's in trouble. In this culture of two careers, of husband and wife as breadwinners both, woman as "only" wife and mother is all too often seen as a relic from patriarchal days. Where is her claim to fame? What has she achieved on her own? What is she in her own right? How dare she perpetuate stereotypes—man as the doer out there in the world, woman as the nurturer back here in the home? What sort of role model can she possibly be?

Please understand me. I am not downgrading women on Wall Street, sister CEOs, congresswomen, female heads of state. I am not insinuating that motherhood and career are incompatible. I do deplore the refusal of *some* female yuppies to be challenged, the assumption that someone who is just or primarily wife and mother has nothing constructive to offer to the upward bound.

It is not within my time and competence to argue motherhood versus career. In that complex realm more depends on concrete circumstances than on abstract principles. I shall not romanticize motherhood; nor shall I wave the imaginative banner that read "Eve was framed." Rather, on a day dedicated to mothers, I shall suggest down-to-earth responses to this day, four ways of celebrating a unique vocation. Since a homily is liturgy, I shall arrange my reactions under what we older Catholics called four types of prayer: praise and thanksgiving, petition and contrition.

First, praise. Glory be to God for life-givers! Glory to God who has shared with women so divine a power. Glory to God for shaping in God's image humans who reveal the female face of God, give life at peril to their own.

Second, thanksgiving. Gratitude to God for a vocation second to none—not second to priest or president, to CEO or CPA. I am grateful not only because without my mother my very existence would be "doubtful." Grateful as well for all that goes into mothering: cleaning my bottom and thrashing it, tolerating adolescent antics and temper tantrums, pampering the moods of puberty, supporting my growing to freedom and independence, suffering somehow my focus on myself, surrendering present pleasure for my future, doing without so that I might have, might grow, like Jesus, "in age, in wisdom, in favor with God and humans" (Lk 2:52).

Third, petition. Let us storm heaven for mothers in our fair land who must mother below the poverty line, who have to watch one out of five children grow up with minds stunted and bodies shriveled. Cry to heaven for mothers too young to mother. For mothers who pass on their drug dependency to their children. For mothers in Ethiopia watching their babies starve, mothers in Belfast watching their children play with hate in their hearts. For mothers who see their young pimped or angel-dusted or sucked into crime. For mothers who have to play father as well.

Fourth, contrition. Let us ask forgiveness for our blindness. Let us sorrow for our failure to support poverty-stricken mothers, for a minimum wage that forces mothers onto relief, for crowding homeless mothers into rat-infested hovels. Forgiveness for the feminization of poverty, unequal wages, low retirement benefits, epidemic violence against women, machismo, clergy attitudes that would bring tears to the eyes of Jesus. Sorrow for a way of life where the food D.C. throws away in a day could feed all our hungry that day. Sorrow for an infant-mortality rate that shames our vaunted medical care.

Good friends in Christ: I suspect you may find my approach a strange way to celebrate Mother's Day. But I would be less than honest with an intelligent congregation (1) if I kept you in ignorance of God's female face, of our Father as Mother; (2) if I did not suggest what the best of theology is discovering about the mothering of Mary, about Mary as our mother too; (3) if I refused to reveal not only my deep delight in the mothers I have known through 75 years, but my dreadful distress at the unchristian misery of a million mothers across the earth.

This Mass today I offer in deep devotion to mothers—beginning with a single mother 75 years ago and reaching down the decades to so many of you before me now. For, like the mother of Jesus, you ceaselessly reveal to me the female face of God. For this I expect to be, in a literal sense, eternally grateful. Eternally.

Dahlgren Chapel
Georgetown University
and
Holy Trinity Church
Washington, D.C.
May 13, 1990

NOTES

Homily 1

1. St. Augustine, *Confessions* 8, 7; tr. F. J. Sheed, *The Confessions of St. Augustine* (New York: Sheed & Ward, 1943) 170.
2. *Confessions* 8, 12; tr. Sheed 179. The Pauline text was Rom 13:13–14.
3. Reference to the professional basketball team in Charlotte, N.C., where this homily was delivered.
4. Reference to a well-known department store in Charlotte.
5. Reference to the highest peak in the eastern United States.

Homily 2

1. This homily accompanied my presentation of the Tenth Annual Cardinal Newman Lecture, sponsored by The Oratory: A Center for Spirituality, Rock Hill, S.C., March 3, 1990. It was the Saturday after Ash Wednesday, hence the homily's connection with Lent.
2. *Time* 134, no. 23 (Dec. 4, 1989) 11.

Homily 3

1. On this difficult passage, see the succinct remarks of Myles M. Bourke, "The Epistle to the Hebrews," *The New Jerome Biblical Commentary,* ed. Raymond E. Brown, S.S., Joseph A. Fitzmyer, S.J., and Roland E. Murphy, O.Carm. (Englewood Cliffs, N.J.: Prentice Hall, 1990) 60:62, pp. 939–40.

2. From the Catholic News Service as reported in the *St. Louis Review,* June 23, 1989, 9.
3. Karl Rahner, "Following the Crucified," *Theological Investigations* 18: *God and Revelation* (New York: Crossroad, 1983) 155–70, at 165–66.
4. See ibid. 169–70.
5. Regrettably, I no longer have the reference for this strong quotation.

Homily 4

1. By "extract" I mean that I am borrowing, often verbatim, from Lenten homilies previously preached to the Dahlgren and Holy Trinity communities and published in one or other of my collections. My justification is that I am here putting together in a single homily what I might call the cream of my reflections on the repentance/joy, dying/rising aspect of Lent.
2. A reference to Johannes Quasten, dear friend and expert in patristics, early liturgy, and Christian archeology, who died March 10, 1987.
3. Constitution on the Sacred Liturgy, no. 7.
4. A reference to a well-known wheeler-dealer in the TV serial "Dallas."
5. Eugene O'Neill, *Lazarus Laughed,* Act 1, Scene 1; in *The Plays of Eugene O'Neill* (New York: Random House, 1955) 280.

Homily 5

1. For scholarly information on the parable, and for much of its religious interpretation, I am deeply indebted to Joseph A. Fitzmyer, S.J., *The Gospel according to Luke (X–XXIV)* (Garden City, N.Y.: Doubleday, 1985) 1082–94.
2. A reference to a play on Broadway not many years ago.
3. *B. Qam.* 82b, quoted by Fitzmyer (n. 1 above) 1088.

Homily 6

1. G. A. Studdert-Kennedy, "Indifference," in Donald Kauffman, ed., *Treasury of Religious Verse* (4th ed.; New York: Pyramid, 1973)) 71. I have presumed to make a handful of slight changes in the text, primarily for rhythmic reasons.
2. Francis Thompson, "The Hound of Heaven," in Wilfred Meynell, ed., *Francis Thompson, Poems and Essays* (Westminster, Md.: Newman, 1949) 112.
3. I have borrowed this phrase from Karl Rahner, *Schriften zur Theologie* 15: *Wissenschaft und christlicher Glaube* (Zurich: Benziger, 1983) 20.

4. See H. Chirat, "Cross, Finding of the Holy," *New Catholic Encyclopedia* 4 (1967) 479–82.
5. In *The New Jerome Biblical Commentary*, ed. Raymond E. Brown, S.S., Joseph A. Fitzmyer, S.J., and Roland E. Murphy, O.Carm. (Englewood Cliffs, N.J.: Prentice Hall, 1990) 54:16, p. 880, Maurya P. Horgan prefers the translation, "I complete what is needed of the Christian sufferings in my flesh for his body," i.e. "This verse reflects the belief that those who proclaim the gospel would have to endure hardships and afflictions."
6. Homilists and others intrigued by Mt 25:31–46 should be aware of recent interpretations that reject the classical identification of the "least brethren" with "all the needy"; see John R. Donahue, S.J., "The 'Parable' of the Sheep and the Goats: A Challenge to Christian Ethics," *Theological Studies* 47 (1986) 3–31.
7. See ibid. 31.
8. For what follows I am indebted to the article by Tom Fox, "A Public Journey of Faith: The Gift of Penny Lernoux," *Sojourners*, December 1989, 14–17.
9. Garden City, N.Y.: Doubleday, 1980.
10. Fox, "A Public Journey of Faith" 15. The letter was written to Fox.

Homily 7

1. Here I am indebted to a revealing article by Christopher F. Mooney, S.J., "Cybernation, Responsibility, and Providential Design," *Theological Studies* 51 (1990) 286–309, at 289–90.
2. New York: Knopf, 1971, 172–73.
3. To understand how a book like Qoheleth (Ecclesiastes) could be included in the inspired Bible, see the commentary by Addison G. Wright, S.S., "Ecclesiastes (Qoheleth)," *The New Jerome Biblical Commentary*, ed. Raymond E. Brown, S.S., Joseph A. Fitzmyer, S.J., and Roland E. Murphy, O.Carm. (Englewood Cliffs, N.J.: Prentice Hall, 1990) 489–95.
4. Francis Thompson, "The Hound of Heaven," in *Francis Thompson, Poems and Essays*, ed. Wilfred Meynell (Westminster, Md.: Newman, 1949) 107.

Homily 8

1. From Gerard Manley Hopkins, "The Wreck of the Deutschland," in W. H. Gardner and N. H. MacKenzie, eds., *The Poems of Gerard Manley Hopkins* (4th ed.; London: Oxford University, 1970) 63, stanza 35.
2. Emil J. Freireich, "The Best Medical Care for the 'Hopeless' Patient," *Medical Opinion*, February 1972, 51–55.

Homily 9

1. I am using the edition *John Henry Newman: Parochial and Plain Sermons* (San Francisco: Ignatius, 1987) 196–205.
2. Ibid. 196.
3. Ibid. 197.
4. Ibid.
5. Ibid. 198.
6. New York: Hawthorn, 1973.
7. International Theological Commission, "Human Development & Christian Salvation," tr. Walter J. Burghardt, S.J., *Origins* 7, no. 20 (Nov. 3, 1977) 311.
8. A popular TV series.
9. See Decree on Ecumenism, no. 6.
10. For this shift from the rhetoric of sin to that of woundedness, I have been stimulated by the article of James E. Hug, S.J., "Social Sin, Cultural Healing," *Chicago Studies* 23 (1984) 333–51.
11. See Robert N. Bellah, "Religion & Power in America Today," *Commonweal* 109, no. 21 (Dec. 3, 1982) 650–55.
12. Dayton Hudson Corporation; cited in Leo Ryan, "The Wave of the Future," (London) *Tablet* 242 (Dec. 10, 1988) 1423.
13. Frederick Buechner, *The Hungering Dark* (New York: Seabury, 1969) 45–46.

Homily 10

1. The title is "Love Don't Need a Reason"; words and music by Peter Allen, Michael Callen, and Marsha Malamet.
2. See Richard Kugelman, C.P., "The First Letter to the Corinthians," in Raymond E. Brown, S.S., Joseph A. Fitzmyer, S.J., and Roland E. Murphy, O.Carm., eds., *The Jerome Biblical Commentary* (Englewood Cliffs, N.J.: Prentice-Hall, 1968) 2:254.
3. For problems associated with this "Christ faction," see Kugelman, ibid. 256.
4. See William Dameshek, "Blood," *World Book Encyclopedia* 2 (1975 ed.) 324–28, at 325.
5. See the delightfully informative book by Richard Selzer, *Mortal Lessons: Notes on the Art of Surgery* (New York: Simon and Schuster, 1976) 106 and 118.
6. A reference to a horrible December 1988 earthquake that killed over 50,000 and left more than half a million homeless.
7. A reference to a powerful film on racism in the 60s, described by critic Richard Corliss as "a big, bold bolt of rabble-rousin', rebel-razin' movie journalism" ("Fire This Time," *Time* 133, no. 2 [Jan. 9, 1989] 56–62, at 57).

8. The autobiographer is Cab Calloway; the quotation is excerpted from *Time* 133, no. 2 (Jan. 9, 1989) 69.

Homily 11

1. This verse sounds somewhat Pelagian—as if we could lift ourselves to God by our bootstraps. A more nuanced Christian thesis holds that all salutary acts, i.e. free acts that positively conduce to salvation, including the decision to love, obey, and cleave to God, are possible only with God's grace.
2. Jerome Murphy-O'Connor, O.P., "The First Letter to the Corinthians," *The New Jerome Biblical Commentary*, ed. Raymond E. Brown, S.S., Joseph A. Fitzmyer, S.J., and Roland E. Murphy, O.Carm. (Englewood Cliffs, N.J.: Prentice Hall, 1990) 49:19, p. 802.
3. Useful information is provided by Warren S. Kissinger, *The Sermon on the Mount: A History of Interpretation and Bibliography* (Metuchen, N.J.: Scarecrow, 1975).
4. Here my presentation has been stimulated by the commentary of Patrick J. Ryan, "Radicalization," *America* 162, no. 4 (Feb. 3, 1990) 111.
5. Benedict T. Viviano, O.P., "The Gospel according to Matthew," *The New Jerome Biblical Commentary* 42:29, p. 642. See also Donald Senior, *Invitation to Matthew* (Garden City, N.Y.: Doubleday Image Books, 1977) 68–69.
6. It might help the homilist, and others, to read the provocative book by John Giles Milhaven, *Good Anger* (Kansas City, Mo.: Sheed & Ward, 1989).
7. Senior, *Invitation to Matthew* 69.
8. Ibid. 70.
9. A reference to a popular TV series.

Homily 12

1. This introductory paragraph was used only for the Holy Trinity parish homily, not in the homily preached the same day in Dahlgren Chapel on the campus of Georgetown University.
2. The reference is to a first-rate British mystery writer who crafts intriguing plots, builds real-life characters, and provides believable solutions—all in high literary style.
3. Here I am borrowing from my sermon "The Trinity: Mystery of Love," in my first book of sermons, *All Lost in Wonder: Sermons on Theology and Life* (Westminster, Md.: Newman, 1960) 3–8, specifically 5–7, material reproduced substantially in my 1986 baccalaureate homily at George-

town University, published in my collection *Lovely in Eyes Not His: Homilies for an Imaging of Christ* (New York/Mahwah: Paulist, 1988) 143–48, at 144.

4. So Raymond E. Brown, S.S., *The Gospel according to John (xiii-xxi)* (Garden City, N.Y.: Doubleday, 1970) 752.

5. Here I am indebted to a remarkable essay by Karl Rahner, "Following the Crucified," *Theological Investigations* 18: *God and Revelation* (New York: Crossroad, 1983) 157–70.

6. From "Bob Geldof: The *Rolling Stone* Interview," by David Breskin, *Rolling Stone* no. 462 (Dec. 5, 1985) 26–34, 60, 63–67, at 28.

Homily 13

1. Here I have been helped by two "ancient" articles: James Denney, "The Word 'Hate' in Luke xiv. 26," *Expository Times* 21 (1909–10) 41–42; T. Campbell Finlayson, "Christ Demanding Hatred: Luke xiv. 26," *Expositor* 9 (1879) 420–30.

2. To avoid entangling the homily in less than useful nuances, I have not spoken of situations where the word "hate" is not quite an exaggeration. See, e.g., Joseph A. Fitzmyer, S.J., *The Gospel according to Luke (X-XXIV)* (Garden City, N.Y.: Doubleday, 1985) 1063: "One is called to such 'hatred' to the extent that such persons would be opposed to Jesus; the choice that the disciple has to make is between natural affection for kin and allegiance to Jesus. 'In most cases these two are not incompatible; and to hate one's parents *as such* would be monstrous. . . . But Christ's followers must be ready, if necessary, to act towards what is dearest to them as if it were an object of hatred. . . . Jesus, as often, states a principle in a startling way, and leaves His hearers to find out the qualifications' (A. Plummer, *The Gospel,* 364)."

3. For more detailed treatment, see the homily "Easier for a Camel," in my *Still Proclaiming Your Wonders: Homilies for the Eighties* (New York/Ramsey: Paulist, 1984) 134–38, with references to pertinent literature (240–41).

4. See, e.g., Joseph A. Fitzmyer, S.J., *Luke the Theologian: Aspects of His Teaching* (New York/Mahwah: Paulist, 1989) 137: "No other New Testament writer, save perhaps the author of the Epistle of James, speaks out so forthrightly as does Luke about the use of material possessions by Christian disciples. More than the other evangelists Luke either preserves sayings of Jesus about this topic *or puts on his lips* statements that concern wealth, money, and material goods in general" (italics mine).

Homily 14

1. The second Future of the American Church Conference, with its theme "Empowerment in the Church," was held at the Omni Shoreham Hotel in Washington, D.C., Sept. 29–30 and Oct. 1, 1989.
2. For factual information I have profited, as frequently, from Joseph A. Fitzmyer, S.J., *The Gospel according to Luke (X–XXIV)* (Garden City, N.Y.: Doubleday, 1985) 1124–36.
3. For this insight I am indebted to John R. Donahue, S.J., *The Gospel in Parable: Metaphor, Narrative, and Theology in the Synoptic Gospels* (Philadelphia: Fortress, 1988) 171, 176.
4. Department of Housing and Urban Development.
5. See the *Washington Post,* Sept. 28, 1989, 1.
6. Cf. Donahue, *The Gospel in Parable* 171.
7. Worth reading in this connection is a short commentary on this Sunday's readings by Patrick J. Ryan, "Against Complacency," *America* 161, no. 7 (Sept. 23, 1989) 175.
8. This homily was actually delivered on Saturday evening, September 30, the feast of St. Jerome.
9. Jerome, *Letter 22* 17.

Homily 15

1. For a brief summary, see R. Mercurio, "Sadducees," *New Catholic Encyclopedia* 12 (1967) 843–44. More liberal were the Pharisees, who believed firmly in the resurrection of the body; see R. Mercurio, "Pharisees," ibid. 11 (1967) 252–53.
2. See the brief, informative, stimulating treatment of this Gospel by Patrick J. Ryan, "Death Threats," *America* 161, no. 13 (Nov. 4, 1989) 307.
3. The reference is to a popular TV serial.

Homily 16

1. A reference to Willard Scott, who has created a fresh image for those who scan the skies for TV.

Homily 17

1. A reference to the large number of Frans's family and relatives who flew to the States for the wedding.

2. See, e.g., Bruce Vawter, *On Genesis: A New Reading* (Garden City, N.Y.: Doubleday, 1977) 53–60.

3. What follows is a replay, quite different in details, of a theme I developed four years ago in the wedding homily "Love Never Ends?" in my *Grace on Crutches: Homilies for Fellow Travelers* (New York/Mahwah: Paulist, 1986) 175–78, at 176–77.

4. It should be clear from my brief treatment that I am not exhausting the meaning of the Beatitudes; I am only highlighting some aspects which seem particularly pertinent for a man and a woman entering on Christian marriage. For detailed information see Jacques Dupont, *Les Béatitudes* 1: *Le problème littéraire—Les deux versions du Sermon sur la montagne et des Béatitudes* (new ed.; Louvain: Nauwelaerts, 1958) 209–23; more succinctly, J. A. Grassi, "Beatitudes (in the Bible)," *New Catholic Encyclopedia* 2 (1967) 193–95, and John L. McKenzie, "The Gospel according to Matthew," *The Jerome Biblical Commentary* (Englewood Cliffs, N.J.: Prentice-Hall, 1968) 43:30–32.

5. Tertullian, *To His Wife* 2:8 (tr. William P. Le Saint, S.J., in Ancient Christian Writers 13 [New York, N.Y./Ramsey, N.J.: Newman, 1951] 35).

Homily 18

1. From the introduction to Tobit in *The Oxford Annotated Bible with the Apocrypha: Revised Standard Version,* ed. Herbert G. May and Bruce M. Metzger (New York: Oxford University, 1965) [63].

2. More accurately Khalil, as more faithful to the original.

3. So Suheil B. Bushrui in *An Introduction to Kahlil Gibran,* ed. and selected by Bushrui (Beirut: Dar El-Mashreq, 1970) xiv.

4. Mikhail Naimy, ibid. 153.

5. Kahlil Gibran, *The Prophet* (New York: Knopf, 1961) 15–16.

6. Ibid. 15.

7. Walter Kerr, *The Decline of Pleasure* (New York: Simon & Schuster, 1962) 245.

8. *The Prophet* 15–16.

Homily 19

1. Frederick Buechner, *Telling the Truth: The Gospel as Tragedy, Comedy, and Fairy Tale* (San Francisco: Harper & Row, 1977) 49–50.

2. *Love in the Ruins* is the title of a novel by Walker Percy.

Homily 20

1. A popular TV serial.
2. See R. E. Murphy, "Canticle of Canticles," *New Catholic Encyclopedia* 3 (1967) 68–69, at 69.
3. Jean Mouroux, *The Meaning of Man* (New York: Sheed & Ward, 1948) 108.

Homily 21

1. See Joseph A. Fitzmyer, S.J., *Paul and His Theology: A Brief Sketch* (2nd ed.; Englewood Cliffs, N.J.: Prentice Hall, 1989) 89–90.
2. Immediately from the musical *Godspell*, but more remotely from a prayer of a 13th-century English bishop, St. Richard of Chichester.
3. At this point Mary was pursuing a doctorate in theology at the University of Chicago; Louis was into economics, but with a yearning for history studies and possibly a teaching career.
4. Gerard Manley Hopkins, "God's Grandeur," in W. H. Gardner and N. H. MacKenzie, eds., *The Poems of Gerard Manley Hopkins* (4th ed.; London: Oxford University, 1970) 66.

Homily 22

1. A well-known sports center in Atlanta.
2. I am using "Isaiah" as a convenient term for the author of this section (chaps. 40–55). For a useful discussion of the three "Isaiahs," see John L. McKenzie, *Second Isaiah* (Anchor Bible 20; Garden City, N.Y.: Doubleday, 1968) xv–xxiii.

Homily 23

1. Here I have profited from W. A. Wallace, "Friendship," *New Catholic Encyclopedia* 6 (1967) 203–5.
2. *Confessions* 4, 6, 11.
3. See *Summa theologiae* 1–2, 26, 3–4.
4. I am not implying that God is absent from friendships outside of marriage; I am simply insisting on a presence of God within Christian marriage that is "singular," inasmuch as it is focused on the needs of a relationship that St. Paul called "a great mystery" symbolizing the intimate union of Christ and his Church (Eph 5:32).

5. Besides my own experience, I am indebted here to the article "Calvary Hospital—A Resounding Affirmation of Life at a Hospital for the Dying," *Catholic Health World,* Nov. 15, 1987, 6–7.
6. Ibid. 7.
7. A reference to a highly popular TV show.

Homily 24

1. Title of a popular TV series.
2. *The Love Letters of Phyllis McGinley* (New York: Viking, 1954) 12–16, at 14.
3. Kahlil Gibran, *The Prophet* (New York: Knopf, 1961) 15.

Homily 25

1. From a brief reflection by Phil Burroughs, S.J., "Vulnerability and Not Competency. . . ," *Studies in the Spirituality of Jesuits* 21/2 (March 1989) 45–46, at 46.

Homily 26

1. The context of this marriage ceremony: ten years of a remarkably happy marriage (Catholic/Protestant) celebrated outside the Catholic Church, annulment of husband's first marriage, his instructions for full communion with the Catholic Church, scheduled for the Easter vigil a month after this ceremony.
2. See Evelyn Whitehead and James D. Whitehead, "Christian Marriage," *U.S. Catholic* 47, no. 6 (June 1982) 9.
3. For the record, this homily was not actually delivered. A severe laryngitis imposed total silence on the homilist.

Homily 27

1. The conference in question, organized by Georgetown University's Committee on Catholic Studies, took place at Georgetown March 8–10, 1990.
2. For details on the four enslavements in Paul, see Joseph A. Fitzmyer, S.J., *Paul and His Theology: A Brief Sketch* (2nd ed.; Englewood Cliffs, N.J.: Prentice Hall, 1989) 67–68, 71–74, 74–82, 82, 85–86, 139–40.
3. See William F. Arndt and F. Wilbur Gingrich, *A Greek-English Lexicon of*

the New Testament and Other Early Christian Literature (Chicago/Cambridge: University of Chicago/Cambridge University, 1957) 277–78.

4. Second Vatican Council, Decree on Ecumenism, no. 6.
5. This section is deeply indebted to John Courtney Murray's penetrating article "Freedom, Authority, Community," *America* 115 (1966) 734–41. See my article "The Authority Crisis in Catholicism: Analysis and Prognosis," in *Hope: Psychiatry's Commitment*, Papers Presented to Leo H. Bartemeier, M.D., on the Occasion of His 75th Birthday, ed. A. W. R. Sipe (New York: Brunner/Mazel, 1970) 203–14, where I sum up Murray's essay.
6. Murray, "Freedom" 741.

Homily 28

1. Patrick W. Collins, "The Cathedral of Peoria" (unpublished dissertation for the degree of master of arts, St. Paul Seminary, 1962) 56–57.
2. All information on St. Mary's past has been derived from the Collins dissertation (n. 1 above).
3. Fr. Benedict Joseph Spalding began work on the new cathedral church but did not live to see it completed; he died Nov. 28, 1887, only 38 years old.
4. Collins, "The Cathedral of Peoria" 128; *Western Catholic,* consecration issue, no date.
5. For a creative, eye-opening presentation of this movement to a world church, see Karl Rahner, S.J., "Towards a Fundamental Theological Interpretation of Vatican II," *Theological Studies* 40 (1979) 716–27.
6. The reference is to Most Reverend Edward W. O'Rourke, who was consecrated July 15, 1971.
7. Peoria, Tazewell, and Woodford.
8. Text in Collins (n. 1 above) 43–45; *Peoria Journal,* June 29, 1885.

Homily 29

1. This homily celebrated the 150th anniversary of the third church (begun in 1838, consecrated and dedicated Feb. 11, 1839) and was delivered on the First Sunday of Lent (1989), when the catechumens' names were inscribed in the Book of the Elect.
2. I have developed this point at greater length in my homily "Lent Is for Listening," in my collection *To Christ I Look: Homilies at Twilight* (New York/Mahwah, N.J.: Paulist, 1989) 35-40, at 36–37.

Homily 30

1. Gerard Manley Hopkins, "S. Thomae Aquinatis Rhythmus ad SS. Sacramentum," in W. H. Gardner and N. H. MacKenzie, eds., *The Poems of Gerard Manley Hopkins* (4th ed.; London: Oxford University, 1970) 211.
2. This succinct sentence should not be interpreted as implying that the Church is not the (Mystical) Body of Christ. It is indeed, but the demands of this homily call for a simpler way of speaking.
3. See, e.g., Robert N. Bellah, "Religion & Power in America Today," *Commonweal* 109, no. 21 (Dec. 3, 1962) 650–55.
4. See *Time* 128, no. 10 (Sept. 8, 1986) 57; the institution is Harvard.
5. William Raspberry, " 'A Rising Tide of Materialism,' " *Washington Post,* Feb. 1, 1988, A15, reporting a survey sponsored by the American Council on Education and UCLA.
6. Joseph Nocera, "The Ga-Ga Years: Money Love, Market Lust, and the Seducing of America," *Esquire,* February 1988, 79–90, at 80.
7. The expression is taken from the title of Bonnie Angelo's interview with Pulitzer Prize winner Toni Morrison, *Time* 133, no. 21 (May 22, 1989) 120–22, at 120.
8. Frederick Buechner, *The Magnificent Defeat* (New York: Seabury, 1966) 23. I have used this material in a baccalaureate homily at Boston College, "Poet, Lunatic, Lover," published in my collection *Grace on Crutches: Homilies for Fellow Travelers* (New York/Mahwah: Paulist, 1986) 179–84, at 184.
9. A reference to the location (University Heights) of John Carroll University.

Homily 31

1. "St. Luke: Sanctity and Medicine," in my *Saints and Sanctity* (Englewood Cliffs, N.J.: Prentice-Hall, 1965) 129–39.
2. Richard Selzer, *Mortal Lessons: Notes on the Art of Surgery* (New York: Simon and Schuster, 1976) 46, 48.
3. For details see "Calvary Hospital—A Resounding Affirmation of Life at a Hospital for the Dying," *Catholic Health World,* Nov. 15, 1987, 6–7.

Homily 32

1. Lawrence J. Madden, S.J., "Is the Folk Mass America's Only Contribution to Liturgy?" *Pastoral Music* 13, no. 4 (April-May 1990) 53–55, at 54.

2. The title is "Love Don't Need a Reason"; words and music by Peter Allen, Michael Callen, and Marsha Malamet. See the opening paragraph of Homily 10, "What We Don't Have Is Time," in the present volume.

3. See *Time* 132, no. 4 (July 25, 1988) 69.

4. Second Vatican Council, Constitution on the Sacred Liturgy, no. 112 (tr. *The Documents of Vatican II*, ed. Walter M. Abbott, S.J. [New York: Herder and Herder/Association, 1966] 171).

5. For useful background in short space, see the articles by R. G. Weakland, E. Thurston, G. Reese, A. Milner, F. J. Moleck, R. M. Longyear, and F. J. Burkley under the general heading "Music, Sacred, History of," *New Catholic Encyclopedia* 10 (1967) 105–29.

6. See Weakland, ibid. 105: "It is difficult to determine whether in Eph 5.19 St. Paul is referring to three different types of musical pieces in the Christian community or is using three terms to describe one and the same phenomenon. . . . In Col 3.16 he uses, however, the same division."

7. John Milton, *Il Penseroso.*

8. Robert J. Batastini, "Let's Be Practical" [Comments on the Nov. 5, 1987 letter of the Congregation for Divine Worship, "Concerts in Churches"], *Pastoral Music* 12, no. 4 (April-May 1988) 37–39, at 38. My phrase "as you will shortly sense" referred to a concert which the church's organist, Paul Skevington, D.M.A., gave after my homily to celebrate the blessing of the Steiner-Reck 29-rank tracker anniversary pipe organ in St. Rita's Church.

9. The quoted words here and in the rest of this paragraph are from well-known hymns.

10. The reference here is to the concert (n. 8 above), which included selections from Bach and Pachelbel; towards the end of the concert the congregation joined the choir in the last two stanzas of "Holy God, we praise thy name."

Homily 33

1. For a useful swift account of this episode, see Richard J. Dillon, "The Acts of the Apostles," *The New Jerome Biblical Commentary,* ed. Raymond E. Brown, S.S., Joseph A. Fitzmyer, S.J., and Roland E. Murphy, O.Carm. (Englewood Cliffs, N.J.: Prentice Hall, 1990) 44:43, pp. 739–40.

2. It was the annual celebration of Mother's Day.

3. *Osservatore romano,* Sept. 21, 1978, 2.

4. Elizabeth A. Johnson, C.S.J., "The Incomprehensibility of God and the Image of God Male and Female," *Theological Studies* 45 (1984) 441–65, at 447.

5. Ibid.
6. Raymond E. Brown, S.S., *The Gospel according to John (xiii–xxi)* (Garden City, N.Y.: Doubleday, 1970) 925–26.
7. Gerard Manley Hopkins, "The Blessed Virgin Compared to the Air We Breathe," in *The Poems of Gerard Manley Hopkins,* ed. W. H. Gardner and N. H. MacKenzie (4th ed.; London: Oxford University, 1970) 93–97, at 95.